Sexual Abuse in Nine North American Cultures

Sexual Abuse in Nine North American Cultures

Treatment and Prevention

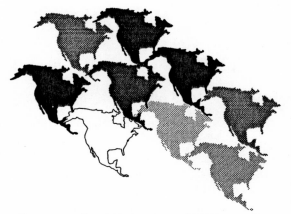

Lisa Aronson Fontes
Editor

Foreword by Eliana Gil

SAGE Publications
International Educational and Professional Publisher
Thousand Oaks   London   New Delhi

For information address:

SAGE Publications, Inc.
2455 Teller Road
Thousand Oaks, California 91320
E-mail: order@sagepub.com

SAGE Publications Ltd.
6 Bonhill Street
London EC2A 4PU
United Kingdom

SAGE Publications India Pvt. Ltd.
M-32 Market
Greater Kailash I
New Delhi 110 048 India

Printed in the United States of America

Library of Congress Cataloging-in-Publication Data

Main entry under title:

Sexual abuse in nine North American cultures: treatment and prevention /
edited by Lisa Aronson Fontes.
    p.   cm.
  Includes bibliographical references and index.
   ISBN 0-8039-5434-4 (acid-free paper).—ISBN 0-8039-5435-2 (pbk.:
acid-free paper)
    1. Child sexual abuse—United States—Cross-cultural studies.
I. Fontes, Lisa Aronson.
HV6570.2.B74 1995
362.7′62′0973—dc20

                                                            95-5105

This book is printed on acid-free paper.

00 01 10 9 8 7 6 5

Sage Production Editor: Diana E. Axelsen
Sage Typesetter: Andrea D. Swanson

This book is dedicated to the child
whose first words to me were,
"It is hard to be a 5-year-old named Jamie."
I hope you are safe.

Contents

Foreword

ELIANA GIL

I experienced my first quandary about race and class at the age of seven, when I was living with my extended family in Guanyaquil, Ecuador. The circumstances remain vivid as I describe them now. Chavita was a girl my age whose family had brought her to be raised by my grandmother. Chavita's family had limited resources and felt that she had a better chance of getting good care and an education with our family. In return, she would lead a life of service like her parents, grandparents, and extended family. Because she was so young, her job was to be my maid, my playmate, and my companion.

I did not realize there were strict boundaries imposed on my relationship with Chavita. So, when she cried because she missed her parents, I would comfort her; when she was frightened, I would reassure her. Slowly our friendship deepened, and I grew to love her as the sister I did not have. Chavita always seemed to sense what I did not: that others would disapprove intensely of our friendship. Often I noticed her withdraw when others observed our play from afar. During the night, we waited until my grandmother opened the door to check that we were asleep; then Chavita would climb into my bed. Before falling asleep, we often talked into the early hours of the morning; but Chavita always woke up in time to get on the floor where she was supposed to sleep.

One morning my grandmother found her sleeping with me and yanked her out of bed to be awakened by a harsh beating. "Who do you think you are?" she demanded. She threw Chavita out of the room and scolded me for allowing that "filthy child" to get into my bed. When I protested that I had *asked* Chavita to sleep in my bed, my grandmother explained that we were not the same; Chavita was a servant, and I had to "command respect" or she would take advantage of me.

When I think about this shocking experience now, I realize that my grandmother's attitude toward Chavita was an expression of the Latin traditions that she had followed all her life. She was teaching me about race and class in the same way her mother had taught her. She was convinced that Chavita was somehow subhuman because her skin was darker than mine and because our family enjoyed a life of privilege, partly at the expense of those around us whose lot in life was to focus on our needs.

It's hard to know why children accept or reject the things they are taught by their elders—I've often wondered why my experience of that event shaped me in exactly the opposite way from what it was designed to do. Nevertheless, from the outside, I found it impossible to accept that people could be deemed inferior because of their skin color, gender, or class.

When I was 14, our family moved to the United States. I felt mortified that I was not allowed to have the traditional "coming out" party at 15 that I would have had in Ecuador. But at the same time, I was excited to return to Washington, DC, where I had lived for one year when I was younger.

I liked many things about living in America, particularly what I perceived as greater independence, which came about in part because our social status changed dramatically. In Ecuador, we were economically privileged, we had servants, and our mother stayed home. In the United States, there were no servants in our house; my brother and I were left alone until my mother returned from work; and most importantly, I had the freedom to choose my friends and my activities. Suddenly, my mother's efforts to restrict my contact to people of "my class" were no longer successful because I went to school with children from divergent cultures, ethnicities, and classes. In spite of some difficulties adapting to expectations that I clean my room, wash my clothes, and cook some of my meals, this lifestyle felt more congruent to me, and I'm sure these initial impressions influenced my later choice to remain in the United States.

The transition from life in Ecuador to life in the United States was fraught with a range of emotions, including tension, confusion, and significant feelings of inferiority and isolation. I was on the receiving end of racism for the first time in my life, and I empathized with Chavita even more. Kids laughed at my English and made fun of my name. Teachers called attention to me by asking me to pronounce my name. Eventually the school records changed my name to Elaine, and I was called by this name for years. In a way, the fact that it was easier to pronounce gave me the anonymity that signified acceptance. The most difficult change was feeling like an outsider who was thought to be less intelligent (often people who don't speak English are thought to be less bright) or who was always chosen last (almost as an afterthought).

Partly because children are resilient and partly because I gravitated toward the differences I perceived in the United States, I acculturated fairly quickly, so much so that I created tension at home when I asserted my independence by becoming verbally defiant. In the United States, most people assume that I am American unless I make a formal announcement that I am Latin. Many colleagues assume that I am American, because I no longer have an accent and because my skin color is not as dark as the U.S. mainstream stereotype of Latin people. I have become fully bicultural, able to walk in both worlds. This capacity to shift is a result of complex and varied processes, both unconscious and conscious, that clarify and verify the realities, nuances, and influences of culture.

To walk in both cultures means that my identity developed as a result of my integrating values, traditions, attitudes, beliefs, expectations, and histories of both cultures. I am as familiar with the political and social revolutions of my adopted country as I am with the struggles of my birth country. Cultural identity greatly influences individual identity formation, through exposure, identification, and experience. Initially, our truths are the truths of those around us, because the people around us direct our attention and define our thinking. Eventually, we may disagree with and discard part of the surrounding tradition, defining an identity entwined with but separate from our cultural heritage.

Culture is a concept that encompasses a great deal. It is tempting to think of culture as ethnicity; but cultures include diverse ethnicities, languages, and family structures; perceived differences among people based on class, gender and gender roles, or skin color; views of mainstream culture and its public agencies; political histories; moral and religious principles; lifestyles; child-rearing practices; the ways emotions are expressed; and who the accepted healers are. Culture also includes the ways individuals and communities regard issues of violence and sexual assault against its vulnerable members (who may be men), and what level of action is taken when violence and sexual assault occur. Cultures have unique narratives, unique ways of resolving survival and extinction issues, and composite identities which result from formative experiences. To separate an individual from his or her cultural background is like prying roots from the dirt that surrounds them.

Cultures convey expectations, make demands of their members, and provide more or less rigid rules with consequences for compliance or dissension. Individual differences may be encouraged, tolerated, or prohibited. In some cases, group norms are overridden in favor of protection of individual rights.

Sexual Abuse in Nine North American Cultures has been masterfully sculpted to give us individual perceptions of cultures by professionals who were influenced by and who currently provide services to families and communities in distress. It becomes painfully clear that individuals participate in collective histories of toil and redemption; along the way, unity becomes a strengthening strategy for survival. Individual pain and crisis must be viewed against the backdrop of sociocultural development, which often has a cumulative impact that can reinforce feelings of oppression, hopelessness, or futility.

There are unique aspects in every culture. The authors repeatedly encourage clinicians to affirm and strengthen their cultural competence, postulating that a thorough understanding of culture and of how individuals interact with their cultural heritage is critical in providing useful mental health services. Clinicians must take the initiative to research the cultural backgrounds of their clients; it is unrealistic to place this burden on troubled individuals seeking help. Fortunately, health care professionals, including the contributors to this book, are taking on this task. The authors have summarized relevant information which facilitates learning about a variety of cultures.

This book makes a significant contribution both by heightening awareness of cross-cultural issues and by augmenting a spotty knowledge base regarding child sexual abuse within different cultural groups. The field of child abuse prevention and treatment has maintained a simplistic approach to cross-cultural concerns, often ignoring ethnocultural information in research studies or treatment approaches. In some cases it has inadvertently contributed to stereotypes by demanding that cultural issues be appraised without offering specific training in how to make those appraisals. The end result is that professionals in the child abuse field (mental health, public health, law enforcement, medicine, and social work) either over- or underreact to cross-cultural diversity. It is as dangerous to exaggerate cultural differences to the point that there is a likelihood of overidentification of problems as it is to minimize them, relegating abusive behavior to expectable or tolerable behavior within cultures.

As diverse as cultures are, unifying themes contribute to the establishment of cultural identity. These themes include organization of the family unit; the relative value of interdependence compared to autonomy and differentiation; the treatment of female sexuality; childrearing practices; work ethics; the relationship between religion and sexuality; gender roles; interpersonal boundaries; level of tolerance for emotionalism; and the extent to which cultures are ideocentric (organized around individual needs) or allocentric (group oriented). This book explores these themes as they are expressed in nine North American cultures.

Cultural issues are relevant to child sexual abuse in three major ways: how cultural beliefs or attitudes contribute to family climates in which children can be abused; how cultural organization prohibits or hinders disclosure; and how culture plays a role in seeking or accepting social service or mental health assistance. These issues must be addressed if families are to be helped. These three dimensions are amply discussed in this book, which offers invaluable insights that raise our consciousness in addition to providing specific strategies that can be implemented in practice. The book furthers our understanding of how cultural beliefs are both supported by and contribute to individual behaviors and family interactions. Specifically, when assessing the development of child sexual abuse within families, the authors argue for an ecosystemic view that discourages confining the focus to individuals and champions an amplified view of the individual as he or she interacts, adapts, or separates himself or herself from family, community, and cultural contexts.

This volume is provocative, personal, and professional; it is both abstract and concrete. It struggles with how to discuss the diversity within cultures without wavering from its overall goal of providing basic historical premises for diverse cultures. Although not all major ethnic groups in the United States are discussed, the book does provide a framework within which such work can be extended to cover, for example, Native American cultures. It also provides an uncharacteristic view of culture which reaches beyond race and ethnicity. For example, both homosexuality and Seventh-Day Adventists are discussed as unique cultures—these chapters are written with great candor and clarity. Such analysis is badly needed and in the future might be explored with respect to the culture of persons who are disabled and who struggle with the identification and treatment of child sexual abuse.

The contribution of the book is not only in the information it so aptly presents but also in the way it encourages the reader to think and in the assertion that clinicians must enlighten and empower themselves when working cross-culturally, approaching issues of culture with rigorous attention and sensitivity. Clinicians are challenged to recognize strengths and utilize the internal resources of each culture, rather than pathologizing what is unfamiliar or imposing treatment goals that are inconsistent with or incongruous to individuals of diverse cultures. These internal resources include helpers such as indigenous healers; priests, rabbis, or ministers; curanderos; and incorporation of traditional healing rituals such as sweat lodges or sitting *shivah*. By drawing on these resources, clinicians optimize their chances of meeting their stated goal: to be of assistance to families so that the quality of their lives is improved and children are safe and nurtured.

Preface

LISA ARONSON FONTES

A s a student in 1985 at a major teaching hospital in a Latino neighborhood in New York City, I attended grand rounds, where a case was presented of a 10-year-old Dominican girl who misbehaved in school, washed herself constantly, masturbated in public, and engaged in other behaviors that puzzled the multidisciplinary team that had been charged with her care. The team members discussed their various hypotheses and the medications that had been tried. Finally, a specialist in sexual abuse stood up in exasperation and suggested that this girl was showing classic signs of sexual molestation. The team leader looked irritated and, with an attitude of, "Why does this guy always raise that issue?" replied, "We could not really communicate with the family because the girl was the only one who spoke English, and that was minimal, but the father seemed like a nice guy so we ruled out sexual abuse."

I was astounded. The team seemed to have no understanding of the "nice guy" veneer of many people who abuse children. Even more alarming was their willingness to attempt drastic interventions with little awareness of their patient's family, community, or cultural context. If this was the care given at one of the top settings in the country with a large Latino population, how were Latinos, immigrants, and members of other minority groups treated elsewhere? How many people experiencing sexual abuse were being overlooked or mistreated because of cultural or linguistic misunderstanding, or downright racism or homophobia? Additionally, I wondered about the ways in which culture affected people's experiences of sexual abuse.

My experiences that morning set me on a path of research and clinical work that has now given birth to this book. Thankfully, we know much more about sexual abuse now than we did 10 years ago. However, the impact of culture on sexual abuse intervention is only beginning to form part of the discussion. At some conferences on sexual abuse today, practitioners can learn culturally sensitive approaches to child protection and therapy for sexual abuse. Increasingly sophisticated research is emerging about culture and sexual abuse. At conferences dedicated to multicultural therapy, however, issues of family violence and sexual abuse are still rarely broached.

The heart of this book is a collection of nine original chapters by authors from a variety of cultural groups who are experts in treating sexual abuse among members of their group. The culture-specific chapters present the strengths and challenges of each cultural group. They consider ways that cultural norms can be used to protect children and promote healing from abuse.

This book is solution oriented. Much of the culture-specific writing today seems to ascribe to a deficit-pathology model, stressing what appears to be "different" or "lacking" about cultures that are in the minority in the United States. Simultaneously, much writing about culture fails to examine or challenge the all-pervasive norms of the dominant United States culture. This book offers us opportunities to learn from minority cultures. The chapter on sexual abuse in Anglo American families also helps us understand the cultural contributions to sexual child abuse (and recovery!) that are written into the very fabric of the dominant culture—usually neglected as a culture because it surrounds us so completely.

Considering culture is crucial but not sufficient in the treatment of sexual abuse. We must also examine how social status due to sex, race, proficiency in English, economic class, religion, national origin, and sexual orientation partially determine the way people are treated by the various social systems that intervene when sexual abuse comes to light. After discussing cultural norms, each chapter discusses oppression issues that emerge in encounters with the social service system and how professionals can help families work to counteract this oppression.

The sexual abuse of children happens in all sectors of the population. Interventions that are tailored to the specific ways sexual abuse is handled by members of a given group—and the meanings people from that group ascribe to both the abuse and interventions—will be more effective than interventions that are "generic" (that is, based on the lives of heterosexual, middle-class, White, European American, Christian, female clients).

In my introduction, I suggest ways in which culture can contribute to an ecosystemic context for understanding the prevention, occurrence, detection, and recovery from sexual abuse.

Nine chapters devoted to specific cultural groups follow. The word "culture" has been interpreted broadly here to mean people bound by common beliefs, history, and practices. Although it is somewhat unusual to include lesbian and gay male cultures on the same level as the other cultures discussed in this book, I believe readers will find these chapters helpful in thinking about the impact of history, discrimination, and group norms on interventions for sexual abuse with gay and lesbian clients and their families. These chapters complement the others by addressing the ways that sexual orientation affects experiences of sexual abuse. Each of us participates in a culture shaped by our sexual orientation, although most of the literature on sexual abuse assumes the heterosexuality of the people discussed rather than addressing sexual orientation explicitly.

In the concluding chapter, I discuss some of the general promises and pitfalls of attending to culture in providing services for sexual abuse. I offer a view on the general issue of matching clients and service providers for ethnicity (which is also discussed in culture-specific chapters), and provide some suggestions for those who set the policies that shape the lives of those who research and intervene in sexual child abuse, as well as those who are affected personally by it.

I commend the authors of these chapters for their courage. In conversations, e-mail, and letters, the authors described sleepless nights and knots in their stomachs as they risked writing publicly about a topic that most of us fear examining even with members of our own group: How does membership in *my* culture put children at risk for abuse?

Every culture has norms that raise the risk of sexual abuse for children, as well as values that have the potential to protect children from sexual abuse. How do we bring about change? The first step toward change is naming our oppression. In this case, individuals, families, communities, and the wider society must break through denial and label the sexual child abuse in our midst. The second step involves education: speaking out in all possible forums about the existence and harmful effects of sexual child abuse and involving people from all groups and professions in working to protect children and promote recovery. The third step, I believe, is for members of specific groups to organize to change the conditions of their own group that permit or foster sexual abuse. At the same time, members of all groups must band together to change the societal climate that allows sexual abuse to occur.

Although this book discusses members of a variety of groups, it is not all inclusive. This book is meant to advance the discussion on culture and sexual abuse—it is not the last word. Shared contexts facilitate the growth of common coping strategies. Group similarities do not hinge on ethnic origin alone. Those who work with Central American refugees from war-torn countries, for example, may find the chapter on Cambodians as relevant as the chapter on Puerto Ricans. People who work with deaf clients may find important information on languages in the chapter on Puerto Ricans, as well as information on isolation from one's parents in the chapter on lesbians, for instance. In addition, you may find that a prevention or healing practice used by one group will spark ideas for work with your own group. Also, of course, we are all members of multiple reference groups based on our race, gender, class, ethnic origin, religion, sexual orientation, and other factors.

We are guilty here of what I call "ethnic lumping" (Fontes, 1993a). We have collapsed some groups into large categories. For instance, the chapter on Asians includes Chinese, Japanese, Koreans, Filipinos, and Pacific Islanders. Clearly, each of these groups merits a separate chapter, but that is not possible in this volume. In this book, there is only one chapter on Latinos, which focuses on Puerto Ricans. It will certainly inform readers who seek information on working with other Latinos, but there are differences. I do not believe there is one correct way to cut the pie that makes up North American society. The authors helped decide where they would draw the boundaries around their discussions, resulting in dynamic, authoritative, and liberating discussions.

Factors including social class, education, and degree of assimilation contribute to great variability within each of the groups discussed. Readers should proceed with caution in applying ideas suggested here to individual cases. Each individual and family must be assessed for their particular needs and their degree of adherence to cultural norms.

Discussions of culture, sex, and violence tend to put us all on the defensive. I hope readers will approach this book with an open and generous spirit, which is the spirit in which it was written. We hope you will communicate with us about what you like and do not like about it, and what works and does not work. Please let us know about your related local projects.

I am filled with gratitude to the contributors, a brilliant bunch who have worked diligently and have good-naturedly tolerated my numerous editorial suggestions. Thanks to Jerry Weinstein for sharing his computer skills. I am grateful to Carlos Fontes, Linda Baker, Roberto Irizarry, Catherine Taylor, and

Kim Gerrould for their critiques of my work. I am grateful to Tom Herman for his nurturing encouragement; to C. Terry Hendrix, Jon Conte, and Diana Axelsen at Sage—a dream team; to Richard Baldwin, Janine Roberts, Gretchen Rossman, John C. Carey, and Lynn Hoffman for their mentoring and friendship; to my new Purdue "family" for the web of kind challenge which supports me now; and to the colleagues, faculty, students, clients, and friends who have been my teachers. I thank Muriel Fox, Shepard and Eric Aronson for their long-distance cheering, advising, and consoling. Ana Lua, Marlena and Carlos Fontes—you are endless sources of inspiration and the center of my universe.

We give this book to the world in the hope that it will help reduce violence within families and reduce the violence perpetrated by social service systems. It is an honor to participate in this process.

Introduction

LISA ARONSON FONTES

Those of us who work with people affected by sexual abuse have learned that no formula for intervention works every time. Effective interventions require careful, continual assessment of the abuse and of responses to the abuse and to our interventions. These responses are partially shaped by culture: the culture of the client(s) and the treatment providers, and the cultural context of the wider society in which the abuse and the intervention occur.

I advocate for the adoption of an ecosystemic approach to sexual abuse that takes into account individual, familial, cultural, and societal factors. This approach is not difficult to learn or understand. It increases our ability to create prevention programs and intervene in instances of sexual abuse with members of a variety of cultural groups, including our own.

Individuals and Families

The early literature and most of today's writings on sexual abuse concentrate on characteristics of individual victims and offenders. Treatment interventions are geared toward helping individuals (Fontes, 1993a). This emphasis reflects the high value placed on individualism in Western cultures, and it is limiting. We must not fall into the trap of psychologizing social realities (De La Cancela, 1991)—an examination of psychological factors alone is not adequate to intervene successfully in sexual child abuse.

1

In recent years, a body of literature has emerged exploring familial aspects of sexual abuse. These writings include discussions of roles and rules in families with incest, information on how abuse may be repeated across generations, and a fair amount of mother-blaming (Barrett, Trepper, & Fish, 1990; Birns & Meyer, 1993). Articles and books have emerged promoting the use of family therapy in cases of sexual abuse to help families recover from the impact of sexual abuse and the interventions that follow disclosure (Fish & Faynik, 1989; Trepper & Traicoff, 1985). Direct care providers and policy-makers debate the proper balance between ensuring safety for children and keeping families together (Gelles, 1993).

Ethnic Culture

The psychological, social work, medical, sociological, and legal literature on sexual abuse neglects severely the impact of ethnic culture and oppression in the occurrence and treatment of sexual abuse. In much of the early work, the ethnicity of the people discussed is not even mentioned, or all-White samples are used (Fontes, 1993a).

In some groundbreaking research, scholars have looked for racial and ethnic differences in the prevalence or effects of sexual child abuse (Russell, Schurman, & Trocki, 1988). In these studies, *ethnicity* and *race* are considered demographic labels. That is, people from a particular group are found to have a given rate of abuse per thousand, as compared to another group. These studies tend to suffer from methodological problems in definitions and data collection, and their findings are often contradictory (Wyatt & Peters, 1986a, 1986b). In terms of prevalence, the most useful conclusion that can be reached is that sexual child abuse affects members of all cultural groups in the United States. There is some evidence that members of different groups respond differently to disclosures by their children of sexual abuse (Pierce & Pierce, 1984; Rao, Di Clemente, & Ponton, 1992) and that patterns of help-seeking after disclosure differ according to factors such as ethnic group membership, socioeconomic status, marital status, and previous experiences with social service systems (Thompson & Smith, 1993).

Meaning—not skin color—shapes culture. Although researchers some-times consider race and culture as demographic labels, culture as a complex web of behaviors, values, and attitudes has hardly been discussed in relation to sexual abuse (Fontes, 1993a). Consider all the messages we receive while growing up about our bodies, virginity, gender roles, sexuality, shame, power, and help-seeking. These are all highly influenced by our ethnic cultures. Therefore, it is natural that there would be some variability by ethnic culture in experiences of sexual abuse and in responses to interventions.

Societal Contexts

Even as we learn to acknowledge the impact of culture on our clients and ourselves, we must also acknowledge that feelings and behaviors may result from experiences of oppression, and not culture per se. For example, if an African American mother decides not to contact the police about the rape of her child, this decision may stem from knowledge of oppressive police brutality against her group, not a culturally based reticence. Similarly, if a Mexican American family fails to show up for therapy appointments, this may stem from the oppression of poverty—which makes child care and transportation to sessions difficult—not a cultural aversion to therapy. The seeming passivity that a Cambodian family shows in permitting authorities to remove a child from their home may be due to disempowering experiences with authorities in Cambodia, Thailand, and the United States, not from cultural fatalism or a lack of concern for the child. When working with people of a different cultural group, it is easy to assume that behaviors that defy our expectations are cultural and therefore not easily amenable to change. We must not ignore the systemic variables that may foster or maintain these behaviors. When in doubt, ask both the clients and other cultural informants about the source of the behavior.

At times, it may be difficult or impossible to separate issues of culture and oppression. Cultural norms do not emerge in a vacuum. Payne (1989), Wilson (1994), and Fontes (1992) describe ways in which Black Caribbeans, African Americans, and Puerto Ricans, respectively, often adopt child-raising norms that involve corporal punishment and unquestioning obedience to authority. These norms may have emerged to help children survive the brutalities of racism and slavery, and now appear as "part of the culture."

Some of the writing on sexual child abuse concludes that the problem extends well beyond individuals and families, and is rooted in patriarchy (Herman, 1981; Sommers-Flanagan & Walters, 1987). How patriarchy might reach into the lives of individual people and cause them to molest children has not been explicated. In addition to the concept of patriarchy, which affects members of all cultural groups, specific cultural groups face differing experiences in the wider culture because of their economic and social status. These factors in part determine access to treatment, likelihood of legal intervention and family separation, and the probable attitudes of representatives of various systems. Little has been written about the impact of the wider culture on the prevention, disclosure, or treatment of sexual abuse (Fontes, 1993a), and even less about how culture and oppression might interact in their impact on sexual abuse.

Contextualizing Vulnerability to Incest

In an excellent series of publications, Trepper and Barrett (1986, 1989) have developed a vulnerability to incest model in which they hypothesize that all families have a degree of vulnerability to incestuous abuse that can be exacerbated by precipitating factors and mitigated by coping mechanisms (Barrett et al., 1990, p. 159). According to this theory,

> there is no one cause of incestuous abuse. Instead, all families are endowed with a degree of vulnerability based upon environmental, family, individual, and family-of-origin factors, which may express as incest if a precipitating event occurs and the family's coping skills are inadequate. (Trepper & Barrett, 1989, p. 15)

I will use this model as background for a discussion of the role of culture and oppression in the occurrence of sexual abuse inside and outside the family.

To place responsibility where it belongs, sexual child abuse will not occur without the presence of someone with offending tendencies who chooses to act on those tendencies and has access to a child. As we examine systemic factors in sexual abuse, we must not overlook the role of the individual person who chooses to offend. However, systemic factors are important in the following ways: They may contribute to the existence of offending tendencies, they affect access to specific children, they partially shape community protective factors, and they contribute to the likelihood of revictimization or recovery.

Vulnerability Factors

Socioenvironmental Factors

According to Trepper and Barrett (1989), certain socioenvironmental factors increase vulnerability to incest. These include acceptance of male supremacy, the socialization of men toward aggressive sexuality, the valuation of younger and less powerful females by males, and lack of caretaking experience by fathers of young children (Trepper & Barrett, 1989, pp. 78-84). The multicultural applicability of some of these notions merits research but in general is supported by the authors of this volume. *It is crucial to remember that cultures that may seem to create high vulnerability to incest in their members according to the above criteria may also provide protective factors that reduce the likelihood of sexual abuse.* If we fail to recognize these protective factors or coping mechanisms, we may fall into the trap of whole-sale condemnation of cultures without recognizing their unique strengths.

As you read these chapters, you will discover that every culture has attitudes, beliefs, and practices that seem to put children at risk for sexual abuse, and others that seem to protect them. In most cases, the same quality can be used either as a rationalization for abuse or as a lever to help families and communities protect their children. For example, Marian Schmidt identifies the traditional Anglo American emphasis on individual rights and needs as a possible rationalization for abusive behavior. Somewhat paradoxically, perhaps, Amy Okamura, Patricia Heras, and Linda Wong-Kerberg identify pressures on Asian children to sacrifice their individual needs for the good of the family as contributing to sexual abuse among Asian Americans. Either of these values also could be harnessed for child protection, which would require cultural competency on the part of the service providers.

Another socioenvironmental factor described by Trepper and Barrett (1989) is tolerance of incest in the family's community. Although no cultural group in North America condones overtly the sexual abuse of children, pornography, other mass media, and many subcultures idealize innocent, barely pubescent females (or males) as sexual objects and portray adult bodies (and particularly aging female bodies) as spoiled or repugnant (N. Wolf, 1991). Additionally, coercion, persuasion, and even overt violence are linked to sexuality in films and advertising. These create an atmosphere in which a potential offender may see turning to children for sexual gratification as normal and acceptable (Brady, 1993).

Other socioenvironmental factors described by Trepper and Barrett (1989) include social isolation and chronic stress. Fontes (1993b) describes factors that contribute to the social isolation of immigrants, including discrimination, migration, poverty, lack of bilingual services, and alienation from professionals due to cultural differences. The chapters here describe the social isolation experienced by members of several oppressed minority groups in this country, including gay men and lesbians, as well as the social isolation imposed by norms of Anglo American culture and membership in religious minorities.

Finally, each chapter describes the chronic stressors that hobble members of various groups to different degrees, including, but not limited to, ill health, poverty, police brutality, poor housing, street crime, discrimination, homophobia, anti-Semitism, colonization, and xenophobia. The authors describe the ways they have seen these stressors affect the occurrence of sexual abuse and responses to that abuse.

Family Factors

Trepper and Barrett (1989) describe family factors that they believe contribute to the occurrence of incest. These include factors in the parents' family of origin, as well as family styles, structures, and communication patterns. Multicultural research is needed to assess the applicability of these factors to families from a variety of cultures.

Individual Factors

Although we do not fully understand why some people molest children and most do not, factors including individual history, psychopathology, personality, cognitive distortions, and sexual orientation toward children seem important. With due caution about the danger of overgeneralization, particularly without adequate research, it may be that the types of experiences that predispose adults to sexually abusive behavior vary for different groups. These could include multiple traumas; addictions; exposure to child pornography; a history of sexual abuse by soldiers, clergy, teachers, camp counselors, or scout troop leaders; rape in prison; and sexually exploitative experiences in school. Although these factors should not lead us to expect higher rates of sexual abuse among some groups rather than others, they might determine the nature of the abuse that does occur. In addition, as the chapter authors state again and again, the multiple disempowering traumas of living as members of oppressed groups can contribute to lack of protection by nonoffending parents, school staff, police, and other adults.

Precipitating Events

Trepper and Barrett (1989) write, "Precipitating events are not vulnerability factors per se, but occurrences that may act to trigger an already vulnerable family into incestuous episodes (p. 100). (I object somewhat to the phrasing here because the *potential offender* is triggered into committing incestuous assault, not the "family"). Some of these precipitating events include alcohol or substance abuse, opportunity factors in which the potential offender and potential victim are left alone together for extended periods of time, and acute stressors. The chapter authors describe the circumstances that might contribute to precipitating events for families from particular cultures. For instance, the horrific trauma of the Cambodian Holocaust has led to high rates of posttraumatic stress disorder (PTSD) among Cambodian refugees in the United States (86% in a study by Carlson and Rosser-Hogan, 1993). The symptoms of PTSD can lead to disorganized behavior, dissociation, and increased use of substances, which are precipitating factors for offenders and contribute to diminished protection by nonoffending adults.

Coping Mechanisms

According to Trepper and Barrett (1989, p. 102), even a potential offender in a family that is vulnerable to incest and has precipitating events will not engage in incestuous behavior if coping mechanisms are in place. These coping mechanisms include social networks, religious belief systems, and therapy. To this list I would add cultural beliefs that might counterbalance those listed as vulnerability factors, including a high value placed on children, a rejection of violence in general and sexual violence in particular, and a belief that children are fully human and have a right to their own voice. In addition, I suggest that sex education, abuse prevention education, economic security, regular contacts with caring adults outside the family, and knowledge of social service systems can serve as protective factors. The chapters here describe the protective factors available in each culture and how they can be harnessed to reduce vulnerability to sexual abuse.

The Vulnerability Model and Extrafamilial Sexual Child Abuse

Although Trepper and Barrett have developed their model to apply to incest, I believe it also illuminates issues of extrafamilial sexual abuse, with special attention to culture. For instance, if we examine the vulnerability and precipitating factors discussed above, many of these would make potential offenders more likely to offend outside the family as well as within it. The family vulnerability factors would make families less able to protect their children or respond to the sexual abuse of their children whether the offender is inside or outside the family. Additional factors that would make children vulnerable to sexual victimization from people outside the family might include lack of adequate adult supervision, family separation due to immigration, residence in crime-ridden neighborhoods or war zones, parents' inability to understand English or the workings of the dominant culture, overdependence on others for economic or social support, and lack of affection or warmth in the family. Diminished coping mechanisms can contribute to sexual victimization of children by people both inside and outside the family.

Sexual abuse itself may be seen as a (dysfunctional) coping mechanism (Linda Baker, personal communication, June 30, 1994). Adults who abuse children may be coping as well as they can with memories of their own sexual torture, with desperate feelings of powerlessness, with crushing depression, or with making sense of sexual urges that seem to make no sense. These adults need to be given alternative coping mechanisms that do not endanger others. Sadly, in most areas, there are no offender treatment programs for offenders who do not speak English or who are deaf, and few treatment programs that are sensitive to issues of culture. Such offenders (including sexually reactive children and adolescents) are usually either incarcerated—where they have increased time to masturbate to fantasies of molesting children—or given no treatment whatsoever (Fontes, 1993b).

Vulnerabilities, Strengths, and This Book

Each chapter in this book highlights the vulnerabilities to incest that are characteristic of specific cultural groups in North America, as well as coping mechanisms that would reduce that vulnerability. Each chapter may be seen as an ecosystemic portrayal of sexual child abuse in certain communities in North America, with numerous suggestions for intervention that make sense *in context*.

This book supports a "stew" rather than a "melting pot" approach to diversity. That is, this book reflects what I believe is true of the United States and Canada—although members of a variety of cultures are all together in the same pot, drenched in the same stew of the dominant North American culture, each retains its unique shape and flavor and makes an important contribution. To support this value, I have encouraged the chapter authors to emphasize what they believe is most important for their group, rather than conforming rigidly to a standard model.

You will notice that some chapters seem more anthropological in their discussion of culture, whereas others emphasize issues of oppression. Several chapters emphasize historical issues in creating contexts for cultural groups in North America today, and the influence of these historical issues on individual and family behavior. The chapter on Anglo Americans discusses cultural issues that are so pervasive, they are rarely noticed or discussed.

Although this book will neither please nor meet the needs of all readers, we believe it is an important step in advancing the discussion of culture and oppression issues in overcoming sexual child abuse. We expect it to be useful to therapists; protective workers; law enforcement, legal, medical, and school personnel; and policymakers. We hope you will find it practical and provocative.

African Americans
and Sexual Child Abuse

VERONICA D. ABNEY
RONNIE PRIEST

The number of research and clinical articles addressing childhood sexual victimization in African American communities is increasing, but it still remains sparse (Pierce & Pierce, 1984; Priest, 1992; Russell, 1986; Wyatt, 1985, 1988a, 1990; Wyatt & Mickey, 1988). In addition, significant segments of the African American community have traditionally taken a twofold thematic variation of "see no evil, hear no evil." On one hand, sexually abusing children is something other ethnic groups do. On the other hand, if, in fact, African Americans do engage in incestuous acts or other sexually abusive behavior with children, it is not to be talked about because it is thought that acknowledging sexual child abuse will be used in some damnable way to further exclude African Americans from the American mainstream. Unfortunately, the failure of the community at large to acknowledge child sexual victimization compounds the survivors' psychological distress.

For the purposes of clarity, child sexual victimization is defined as the sexual manipulation and/or coercion of a dependent child or adolescent by a dominant authority figure in which the child or adolescent is unable to give informed consent. Child sexual victimization and sexual child abuse are used interchangeably here.

This chapter is an attempt to explore the issue of sexual abuse as it relates to African Americans. It includes a brief look at the history of African

Americans in the United States. In addition, it addresses the impact of culture on several factors, including the African American family, sexuality, homophobia, attitudes toward disclosure and the reporting of sexual abuse, and the effects of sexual abuse. Case examples are used to discuss treatment, and prevention is examined.

Any discussion of intervention considerations with African American clients should first recognize that there is no such thing as a "generic African American client." African American clients are not necessarily homogeneous and may demonstrate "in-group" cultural distinctiveness based on, among other things, gender, socioeconomic status, and level of acculturation to European American norms (Baldwin, 1991). It has been suggested that the component that most closely serves as a cultural solidifying factor among African Americans is the experience of racism perpetrated by the majority culture (Jackson, 1992).

Sociopolitical History

In general, African Americans have not been afforded equal access to the "American Dream." The history of African Americans is heavily steeped in economic, political, social, and sexual exploitation compounded by racism and the denial of equal education and mental health opportunities (Baldwin, Brown, & Hopkins, 1991; Clark & Harrell, 1992; Pinderhughes, 1982). This oppression and discrimination date back to the arrival of the first Blacks from Africa, brought against their will as slaves to Jamestown, Virginia, in 1619. Blacks remained slaves until 1865, nearly 250 years later, when the Thirteenth Amendment abolished slavery in the United States. This, however, did not bring true freedom or opportunity. A racial caste system continued to exist, depriving African Americans of equal civil rights. In 1955, the civil rights movement began, culminating in the passage of the 1964 Civil Rights Act and the Voting Rights Act of 1965. The former outlawed racial discrimination in federally assisted programs and declared discriminatory employment practices illegal, whereas the latter provided protection and enforcement of the voting rights of African Americans.

African Americans moved out of the 1960s with a sense of great hope. Affirmative action programs were promoted as a way to guarantee equal opportunity in education and employment. These programs, however, were viewed by some Whites as reverse racism, and by the mid-1970s, a backlash became apparent. This backlash, combined with a general conservative political trend, has slowed and even reversed some of the gains of African Americans, evident in high rates of unemployment and decreased educational opportunities (Gibbs, 1991). As a result, 50% of African Americans continue to live in poverty as second-class citizens despite the advances made by others. African Americans who consistently experience racism and are on the bottom rungs of the socioeconomic ladder may see themselves as victims, rather than citizens having equal stature to European Americans.

Culture

The African American Family

Many have commented on the alleged negative impact of almost 400 years of oppression and discrimination on the African American psyche and family. This trend led to stereotyping, pathologizing, and overgeneralizing about the African American family, which was erroneously believed to have a matriarchal structure. Meyers (1982) points out that myths about the African American family have been perpetuated by three principal, but false, assumptions historically made in research: "1) the assumption of equivalence of culture, color and class, 2) the assumption of the homogeneity of the Afro-Americans and of their communities, and 3) the assumption of general cultural equivalence" (p. 40).

Research on the African American family did not begin to shift until the works of Billingsley (1968) and Hill (1972). Billingsley explored the complexity of the African American family by viewing it as a multistructured, ethnic subsociety, and Hill was the first to emphasize the strengths of the African American family. The myth of the "black matriarchy" was refuted in a number of studies reviewed by Meyers (1982). Others have continued to explore the positive adaptation of the African American family: its strengths, its flexibility and resilience, its African cultural origins, and its interactions with the majority American culture (Hale, 1982; McAdoo, 1981; Nobles, 1978; Ogbu, 1981; Staples & Mirande, 1980; Wilson, 1992).

Currently, there is no homogeneous African American family. For the most part, African American families fall into one of three groups (Billingsley, 1968): nuclear, extended, or augmented. Nuclear families consist of one or both parents and children, and comprise 66% of African American families.

Extended families, which comprise 25% of African American families, are those that include other relatives living in the home of the nuclear family. Augmented families are those that include nonrelatives in the home of the nuclear family and constitute approximately 10% of African American families.

Hill (1972) pointed out six cultural themes in African American culture that he identified as strengths: adaptability of family roles; strong kinship bonds; strong work, education, and achievement orientation; strong religious orientation; a humanistic orientation; and endurance of suffering. In reviewing these, it appears that five of these themes/values may function to either protect African American children from sexual abuse or aid in the recovery of the African American family when sexual abuse has occurred.

Roles in the African American family are adaptable and flexible as a result of the historical and economic need for mothers to work and the fact that African American women have had greater access than African American males to employment (although their wages are lower on average than those of men from all groups and those of White women). With a mother and/or father working, older children often must assume responsibility for younger children, and each parent must be flexible in the roles that he or she assumes. Role flexibility is crucial to families that have been shattered by sexual abuse and can greatly enhance their adjustment. Ho (1992b) states, "If the roles in a particular family are flexible, then the family is more likely to be able to cope with changes in circumstances" (p. 77).

The strong kinship bonds found in African American families can be traced to African cultural roots (Hill, 1972) and have had a profound positive impact on the African American's adaptation to slavery, oppression, and institutional racism. When the disclosure of sexual abuse breaks up the nuclear family, there is increased reliance on extended family. Strong kinship bonds can facilitate the provision of functions and services to African American families who are experiencing a crisis. Because of their importance, extended family members may need to be involved in the treatment of sexually abused African Americans. In addition, these strong kinship bonds may serve as positive and negative influences in reinforcing or challenging the nonabusing parent's decision about separating from a sexual offender.

Despite myths to the contrary, the literature documents a strong work, education, and achievement orientation found in African American families (Looney & Lewis, 1983). Hard work and education are viewed as ways out of poverty and aid African Americans' struggle to cope with racism. This work ethic can provide survivors and their families with the motivation to "keep on keeping on" despite adversity.

The strong religious or spiritual orientation held by many African American families has its roots in African cultures, where religion is an essential part of the human existence. African American churches played a crucial role in the fight against slavery and during the civil rights movement. Also, the church has traditionally been a source of spiritual and material support for African Americans when coping with life's mundane problems. A strong sense of spirituality may enhance the African American family's or individual's recovery from sexual abuse. Courtois (1988) points out that spirituality can be therapeutic and "can be a calming source of support and strength during stress" for sexual abuse survivors (p. 202).

The strong humanistic orientation of African American families, evidenced by a concern for others and spontaneous and natural interactions, is related to a strong sense of spirituality (Ho, 1992). Sexual abuse and humanism seem incompatible because of the narcissism inherent in sexually abusive behavior. Therefore, one could hypothesize that children in families where humanism is highly valued might be less vulnerable to sexual abuse by a family member. In addition, such a family might respond in a more empathic and attuned fashion after a child discloses sexual abuse to family members.

A strong tolerance for or endurance of suffering is highly valued in the African American culture. Ho (1992b) points out, "In adjusting to the victim system and adversity, Black Americans have developed great tolerance for conflict, stress, ambiguity, and ambivalence" (p. 78). African American women are particularly noted for their strength. Out of the myth of the "Black matriarchy" has come the belief that "Black women can handle it":

> Black women are strong and can handle anything life throws at them—whether rape at the hands of white slaveowners; the trauma of being separated from their children in slavery; racism; violence against us within our communities; or sexual abuse. (M. Wilson, 1994, p. 10)

A high value placed on the endurance of suffering may hurt the survivor of sexual abuse. First, it may function to minimize the concern of both the African American and White communities about the problem of sexual abuse for African Americans because if African Americans, particularly women, can endure such great suffering, they can handle being sexually abused. Second, such a value may hinder sexually abused African Americans of either gender from pursuing treatment.

Ho (1992) adds that valuing an endurance of suffering may well be connected to strong religious or spiritual orientation, which often includes a belief that seeking help in any way other than through prayer is an indication of a lack of faith in God. This value may lower disclosure rates among African Americans who seek their solace in prayer, friends, and the church, and not through mental health or social service avenues. Some African American victims of sexual abuse may decide to suffer in silence to protect the African American male perpetrator, who is likely to receive more severe legal penalties for his behavior than a White male.

Low-income African American families tend to use physical discipline to keep their children in check. As the socioeconomic status of African Americans improves, their child-rearing behaviors tend to approach those of Whites. However, there are differences that do not seem to be significantly affected by socioeconomic status. D. K. Lewis (1978) finds that African American parents tend to share child care and decision making about child rearing; encourage assertiveness, willfulness, and independence; and train children to be receptive to people, putting less emphasis on mastery of the physical environment.

In a study of preschool children, Baumrind (1972) found that African American parents used authoritarian child-rearing practices but, despite this, raised very assertive children. The authoritarian African American parents seemed to lack the repressed hostility, dogmatism, and rejecting behavior characteristic of the authoritarian personality. Gillum, Gomez-Marin, and Prineas (1984) found that, compared to White families, African American families expressed less open conflict, exercised more control, demanded more organization, and put more emphasis on achievement and religious orientation.

Divorced and Never-Married Single Mothers

Martin and Burpass (1989) and McKenry and Fine (1993) have discussed the increased incidence of divorce in African American communities. McKenry and Fine (1993) have suggested that "the state of being married may no longer be normative in African-American communities" (p. 99). McAdoo (1989) conducted macroanalytic divorce research that suggested that divorced African American women remain unmarried for approximately 12 years, compared to an average of 7 years for European American women.

Logically extended, McAdoo's findings suggest that African American children may be exposed to adult males who are not their biological fathers for an extended period of time based on parental dating or live-in arrangements. This extended exposure to males who are not their biological fathers may place children at an increased rate of sexual victimization compared to children who live with both biological parents.

An additional consideration that affects the issue of disclosure by the non-abusing spouse involves the issue of mate selection. A woman whose child or children have been sexually abused by her husband or significant other may question her judgment in men. Questioning her own judgment frequently leads the mother to engage in self-condemnation and intense feelings of inadequacy.

Sexuality

A discussion of sexual abuse and African Americans would be incomplete without a look at the myths and stereotypes perpetuated about African American sexuality since the time of slavery. African American females were sexually assaulted and exploited by their White slavemasters, yet blamed for enticing them. According to L. M. Williams (1986), "The black female came to be viewed as a legitimate (culturally approved) victim of sexual assault" (p. 9). African American males were, and continue to be, thought of as rapists and were feared to be the greatest threat to the chastity of White females.

Despite the end of slavery and the repeal of laws that legitimized the abuse of African American women and the persecution of African American men, African Americans are still viewed as "sexy, hypersexual, permissive people, who have few morals about sexual promiscuity in or out of marriage" (Wyatt, 1982, p. 335). African American males are believed to have larger penises, and African American females are viewed as sexually precocious, always welcoming intercourse and never withholding consent (L. M. Williams, 1986). E. C. White (1985) addresses several paradoxes facing African American women who are viewed as both superhuman (through their long history of enduring suffering and self-sacrifice) and subhuman (seen as wild, hypersexual, and streetwise).

The response to sexual abuse of African Americans finds many of its roots in these myths. Wyatt (1990) makes the point that social scientists' assumptions about the nature of sexual precocity in African Americans and other ethnic groups of color may lead to their mistakenly attributing abusive behavior to voluntary sexual experiences. This may mean that the abuse of African American children may go undetected. Wilson (1994) adds that myths regarding the hypersexuality of African American females lead to a lack of concern from society as a whole about the effects of sexual abuse on African American women.

Accompanying myths regarding African American sexuality is a belief that sexual abuse must be rampant or normal in the African American community. As a result, the issue of sexual abuse in the African American community has been largely ignored and, until recently, neglected by researchers. Sexual abuse appears to be equally prevalent among African American and White women (Russell, 1986; Wyatt, 1985).

Where Whites and African Americans may differ is in their approach to sexuality (Pierce & Pierce, 1984), not in their morals. African American parents have similar behavioral expectations for male and female children; aggressiveness, assertiveness, emotional expressiveness, and nurturing behaviors are encouraged in both girls and boys (D. K. Lewis, 1978). With more flexible gender roles, African Americans' sexual identity seems to be more relational than that of White children. It is based on the way a child relates to members of the other sex and his or her sexual interactions, rather than on gender-typed behaviors (D. K. Lewis, 1978).

Wyatt's (1988c, 1988d) studies on the sexual differences between African American and White American women have given us important data on the sexual behavior of African Americans. African American and White American women do not differ significantly on the mean age of first coitus (Wyatt, 1988a). African American women engage in fewer childhood exploratory sexual behaviors before age 12 (Wyatt, 1988b). Although prohibitions against masturbation have been noted in the past for African Americans (Staples, 1973), Wyatt, Peters, and Guthrie (1988a, 1988b) found that only 10% of African American and White American women recalled receiving prohibitions about masturbation from their families. Wyatt, Peters, and Guthrie's studies also seem to indicate that African American women have fewer homosexual experiences, are less likely to have extramarital sex or to engage in prostitution, are just as likely to use contraception, and are less likely to broaden their sexual repertoires. African Americans also seem to be less likely to discuss personal matters with Whites, particularly issues regarding sexuality, due to a lack of trust in Whites (Pierce & Pierce, 1984).

Homophobia

Any attempt on the part of mental health professionals to assist in the healing process of African American clients who have been abused sexually during childhood should begin with the recognition that African American clients may present unique challenges. For example, the existing literature

(Bolton, Morris, & MacEachron, 1989; Breer, 1992; Hunter, 1990; Lew, 1988) furnishes lucid documentary evidence of the difficulty that males, in general, may have disclosing their childhood sexual victimization. African American males may be confronted with the added burden of an essentially homophobic community. The way this homophobia is manifested in the community may also be uncommon. In African American communities, homosexuality is ostracized, that is, being a "fag," "sissy," or "lesbo" are severe put-downs. The put-downs are tolerated, nonetheless, as long as no one in the speaker's family is gay. An additional variable in whether an individual is homosexual involves whether (a) he was orally copulated (or had to perform fellatio), (b) he was anally penetrated, or (c) he anally penetrated someone else. A distorted belief system exists that suggests that the male who is acting in a sexually aggressive manner with another man is absolved from being classified as gay. A segment of the community believes that aggression somehow lessens the degree of homosexuality. Consequently, for the African American male client who has been sexually victimized as a child, there may be degrees of victimization that have received little attention either in the existing literature or in the intervention considerations of mental health professionals.

Disclosure and Reporting

The current literature (Courtois, 1988; Gelinas, 1988; Haugaard & Reppucci, 1988) related to underreporting of child sexual victimization frequently cites shame associated with sexual abuse, fear of not being believed, fear of being removed from the caretaker's home, and a belief by the victim that disclosing sexual victimization may lead to the dissolution of parents' marriage/relationship (in the case of parental incest) as generic considerations that may lead to suppressed disclosures by sexual child abuse victims. However, there is currently no published research that addresses the qualitative and quantitative differences between African Americans and European Americans around these substantive issues.

Pierce and Pierce (1984) found lower rates of rejection by African American mothers after disclosure, as compared to White mothers. They speculate that these lower rates may be due to one of two factors. First, African American mothers may be less fearful of the male perpetrators because many of these men did not reside in the home or were not the fathers of the children. Second, the African American children had closer relationships to their mothers resulting from a more supportive mother/child dyad.

Reporting of sexual abuse by African Americans is further complicated by the realization that a significant number of African Americans have experienced negative encounters with the police, criminal justice system, and/or social service agencies, which impedes the reporting of child sexual victimization. Notable segments of African American communities are less than enamored with social service providers based on their feelings of being made to wait extended periods of time for delivery of services. Moreover, service recipients also report being treated in a dehumanizing manner by social service workers. The feelings of distrust and dislike toward social service providers may be further complicated by the perception that the helping professionals are in some way aligned with an oppressor group.

It should also be recognized that, depending on socioeconomic status, many members of African American communities are unaware of existing services. Sources of mental health assistance are not generally well publicized in African American communities.

In the case of African American survivors of sexual child abuse, in addition to the issues discussed previously, prior negative experiences coupled with a misguided reluctance to identify an alleged sexual offender of children and subsequently turn the offender "over to the man" may develop in the community. This issue is particularly salient for the African American female survivor or mother of a child sexual abuse victim who may fear that filing criminal charges against an African American male is, or will be seen by others as, a betrayal of and lack of sensitivity for the African American male who suffers harsher legal consequences for criminal behavior in the United States. Feminist writers (E. C. White, 1985; Wilson, 1994) address this issue with great clarity and emotion in their guides for African American women experiencing physical and sexual abuse, respectively. Both agree that protecting African American males in this way serves to keep African American victims of abuse in abusive relationships and takes a toll on African American communities. Both seem to be saying that abuse is not an appropriate demonstration of African American manhood.

Stereotypes of African American sexuality may also affect the African American survivor's disclosure of sexual abuse. The African American survivor's acute awareness of these stereotypes may contribute to the fear of not being believed. In addition, the belief by outsiders that sexual abuse is rampant in the Black community often functions to discourage African American survivors from disclosing their sexual abuse for fear of contributing in some way to such negative and erroneous beliefs. Finally, African American victims of sexual abuse may also hesitate to disclose because of the cultural and religious belief that elders must be respected. Respect for adult perpetrators is then demonstrated by keeping silent about sexual victimization (Fontes, 1993b).

Effects of Sexual Abuse on African American Survivors

Studies that explore the qualitative and quantitative differences in the effects of sexual abuse on African Americans and White Americans have begun to emerge (Russell, 1986; Russell, Schurman, & Trocki, 1988; Wyatt, 1985; Wyatt & Mickey, 1988). Wyatt (1985) found no statistically significant differences in the prevalence of sexual abuse for African American and White American women, as did Russel (1986) in her study of incestuous abuse. Russell, Shurman, and Trocki (1988) found that African American women, as a result of incest, "reported more upset, greater long-term effects, and more negative life experiences" (p. 127) than White American women. Wyatt (1990) suggested that effects of sexual victimization may be compounded for African Americans by other *dimensions of victimization* as a result of racism.

In a further comparison of African American and White female victims of incest, Russell, Schurman, and Trocki (1988), in an attempt to explain the greater effects reported by African American women, found that African Americans were more likely to be abused at the *very severe level* in terms of sex acts; were more likely to have their abuse accompanied by force; had younger perpetrators; were older at the time of their first abusive experience; were more likely to be abused by uncles and less likely to be abused by grandfathers, first cousins, and female perpetrators; and had equal rates of abuse by fathers. There were several hypotheses made regarding the very severe level of abuse perpetrated against African American women in the study. First, the sample was disproportionately poor, and the literature has shown an association between social class and violence. Second, incest by nonblood relatives tends to be more severe, and nonblood relatives are more likely to use force. Third, the older age of the African American sexual abuse victim may account for the increased use of force. Finally, younger perpetrators commit more severe acts of abuse.

Familiarity With Available Services

The existing literature suggests that African Americans do not avail themselves fully of mental health services (Neighbors, 1990; Sussman, Robins, &

Earl, 1987) and have traditionally sought help through informal networks (Martin & Martin, 1985). Veroff, Douvan, and Kulka (1981) determined that African Americans depend on prayer, personal spirituality, and religious individuals (i.e., ministers) to a greater extent than do European Americans. The reliance on ministers means that ministers have a responsibility to obtain training in specific issues related to child sexual victimization, given that seminary study is generally inadequate (Gallagher & Dodds, 1985). Family physicians or family and friends (Neighbors & Taylor, 1985) are also resources for help. The reluctance to turn to mental health and social service professionals stems from a lack of trust in services that in the past were offered almost always by Whites, a belief that one does not air dirty laundry in public, and a lack of such services in the African American community.

Consequently, African Americans do not use mental health services at rates comparable to European Americans. Moreover, African Americans seeking public mental health services are receiving inadequate services, evidenced by a dropout rate of 50% after one session (D. Sue & Sue, 1990). However, African Americans, particularly in urban areas, are increasingly turning to mental health services for help (D. Sue & Sue, 1990), and more than 14% of African Americans will seek mental health services during a crisis (Neighbors & Taylor, 1985).

It should also be recognized that in some segments of African American communities, there is a negative connotation associated with seeking mental health services. Males, for example, are adamant about "not letting someone get inside their heads." In addition, seeking mental health services is seen as a sign of weakness. An individual who seeks counseling is characterized as "not having his or her stuff together" or as "crazy."

Treatment

A systematic assessment of the utilization patterns of mental health services by African Americans should include a consideration of the level of assimilation into European American culture and the socioeconomic status of the client. It can be inferred that the more the client or the client's parents endorse European American cultural values in conjunction with higher socioeconomic status, the greater the probability that the individual will seek treatment.

Counselors, psychologists, social workers, and other professionals have a responsibility to be culturally sensitive to African American clients who have been abused sexually (Bowman, 1992). Courtois (1988) expressed the realization that being culturally sensitive serves the dual purposes of facilitating "trust building between the therapist and client while allowing the client to make an informed decision about whether to continue in treatment with the therapist or to seek a referral to someone who already possesses knowledge of the culture" (p. 277). Courtois's observations underscore the ethical responsibility to attain multicultural competence when working with clients culturally dissimilar from oneself.

CASE HISTORIES

Ellen

Ellen was an 8-year-old African American girl who had been severely sexually abused by a neighbor 2 years earlier. She was an only child who lived with her mother. She initially presented with symptoms of severe posttraumatic stress disorder. Because Ellen was unable to give a consistent account of her abuse, the offender was not indicted.

Ellen continually saw the offender in the neighborhood when she went out to play. She expressed fear of retaliation because the offender had threatened to kill her if she disclosed. Her mother was encouraged to move, but even with the resources provided by Ellen's therapist, she never managed to do so, complaining of financial hardship. Her financial difficulties were real, but it appeared that the refusal to move was due primarily to the mother's poor bond with this child, which did not allow her to empathize sufficiently with Ellen's need to be protected from repeated contacts with the offender.

As the treatment progressed, Ellen's condition deteriorated. She was subsequently placed in residential care, where she disclosed severe emotional maltreatment by her mother. The abuse by her mother was reported to protective services. Mother agreed to continue in treatment and retained legal custody. In placement, Ellen began to show signs of improvement, and home visits were recommended.

Ellen routinely returned from visits in a very agitated and fragmented state. After much exploration, she reported that the visits were frightening because she would see the man who had sexually abused her, and it seemed to her that he was staring at her threateningly when her mother was not looking. The treatment team agreed that home visits should be discontinued until Ellen's mother was able to move. An appointment was scheduled for her to meet with Ellen's therapist and the unit social worker to discuss the recommendation.

Ellen's mother arrived for the session accompanied by her minister and requested that he be permitted to be present in the session. It seemed clear that she anticipated needing support during the session. The social worker, a White female, was somewhat taken by surprise by this request, and felt it would not be appropriate to include the minister. She asked Ellen's therapist, an African American female, for her opinion. Ellen's therapist thought it might be an excellent idea. She knew the minister was intimately involved in the life of this family, often functioned as extended family to the mother and Ellen, and held great influence over the mother. Therefore, she felt it would be important for the minister to understand the team's decision.

To both the mother and the social worker's surprise, the minister completely supported the team's decision, was upset with the mother's procrastination, and offered the mother concrete support. In less than 2 months, the mother moved, using her own resources, and Ellen was able to resume her home visits.

This case illustrates two important points. First, as stated above, the church plays an important role in the lives of many African Americans and can be used as a resource when working with African American families. Ellen's minister was a respected authority figure in the life of this family. His opinions were highly valued and had, in the past, influenced the mother's decisions regarding Ellen. In fact, it was the minister who had initially expressed suspicion and concern that Ellen might have been abused sexually. If Ellen's therapist had considered the minister's potential influence sooner and had included him in the treatment during its initial stages, Ellen might have been spared additional trauma.

The second point illustrated in this case is that flexibility and openness are crucial when working in a cross-cultural context. The White social worker's willingness to consult with Ellen's African American therapist was crucial in creating a context where the minister was invited to participate. Had his participation been denied, due to rigidity or lack of cultural competence, most likely the mother would have felt angry and vulnerable and, consequently, would not have been as open to the team's recommendation. In addition, Ellen would not have benefited from the minister's influence on her mother.

Cara

Cara (not her real name) was a 38-year-old divorced African American mother who had two daughters, ages 10 and 12. She was a college graduate who was working as a registered nurse. Cara entered counseling after her two daughters disclosed to her that they had been sexually victimized by Cara's then-boyfriend for 3 years (from the ages of 7 to 10 and 9 to 12, respectively). Immediately after the disclosure, Cara evicted the alleged sex offender from her home and threatened to kill him if she ever saw him again. Cara's expressed primary concern was for her daughters. Her apprehension was communicated in the context of getting her children to a point where they could "just be okay and be able to get on with their lives." She articulated no problem with having her children in counseling "if it would help them get better."

Cara was extremely reluctant to prosecute the alleged child molester, although she in no way doubted the veracity of her daughters' allegations. During subsequent counseling sessions, Cara disclosed that she had been sexually victimized by her uncle for 7 years, from the time she was 9 until she was 16 years of age. Cara had received no counseling.

Cara stated that she "had" to see her uncle every year at the family Christmas dinner. She reported feeling depressed for weeks after the dinners. She also reported feeling extremely tense during the family gatherings because she maintained a sense of hypervigilance to ensure that her daughters would not be in a compromising situation with her uncle. There was also the attendant pressure of making up excuses for why she did not like her daughters interacting with the uncle when he "had not done anything to them." Cara expressed feeling a great deal of hostility toward members of her nuclear family because the emphasis was continually on her daughters, and no one was able to make the connection that "just maybe" something had happened to her.

Cara initially entered counseling accepting full responsibility for her daughters' victimization. She was clinically depressed and blamed herself for her inability to protect her children and "not being there for them," and "being a poor judge of men." Cara was adamant about not blaming her ex-boyfriend for victimizing her children because "Black men have a difficult enough time in society" without getting placed in jail.

Cara continued in individual counseling and after 1 month was also referred for both family and group counseling. Family counseling was initiated so that any feeling that negatively affected the relationship between Cara and her children could be addressed (e.g., betrayal and/or abandonment).

Group counseling afforded Cara an opportunity to interact with other women who had similar sexually abusive experiences and feelings, in addition to women who were at advanced stages of recovery. Group therapy represented a safe, nurturing environment in which Cara was able to address her concerns and feelings honestly.

An additional benefit of Cara being placed in group therapy was realized when she was able to discuss and confront openly the racial aspects of her sexual victimization in a therapeutic environment. During group counseling, Cara was able to address her conflicted feelings of wanting to "protect" her ex-boyfriend, juxtaposed with the rage she felt toward him for victimizing her daughters. Eventually, Cara pressed charges against her ex-boyfriend, who was convicted for sexually victimizing a minor child.

Calvin

Calvin (not his real name) was a 24-year-old African American college student. He presented in counseling after listening to a guest lecturer talk about incest in one of his classes. Calvin had "been having problems for a while." He reported being sexually victimized by his grandfather from the time he was 5 until he was 17 years of age. Calvin considered himself gay, but he expressed a desire to "no longer act out." He also was concerned that his history of being sexually victimized led to his sexual attraction to other males.

The victimization stopped when his older brother caught the grandfather abusing Calvin. Calvin made his brother promise to never tell their parents. Calvin's inability to disclose the sexual abuse to anyone except his minister was based on a fear of "tearing the family apart" or not being believed because the abuser was his mother's father. Calvin related during a session that he had told his minister of the abuse about 3 weeks after his brother discovered the abusive situation. Calvin vividly reported remembering that when he had asked his minister why he was abused and how he could possibly get over it, the minister replied, "God never puts more on us than we can bear." The minister was undoubtedly attempting to console Calvin, but the statement made him feel that he was somehow unworthy or weak for not being able to simply "get on with his life."

Calvin said he was also afraid that he would be taken away from his parents. He further recounted that it was a strongly held belief in his family that you did not take familial situations outside the family, especially if it would cause the family or a member of the family to face "the system."

Calvin's concerns related to his sexual victimization as a child were further complicated by an additional crucial concern. Calvin reported that since he was 5 years of age, he felt emotionally abandoned by his father. He reported longing to be held and consoled by his father as a child, yet his father remained emotionally distant. In some instances, his father had ridiculed him for expressing a need to be close.

When Calvin initially entered therapy, he was haunted by the prospect that he was somehow responsible for his grandfather sexually victimizing him. He maintained that had he not been so emotionally needy, he would have not have allowed the abuse to occur. (Please note the extent to which Calvin assumed responsibility for his victimization, although he was only 5 years old when he was first abused.) Calvin continually attempted to identify the specific behaviors or needs that he had manifested that might have facilitated his victimization. An important part of Calvin's recovery was teaching him to relieve himself of blame for the abuse and assign responsibility to his grandfather.

Calvin also expressed concern that his adult relationships with partners had invariably deteriorated to some form of emotional abuse. Calvin expressed particular anguish about his seeming need to make his partner submit to him sexually. During counseling, it was necessary to clarify what was meant by "having his partners submit to him" and to determine that Calvin was not victimizing children or sexually molesting adults. Processing his history of sexual abuse helped Calvin reach a psychological and emotional perspective from which he became increasingly comfortable with his self-reported sexual orientation.

Discussion

The clients in the above cases seemingly held cultural values that negatively affected their ability to recover emotionally and psychologically from sexual abuse. Cara incorrectly felt that she had a responsibility to "protect" the individual who had victimized her daughters, based on the offender's shared ethnic and cultural similarity, as well as a belief that, due to the racism experienced by African American males in American society, she should not subject her children's victimizer to the criminal justice system.

Calvin's attainment of psychological wellness was hampered in large measure by a belief that he should not disclose family secrets. He had sought the intervention of an identified spiritual person in the community (in this case his pastor, as is frequently the custom in African American communities) without also seeking a mental health professional. In addition, each client struggled with generic issues frequently reported by survivors of child sexual victimization, including self-blame, a sense of being betrayed by the offender, shame, and low self-esteem.

During the course of counseling, it was crucial to establish a safe therapeutic environment for the clients where they were able to discuss their
feelings and concerns. When engaging these clients in therapy, it was also
important to address their cognitions related to causing distress to sexual
perpetrators in the African American community. Specifically, the clients were
encouraged to examine their beliefs that disclosing their childhood sexual
victimization would in some way betray African Americans. Clearly, there
was a need to hold the offender accountable and for the clients to be accountable to themselves and other potential victims.

A central thematic consideration in addressing child sexual victimization
with African American clients is the issue of responsibility and victim self-
blame. It is not unusual for African American clients to blame themselves for
the victimization, in addition to feeling an unfounded need to shield the
offender from experiencing the consequences of his or her actions. Perhaps
the multiple layers of victimization experienced by African American survivors of sexual child abuse contribute to this self-blame.

African American Offenders

Many insightful texts currently exist related to intervention with adolescents and adults who sexually victimize children (Becker, 1990; Knopp, 1982,
1984; Maletzky, 1991; O'Connell, Leberg, & Donaldson, 1990). However,
the extent to which the articulated interventions of the writers lack any
meaningful discussion of cultural considerations represents a critical void that
must be filled by sound theory, research, and clinical practice.

For example, mental health professionals would be well advised to discern
the extent to which offenders abuse African American children based on a
belief that because these children are devalued in society, offenders will not
be prosecuted for sexual activity with them. It may also prove fruitful for
mental health professionals to investigate the extent to which psychosocial
and economic stressors are contributing factors in sexual offense behavior.

In a Memphis, Tennessee, program, a central part of the intake process
includes interviews with the offender designed to assess the extent to which
the offender devalues African American children. Devaluation of the child is
viewed as a factor contributing to the perpetrator's abusive behavior. In
addition to identifying the offender's faulty cognitions that permitted him or
her to sexually abuse a child, the program also focuses on interrupting the

offender's abuse cycle and replacing erroneous sexual knowledge with precise sexual information.

The program is unique in its Africentric perspective. Offenders are guided through the process of examining the political, psychological, and sociological ramifications of their abusive behavior on the community. This is accomplished by assisting the offender in organizing a cosmology, epistemology, axiology, ontology, and philosophy in a way that enhances the psychological and spiritual well-being of the individual and the community.

The program has not been in place long enough to generate empirical data on its efficacy. Thus far, however, offenders have self-reported (during program exit interviews and 30- and 90-day follow-ups) a sense of self and community that is in keeping with an Africentric perspective. We recognize that offenders often wantonly attempt to manipulate the therapist; consequently, conclusions cannot be drawn until we have obtained empirical verification of the offenders' self-reports.

Prevention

The number of primary prevention sexual child abuse programs that have been conclusively proven effective in general (Plummer, 1984; Tharinger et al., 1988) and effective in African American communities in particular is exceedingly sparse. These programs are rare in African American communities. Historically Black colleges have taken initiatives in this area. Since 1990, Spelman College has supported a collegewide program on child abuse and neglect (Booth, 1993). It is readily apparent that prevention methodologies that represent reasoned, thoughtful, well-researched responses to child sexual victimization should be formulated in African American communities (see Holton, 1993).

For example, increased comprehensive community awareness programs should be considered. These programs can be school-based, church-based, and/or community agency-based. An example of such a program is sponsored by a church in Memphis, Tennessee. The program furnishes children, adolescents, and their caretakers with developmentally appropriate information related to child sexual victimization. Children and adolescents are furnished information and opportunities to develop and internalize skills that will prove beneficial in combating child sexual victimization.

The facet of the program that most strongly recommends its continuation is the emphasis on educating caretakers and parents. Adults enrolled in the program are given an opportunity to discuss possible behavioral indicators of child sexual victimization with mental health professionals who have expertise in counseling sexually victimized children. Moreover, the program also includes a component that addresses appropriate interactions between adults and children.

It is sincerely hoped that additional effective prevention programs exist in African American communities throughout the United States. Unfortunately, these programs have not yet gained sufficient notoriety to be included in this chapter.

It is also crucial that the media (news, television, radio, publications, and popular music) get involved. The reader should recognize that prevention programs similar to those mentioned above may initially cause an increase in the number of disclosures of reported cases of child sexual victimization. The anticipated number of increased disclosures would necessitate that identified victims receive prompt, competent services from mental health professionals and adjunct services.

A great deal more needs to be done if the incidence and prevalence of child sexual victimization in African American communities is to be reduced. The very credibility of the therapeutic intervention used with individuals who sexually abuse children is at stake. Also, society and the victims of sexual child abuse clearly deserve more from helping professionals than we are currently furnishing.

Conclusion

This chapter has provided an overview of child sexual victimization as it pertains to African American clients. Although African Americans respond to sexual abuse in many of the same ways that White clients respond, there are aspects of the experience that are organized differently because of the cultural context. There are cultural factors that both compound the effects of sexual victimization for African Americans and increase vulnerability. However, it is apparent that there are also many aspects of the African American culture that decrease the risk of sexual victimization and enhance the process of recovery. Although sexual abuse is no more prevalent among African Americans than among Whites, it is a phenomenon that must be acknowledged and responded to in a responsible fashion by both the African American community and the society at large.

Puerto Ricans and Sexual Child Abuse

LILLIAN COMAS-DÍAZ

Discrimination and oppression rob individuals of their voices. As a specific type of oppression, sexual abuse represents a Pandora's box for many Puerto Ricans. The threats, cultural taboos, and legal realities tend to silence the voice of the sexually abused client. For some, traditional cultural values inhibit disclosure and recovery.

The Puerto Rican historical and sociopolitical context adds another dimension to the problem of sexual abuse among this ethnic minority group. The past and contemporary colonial condition facilitates the internalization of oppression. Such internalization may lead to revictimization through sexual abuse. The victim mentality characteristic of the colonized condition further cements the oppression of sexually abused clients. As with other types of victimization, sexual abuse often engenders a cycle of abuse.

This chapter discusses sexual abuse among Puerto Ricans. The sociopolitical context and the psychology of colonization provide a frame of reference for the internalization of oppression and victimization through sexual abuse. Puerto Rican ethnocultural values are discussed, highlighting their implications for sexual abuse. Culturally sensitive and gender-informed interventions for working with Puerto Rican victims of sexual abuse are discussed, and

Author's Note:

The author gratefully acknowledges Lisa Fontes's affirming and nurturing editorial contributions to this chapter.

31

clinical material aids in the illustration of these issues. Identifying clinical data are disguised to protect confidentiality.

Puerto Ricans as Ethnic Minorities

Most Puerto Ricans in the continental United States are members of a low-income ethnic group that originates from a country bearing colonial ties to the United States. The island of Borinquén became Puerto Rico, a colony of Spain, in 1493. In 1898, it became a colony of the United States. Puerto Ricans were granted U.S. citizenship in 1917, and at the same time, military service became obligatory for all eligible males. In 1952, Puerto Rico became a commonwealth. Despite this development, political power remains with the U.S. government.

The question of Puerto Rico's uncertain political status—statehood, independence, or commonwealth—reinforces a pervasive national identity crisis. In the 1993 referendum debating the political status of the island, Puerto Ricans voted to keep the commonwealth, mainly for economic reasons. This type of decision-making process perpetuates Puerto Rico's colonial relationship with the United States. Puerto Rico's political status has been considered by the United Nations's Commission on Decolonization on several occasions (Babín, 1973). The island is still considered a classical example of colonialism and imperialism. G. Lewis (1974) has asserted that the North American military occupation, juridical control, and economic exploitation result in a process of deculturation that threatens Puerto Ricans with ethnocide.

As a nation, Puerto Rico has always borne a colonial status. The economic and political oppression has suppressed self-determination. Such a history of colonialism has denied Puerto Ricans their right to control their own economic and political affairs. The colonial government advertises migration to the continental United States as a flexible means of earning a living. Thus those who cannot find work on the island often migrate, resulting in a significant number of Puerto Ricans in the continental United States with limited education and skills.

A growing number of educated Puerto Ricans have been migrating to the United States, creating a brain drain (Turner, cited in Facundo, 1991). Many of the Puerto Ricans with educational and professional skills migrate in search of employment, specialized education, or career advancement. As an illustration, human services professionals from the island are being recruited by agencies serving Puerto Ricans in the continental United States (Facundo, 1991). In addition, Puerto Ricans with professional status also migrate for reasons of politics, specialized health care, or an escape from the island's problems of drugs and crime (Rohter, 1994).

Regardless of socioeconomic status, most Puerto Ricans in the continental United States become an ethnic minority group of color. They are confronted with ethnic and racial prejudice, rejection, discrimination, unemployment or underemployment, and alienation. These types of oppression often lead to feelings of helplessness. Puerto Ricans are readily stereotyped by North Americans, who tend to perceive them as poor, unemployed, politically weak (Betancourt, 1974), colonized, inferior, and as people of color.

Many Puerto Ricans in the continental United States maintain close contact with island Puerto Rican communities through migration and reverse migration. The constant flow between Puerto Ricans on the island and the Ricans (second- and third-generation Puerto Ricans on the mainland) yields a unique Puerto Rican transculturation involving an adaptive and readaptive process (Comas-Díaz, 1987). Transculturation differs from acculturation in that it refers to a process whereby a distinct culture emerges from a conflict in opposing cultural values (De Granda, 1968). Thus transculturation embodies the dynamic, evolving, and dialectical nature of the Puerto Rican culture.

The Psychology of Colonization

The Impact of Colonization on Puerto Ricans

Colonization is a predominant component in the lives of Puerto Ricans. The colonized experience victimization, depersonalization, self-denial, assimilation, strong ambivalence, and a fundamental need for change (Memmi, 1965). For Puerto Ricans, colonialism creates an objective reality and an underlying subjective experience of powerlessness. It has created a condition of profound helplessness causing many Puerto Ricans to perceive themselves as inadequate and ineffective (G. Lewis, 1974). The legacy of colonialism results in feelings of alienation, frustration, and poor self-esteem. Consequently, effective interventions require an understanding of the pervasive impact of colonization on Puerto Ricans.

The colonizer-colonized dynamics *color* the relationship between Norteamericanos and Puerto Ricans, resulting in the creation of a racial collective unconsciousness. Colonized countries are not only exploited and victimized for the benefit of the colonial power but also serve as the quintessential scapegoats. For instance, many people in the United States believe that Puerto Rico represents an economic burden for the United States, without acknowledging the financial exploitation of the island. Social analyses of Puerto Ricans' realities tend to blame the victim. The ethnic and racial visibility of Puerto Ricans in the continental United States facilitates their becoming a target for negative projections and scapegoatism.

The inferior and negative designations of Puerto Ricans as colonized persons appear immutable in the racial collective unconscious of many North Americans. Colonized individuals are often considered savages, slaves, and conquered enemies (Comas-Díaz, 1994). As a result of colonization, Puerto Ricans are often denied their individuality and stripped of their humanity. The colonized condition involves a systematic negation of the colonized, resulting in pervasive identity conflicts for the person of color (Fanon, 1967).

Colonization generates an identity crisis that involves a negative self-definition and low self-esteem for Puerto Ricans (Bird, 1982). This identity crisis further manifests in many Puerto Ricans' inability to identify themselves as Puerto Ricans, Ricans, Americans, Latin Americans, Caribbeans, all of the above, or something else. Puerto Ricans struggle with contemporary colonization (in Puerto Rico) or reside in the colonial nation (United States)—internalizing the colonization experience.

Colonization and Sexual Abuse

Colonization bears gendered effects. Historically, conquered males have been killed, whereas conquered females have been raped, enslaved, and sexually subjugated. The contemporary versions of these dynamics often follow these gender lines: Puerto Rican males frequently struggle with unemployment and underemployment, obliteration due to substance abuse, and active self-destruction, whereas women suffer from sexual-racial objectification and subjugation.

The dynamics of colonization are relevant to the problem of sexual abuse among Puerto Ricans. In discussing domestic abuse among Puerto Rican families, Facundo (1991) asserts that unemployment, exploitation, and discrimination in the North American society may lead Puertorriqueños to develop aggressive survival skills, blurring the boundaries between the external environment and their families. Many Puerto Rican males take their frustrations out on females because they cannot have impact elsewhere (Steiner, 1974). Similarly, sexual oppression and victimization may have been internalized as an aspect of colonization and simultaneously as an identification with its negative effects. In other words, sexual abuse may represent a familiar behavior within the polarities of power and powerlessness, and domination and subjugation. Likewise, the sexual offender may be identifying with the aggressor. Moreover, sexual abuse can be seen as a resistant act—a counter-hegemonic and self-defeating stance taken by members of colonized and oppressed groups. This strategy of resistance fails as an attempt to affirm autonomy and self-determination and results in replication of the colonial gendered exploitation. These processes add complexity to the problem of sexual abuse among Puerto Ricans.

Traditional Ethnocultural Values, Sexuality, and Sexual Abuse

For Puerto Ricans, as with any other ethnic group, the ethnocultural context is crucial for framing behaviors and for delivering effective services. Sexuality and the problem of sexual abuse are embedded in an ethnocultural context (Fontes, 1993a, 1993b). Thus, understanding Puerto Rican cultural values, family dynamics, and beliefs systems, as well as their sociopolitical context, tends to increase providers' effectiveness.

Familismo: *Subordination of the Individual for the Family*

In traditional Puerto Rican families, members beyond the nuclear unit are considered integral to the concept of family (García-Preto, 1982). Many family functions, such as emotional support, financial assistance, problem solving, and child rearing, are shared by members of the extended family. This cultural norm is reinforced by the value of *familismo* (familism), or the tendency to extend kinship relationships beyond the nuclear family boundaries. Due to migration and reverse migration, many Puerto Ricans who do not have their relatives nearby often informally adopt friends as relatives through the system of *compadrazgo* (godparents).

Familism stresses family loyalty by emphasizing interdependence over independence, affiliation over confrontation, and cooperation over competition (Ramos-McKay, Comas-Díaz, & Rivera, 1988). Puerto Rican familism fosters the development of conformity, dependency, and family loyalty (Canino & Canino, 1982; Nieves-Falcón, 1972). The emphasis is on the family rather than on the individual, with a deep sense of family commitment, obligation, and responsibility (García-Preto, 1982). This means that the needs of the individual are subordinated to the needs of the family. The conscious and unconscious reactions toward sexual abuse usually are geared toward maintaining the family's homeostasis. The abuser's threats to the victim that disclosure will disrupt the family's well-being are cemented by the value of familism. Consequently, this cultural value needs to be examined carefully when delivering services to Puerto Rican victims of sexual abuse. Consider the following vignette:

> Rosa, a 40-year-old married woman, was in therapy for an eating disorder. After a year in treatment, she told her clinician that when she was 6 years old, she was sexually molested by a male family friend. The molestation involved the man's touching Rosa's genitals repeatedly over a period of 6 months. Rosa stated that she decided not to tell her mother because the man was her father's boss and *compadre*, and she was afraid of having her father lose his job due to her disclosure.

Family Dynamics: Traditions and Paradoxes

The traditional Puerto Rican family appears to be patriarchal, with an overt authoritarian father and a more submissive mother (Garcia-Preto, 1982). Although Puertorriqueñas are perceived as weak, helpless, and in need of protection (Comas-Díaz & Duncan, 1985), they are expected to be in charge of domestic life. Paradoxically, Puertorriqueñas are expected to obtain power and strength in their overtly "weak" and subordinate position. According to Espin (1986), the Latina enjoys more power at home than her White counterpart.

Traditional male-female dynamics are paradoxical. Indeed, the superficial appearance of the power distribution between Puerto Rican males and females can be deceiving. In a study of sex roles among Puerto Ricans in the United States, Canino (1982) found that on the surface, both husband and wife espoused traditional attitudes. However, when Puerto Rican couples were interviewed more extensively and were observed during actual decision making, most of them shared the decision-making process. Like other Latino families, some Puerto Rican families have an egalitarian power structure, some families have husbands who are domineering, and others have husbands who are submissive and depend on their wives to make major decisions (Falicov, 1982).

Traditional sex roles are undergoing change among Puerto Ricans, particularly for those residing in the United States. Cultural transition provides individuals with plasticity in their gender roles, which allows change. Traditional Puerto Rican sex roles tend not to be reinforced by the mainstream North American culture. For instance, Torres-Matrullo (1976) found that the traditional Puerto Rican family dynamics and gender roles were changing with increased exposure to the mainstream Anglo society. Specifically, she found that whereas the traditional concepts of manhood and womanhood appeared to be changing, the sacredness of motherhood and the importance of children appeared to remain unchanged with increased exposure to the mainstream North American society.

Cultural transition itself often encourages a gender role reversal for many low-income Puerto Rican migrants because it is often easier for the women to be employed or to obtain financial support in the United States (Comas-Díaz, 1982). For example, the mother may become the functional figure in the household, financially aided by welfare, or she may find work in a textile factory, whereas the father becomes peripheral (Colon, 1980). This situation often creates marital and family problems. Notwithstanding the family disruption, role reversal can be used therapeutically to challenge rigid, traditional, dysfunctional sex roles (Comas-Díaz, 1989).

Child Rearing: Patterns and Adaptations

Children are expected within the Puerto Rican family. When a couple gets married, people openly ask them when they are going to have children. Marriages without children are usually seen as an anomaly. If the couple experiences fertility problems, others pity them and give unsolicited advice. Women who are infertile are pejoratively called *machorras* (malelike). A man's maleness is questioned openly if he does not father children, particularly sons. A man who fathers only daughters is pejoratively called *chanchletero* (a man who wears slippers; slippers are considered less valuable than shoes). Those couples who decide to remain childless often encounter anger, resentment, and even ostracism. Consequently, childless couples often hide their decision from family and friends, pretending that they are infertile.

Children are an integral part of the Puerto Rican ethos. Contrary to many White, Anglo-Saxon, Protestant (WASP), middle-class populations, Puerto

Rican children are welcome at social events, including family parties, visits to friends, restaurants, trips, and other activities. Children's presence in daily lives is acknowledged even by strangers. Frequently, people make comments to unknown children and to their parents about the child's beauty and good behavior (*Qué niño lindo y obediente!* What a pretty and obedient child!). Because every adult is a potential authority figure for a child, this scenario complicates Puerto Rican children's ability to protect themselves against sexual abuse.

Consistent with the Puerto Rican tradition, Puertorriqueñas are culturally assigned the role of child rearing. Mothers, grandmothers, *comadres,* and females in general are expected to be involved in child rearing. Motherhood is seen as sacred in Puerto Rican culture. Mothers are also held responsible for the behavior of their offspring. Consider the layers of shame for a mother when her child asserts that he or she has been molested by a sibling.

Given that females are traditionally considered in need of protection, if a daughter is a victim of sexual abuse, the mother is perceived as being responsible for the misfortune:

Juana, 16, was raped on her way home from school. Inés, her mother, responded to the rape in the following manner: *Your father is going to hold me responsible for this. Yo no sé qué voy a hacer.* (I don't know what I am going to do.) Juana consoled her mother by saying that she was fine and that Papi did not have to find out because she would not report the assault.

Within traditional Puerto Rican child-rearing patterns, children are not expected to think about adult issues. Adults can say whatever they want in front of children without expecting them to understand or comment. To demonstrate respect, children should not question authority figures. Moreover, they are expected to be seen but not heard. Indeed, a Puerto Rican saying indicates that children talk when the hens pee (*Los niños hablan cuando las gallinas mean*), which means that they should be silent. Clearly, this type of child-rearing norm further hinders disclosures of sexual abuse (Fontes, 1993b).

Obedience and good behavior are expected from children, particularly in front of adults. People usually blame mothers and shame fathers for the unruly behavior of their children. Likewise, children are given mixed messages about aggression. On one hand, they are taught not to express their anger and aggression directly. On the other hand, males are expected to be machos and defend themselves. These mixed messages often result in the development of passive-aggressive and acting-out behaviors. Within this context, sexual abuse can be interpreted as a dysfunctional acting-out behavior.

The expression of anger is a major problem for Puerto Ricans and is related to the colonial situation. *El puertoriqueño dócil* (The docile Puerto Rican) is both a paradoxical literary icon (Marqués, 1972) and an unrealistic ideal of behavior. Zavala-Martinez (1981) asserts that Puerto Ricans' learned suppression of anger is an adaptive, life-preserving response when the authority to be confronted holds greater power. The learned suppression of anger is further reinforced when Puerto Ricans interact with the more powerful North American individuals and institutions.

In discussing the concept of the Puerto Rican syndrome, or *ataque de nervios* (an episode involving a hysterical release of energy, more common in women), Rothenberg (1964) identifies the long history of colonization as a contributing factor to Puerto Ricans' problem in expressing anger. He postulates that the ataque de nervios represents an adaptation to colonization through the repression and suppression of aggressive and assertive impulses.

Respeto: *Cultural Reaction to Authority*

A cultural value central to Puerto Ricans' sexuality and to the problem of sexual abuse is *respeto* (respect). Respeto governs all positive, reciprocal, interpersonal relationships, dictating the appropriate deferential behavior toward others on the basis of age, socioeconomic position, sex, and authority status. For instance, children are supposed to respect their parents and older siblings, youngers their elders, wives their husbands, students their teachers, and so on.

Respeto is so pervasive in the fabric of the family that an old Puerto Rican saying states that children less than 10 years old should fear their parents; from 10 to 20 years of age, they should respect their parents; and when they are over 20 years of age, they should love their parents (Ramos-McKay et al., 1988). The history of oppression that Puerto Ricans experience both collectively and individually often results in an oversensitivity toward lack of respect.

Respeto may play a central role in the sexual abuse of Puerto Rican children. A child may become the victim of sexual abuse by someone deserving respect. Similarly, a sexually abused child may fear breaking the silence due to respect for the abuser and fear of the consequences of breaking a cultural taboo.

Gender Roles and Sexuality: Machismo and Marianism

In traditional Puerto Rican culture, gender roles tend to be rigidly demarcated. Boys and girls are taught two very different codes of sexual behavior (Nieves-Falcón, 1972). Males are expected to be strong, authoritarian, independent, brave, and in search of sexual conquests. Females are expected to be sentimental, gentle, intuitive, fragile, submissive, and dependent. This rigid demarcation of sex roles encourages a double moral standard for the sexes, exemplified in the *machismo/marianismo* paradigm. Although contemporary gender roles among Puerto Ricans are diverse and fluid, the machismo/marianismo paradigm bears profound implications for sexuality and sexual abuse.

Sexuality is not discussed openly, particularly in cross-gender situations. However, sexuality can be discussed covertly, as illustrated in the predominance of sexual topics in gossip. If sexual matters need to be discussed directly, males prefer other males for discussion and females prefer other females. When confronted with sexual abuse, individuals and families may regress and reidentify with traditional gender roles.

Machismo

Machismo literally means maleness or virility, but culturally it means that the man is the provider and is responsible for the welfare, honor, dignity, and protection of the family. It may be more prevalent among lower socioeconomic classes (Kinzer, 1973), but it influences behavior in all socioeconomic strata of the society (Giraldo, 1972). For the Puerto Rican male, machismo entails a combination of virtue, courage, and fearlessness (Abad, Ramos, & Boyce, 1974). In its extreme form, machismo is manifested through physical dominance of women and excessive alcohol consumption (Giraldo, 1972). Furthermore, machismo dictates that the Hispanic male must constantly signal his sexual availability; seductive behavior is mandatory regardless of marital status (Sluzki, 1982).

Seductive sexual behavior is expected from the Puerto Rican macho when interacting with females who are not members of his extended family (García-Preto, 1982). This component of machismo can lead to problems of sexual harassment and even to sexual abuse under the guise of gender role and cultural expectations. Paradoxically, the macho must protect his female relatives from the sexual advances of other men while making as many sexual conquests as possible himself.

Confronting sexual abuse in his family is a major threat to a Puerto Rican macho. Many Latino families react to rape with grave insult and suffering (Ramos, cited in Espin, 1984). Acting under the value of respect, macho relatives of a female victim are expected to engage in retribution against the perpetrator—to defend the victim's, and thus the family's, honor.

Marianismo and Hembrismo

The counterpart of machismo for women is *marianismo,* a concept based on the Catholic worship of the Mother Mary, who is seen as both a virgin and a Madonna. Marianismo predicates that women are spiritually superior to men and therefore capable of enduring all suffering inflicted by men (Stevens, 1973). Accordingly, unmarried women are expected to be chaste and virginal and not to demonstrate interest in sex once they are married. When they become mothers, Hispanic women attain the status of Madonnas and are expected to sacrifice for their children and husbands. In noting the high incidence of somatic complaints among low-income Hispanic women in psychotherapy, Espin (1985) suggests that these complaints may well be a reaction to the self-sacrifice dictum, especially because somatization is a culturally accepted mode of expressing needs and anxieties.

The *marianista* code often rewards women who adhere to it (Stevens, 1973). Because motherhood is sacred, women who bear children often enjoy a certain degree of power despite their outward submissiveness. Conversely, women who do not conform to the code risk social censorship. As a consequence, a dichotomous classification of women is reinforced (i.e., the Madonna/whore complex). Some Puerto Rican females may present in therapy struggling with issues of sexuality based on these contradictory connotations concerning sexual behavior.

Another sex role characteristic of some Puerto Rican women is *hembrismo,* which literally means femaleness. Hembrismo is a natural reaction to marianismo and shares common elements with the women's movement in the areas of social and political goals (Gomez, 1982).

Hembrismo connotes strength, perseverance, flexibility, and an ability to survive. However, it can also translate into the Puertorriqueña's attempt to fulfill her multiple role expectations as a mother, wife, worker, daughter, and member of the community. This situation can generate stress and emotional problems for the woman behaving in a *hembrista* fashion. The very strategy that gave hembrista women strength in the past can become a barrier to flexibility and problem solving (Zavala-Martinez, 1988). Likewise, many Puerto Rican women may present in treatment with marianista behavior at home and hembrista behavior at work. Indeed, research appears to support this clinical observation. In studying Latinas with professional status, Amaro, Russo, and Johnson (1987) found that Puertorriqueñas who had Puerto Rican male partners were more likely to experience psychological distress while balancing work and gender roles than were their Mexican American and Cuban counterparts.

Gendered Patterns of Sexual Abuse

Machismo and marianismo constitute a system in which one gender role reinforces the other. Machismo can be perceived as men's effort to compensate for their overpresent and suffering mothers, as well as to identify with their psychologically absent fathers (Aramoni, 1982). Machismo can also be seen as a Puerto Rican male's attempt to assert himself in the midst of powerlessness due to colonialism and membership in an ethnic minority group. Indeed, many Puerto Rican females support machismo as a resistance to the sociopolitical emasculation of the Puerto Rican male (Comas-Díaz, 1987).

The machismo and marianismo roles provide a frame of reference for contextualizing sexual abuse among Puerto Ricans. For instance, marianismo dichotomizes women. The female dichotomy of Madonna and whore is highly relevant because sexual abuse is often perceived through this cultural lens. Culturally, the female victim of sexual abuse becomes a whore because she has had sex outside marriage (Fontes, 1993b). When an unmarried woman is no longer a virgin, she is automatically considered promiscuous (Espin, 1986) and thus becomes a fair target for sexual aggression. Revictimization is common:

> Sonia, a 14-year-old Nuyorican (New York Puerto Rican) adolescent was raped by an older classmate. Being English-language dominant, she was seen briefly at a sexual abuse counseling program at the hospital that treated the physical sequelae of rape. Six months after the sexual assault, Sonia's mother went to the program and requested a Latina counselor for her daughter. The intake interview revealed that after Sonia's rape, her paternal uncle began having sex with her. Without acknowledging the uncle's abusive behavior, the mother requested help in dealing with this devastating family problem.

Sexual Abuse of Males

The sexual abuse of males involves several taboos and constitutes a threat to the foundation of machismo. One popular belief is that sexually abused males become homosexuals (Fontes, 1993b). This expectation generates a classic victim-blaming situation for the male survivor of sexual abuse. In general, Puerto Rican society rejects homosexuality (Hidalgo & Hidalgo Christensen, 1979) and is increasingly threatened by male homosexuality due to its association with AIDS (Marín, 1989).

The sexual abuse of males by males may have profound cultural roots and ramifications. Males are considered to have a deep urgent need to satisfy their sexual appetites. Men who act frequently on these needs with a variety of partners are called *bugarrones*. If there are no females available (partly because marianista women are not allowed to have premarital sex), then another male can serve as a sexual partner. Because the *bugarrón* is the aggressor, he is not considered a homosexual, as opposed to the male in the receptive role, who is considered homosexual. People dismiss bugarrones as men who just cannot keep their sexuality in check. The existence of bugarrones in Puerto Rican society may facilitate rape as a contextual behavior of the machismo/marianismo paradigm. A pedophile could take advantage of the existence of the role of the bugarrón as a potential justification for his abusive behavior with children.

A male who has been abused sexually will probably experience several levels of shame. Disclosure will be difficult because it will require admitting that he has been a victim—not an acceptable role for a macho. Disclosing abuse by a male would cast into doubt the firmness of his heterosexuality, and it would be almost impossible for a boy to accuse a woman of sexual abuse because males are expected to "be ready for it" from females at all times.

Regardless of the reinforcement for a man's sexual appetite, the sexual abuse of children is considered one of the biggest taboos in Puerto Rican culture. Unfortunately, this cultural taboo is not always respected. Males convicted of sexually abusing children are often brutally raped and sometimes killed by other inmates in Puerto Rican jails. Frequently, convicted sexual offenders are ostracized from their communities if their victims have been children. Such reactions reflect the high value that many Puerto Ricans place on their children.

Children of color who are sexually abused are often afraid of further damage or death to themselves and their families (due to the perpetrator's threats) if they disclose the abuse. They also cope with other types of victimization, such as institutional racism (Fontes, 1993b). Wyatt (1990) argues that sexually abused children confront multiple forms of victimization, including racial discrimination, stigmatization, and individual and collective violence. She argues that these multiple forms of victimization often result in posttraumatic stress disorder (PTSD). Puerto Rican children are further victimized and their voices silenced because of their sociocultural and linguistic backgrounds, which differ from those of mainstream children. The mainstream institutions do not address Puerto Rican children's needs, often resulting in neglect and further victimization.

Religion and Spiritual Beliefs

Traditional Religious Beliefs

Religion is a pervasive force in influencing behavior, particularly in shaping the expression of sexuality. Most Puerto Ricans are nominally Catholics, but a growing number of Protestant, Pentecostal, and fundamental sects have been proselytizing both on the mainland and on the island. Churches tend to provide support and occasionally substitute for the extended family that has splintered through migration. Indeed, when low-income, Catholic Puerto Ricans migrate to the mainland, they tend to visit the Protestant and Pentecostal churches, where they often find emotional and material support (Ramos-McKay et al., 1988). Protestant and Pentecostal Puerto Ricans facing a sexual abuse problem may tend to confide in ministers for guidance. Thus, to be effective, providers may need to involve the clergy in their work (see Chapters 1 and 6, this volume).

Puerto Ricans' idiosyncratic ways of Catholic worship involve a distrust of organized religion and a personalized relationship with God through a special relationship with the saints (García-Preto, 1982). The Spanish conquistadores used Catholicism as an imperialistic tool to dominate and control their colonies. Consequently, Puerto Rican Catholicism resembles more an imposed cultural behavior than a deeply religious one. For example, attendance at church often functions as a social rather than a religious event.

Folk Beliefs

Puerto Ricans tend to attribute primordial importance to spiritual matters. Belief in spirits is consonant with this value. This belief system can be traced to the Taíno Indian heritage of Puerto Ricans, who believed that everything in nature had a spirit (Steiner, 1974). Some Puerto Ricans believe in *espiritismo* (spiritualism), an invisible world populated by spirits who can penetrate the visible world and attach themselves to human beings. The belief in spirits among Puerto Ricans is best described by the words attributed to a Puerto Rican living in New York City: "If you ever talk to a Puerto Rican who says he or she doesn't believe in spirits, you know what that means? It means that you have not talked to him or her long enough" (Wakefield, 1960).

The Puerto Rican belief in spirits may also be an adaptation to the colonial situation. According to Fanon (1967), the colonized person lives in a state of tension, containing anger that is often released self-destructively or displaced into belief systems of magic and spirits. Faith in magic replaces political action as the feeling of powerlessness is reinforced (Lechner, 1992). Folk beliefs often place the client in a cone of authority, where he or she is assigned to the care and control of a benevolent spirit, exchanging his or her freedom for protection. When political rebellion is not accomplished, passivity and submission function as an adaptation in the form of: "If I can't do it, he (the spirit that possesses me) can do it through me" (Wittoker, 1970). Because Puerto Ricans have been deprived of their freedom of self-determination, many seek protection from powerful spirits.

Curanderismo is the folk healing and belief system prevalent among many Latin Americans that stresses Indian heritage and the use of herbs as medicine. It involves a syncretism of folk Catholicism, 16th-century European medicine, and Mesoamerican and Caribbean Indian practices. Espiritismo and curanderismo are basically Euroamerican in their worldview and social structure. *Santería* is the Afro-Cuban religion and folk belief system consisting of a syncretism between the Catholic saints and the African Orichás, or spirits. Like voodoo in Haiti, shango cults in Trinidad, and *macumba-candomblé* in Brazil, santería is essentially African in worldview and social structure. The African gods and goddesses of santería are of West African origin, specifically Yoruba from Nigeria. Sexual abuse can be interpreted within the santería belief system, as in the following example:

> Juan, a 42-year-old male, was accused of sexually molesting a female neighbor. A santero (santería priest) diagnosed Juan's problem as not attending to his santo Oshun, who controls money and love by protecting the genitals (Martinez & Wetli, 1982). Therefore, the problem of sexual abuse was seen as part of Juan's punishment for neglecting

Oshun. After a series of visits to the santero, Juan was instructed to return to the practice of santería.

There is some controversy as to the adherence by Puerto Ricans to folk beliefs. However, clinicians need to recognize that sometimes—particularly during crisis—many Puerto Ricans, regardless of their transculturation, may adhere to and reidentify with folk beliefs. Similarly, Castro, Furth, and Karlow (1984) compared the belief system about health and illness of less acculturated Latinas of Mexican origin with more acculturated Latinas and Anglo women. Their findings revealed that Latinas have a dual belief system that tends to weaken, but not disappear, with increasing acculturation. Likewise, some Puerto Ricans will seek the services of folk healers while simultaneously receiving professional health and mental health care.

Coping With Sexual Abuse

It is important to be familiar with some of the coping mechanisms that Puerto Ricans may use in dealing with sexual abuse. Sexual abuse represents a traumatic event generating a profound crisis within the Puerto Rican family. Puerto Ricans' styles of coping with sexual abuse are composed of ethnocultural and sociopolitical components.

Cultural Fatalism

Cultural fatalism—the belief that some things are meant to happen regardless of the individual's intervention—is common among some Puerto Ricans. Cultural fatalism reflects an external locus of control in which people perceive the events that happen to them to be the result of luck, fate, or powers beyond their control, rather than due to their own behavior (Rotter, 1966). Some Puerto Ricans with an external locus of control believe that problems are God's way of testing them (*Es una prueba de Dios*). This orientation leads to the acceptance of many events as inevitable, and it removes the personal guilt for failure (Fitzpatrick, 1971).

A cultural fatalistic reaction to sexual abuse may be the response: *Eso tenía que pasar* (It had to happen). Cultural fatalism needs to be examined within the context of colonialism. As a response to historical domination and political control, cultural fatalism may have emerged as a resistance strategy and as a realistic adaptation to the limitations imposed by external realities.

Cultural fatalism appears to be strongly related to socioeconomic class and ethnic identity. Ross, Mirowsky, and Cockerham (1983) found that although persons of Hispanic identity tended to have a fatalistic outlook on life, this fatalism was more pronounced among those individuals from a lower socioeconomic class, as are many Puerto Ricans who reside in the continental United States.

Catholic Endurance and Suffering

The imposition of Catholicism by the colonizing Spaniards has contributed to the development of some coping mechanisms among Puerto Ricans, regardless of their current religion. Denial, repression, and silence about sexual abuse become entangled within this cultural matrix. Many Hispanics' adherence to traditional Catholic values, particularly the religious value placed on enduring human suffering and on self-denial, may prevent some Hispanics from seeking psychological help (Acosta, Yamamoto, & Evans, 1982). The self-sacrifice syndrome, common among women with a marianista gender role, further reinforces the "endure and suffer" attitude: "This is a cross that I have to bear" (*Esto es una cruz que debo de llevar*) (García-Preto, 1990). Providers working with sexual abuse need to recognize clients who have this cognitive orientation and appropriately challenge it or use it in the healing process.

Self-Control

Strongly related to cultural fatalism is the paradigm of self-control. The concept of self-control among many Latinos is different from the one prevalent in the Anglo culture. Castro et al. (1984) argue that a Latin American concept of *controlarse* includes (a) the ability to withstand stress in times of adversity; (b) *aguantarse* (endurance), a passive resignation in which the person accepts his or her fate; (c) *resignarse* (resignation), a more active cognitive coping; and (d) *sobreponerse,* the ability to overcome adversity. In my clinical experience, I have found these coping styles to be prevalent among many Puerto Ricans. However, control is a paradoxical concept for many Puerto Ricans, given the systematic absence of mastery and political control at both the historicopolitical and individual levels.

These coping styles directly affect the help-seeking behaviors of Puerto Ricans. Individuals who embrace the controlarse paradigm are unlikely to seek professional mental health treatment when first facing a problem of sexual abuse. Their help-seeking pathway tends to include family and other support systems first; only as a last resort will they turn to the professional system. Moreover, when faced with sexual abuse—a medicolegal and emotional problem—many Puerto Ricans may be forced to turn to mainstream providers, whereas others may simultaneously resort to folk practices.

Avoidance and Escapism

Sometimes controlarse leads to *no pensar* (avoid thinking about the problem), thus avoiding confrontation and action. No pensar is a distracting response that may shorten the negative effects of depression (Nolen-Hoksema, 1987), and as such, it is a short-term coping mechanism. Similarly, as a mechanism, no pensar is also an attempt to avoid thoughts and feelings associated with trauma. However, no pensar does not address the problem, often leading to avoidance and escapism, another coping mechanism common among some Puerto Ricans. Many Puerto Ricans residing in the continental United States have the dream of returning to the island. The migration and reverse migration reinforces such dreams. Indeed, a common joke among Puerto Ricans is the question: Where are the majority of Puerto Ricans most comfortable: on the island or on the continent? The answer: In the air.

The dream of returning often creates difficulties in adapting to the mainland. The fantasy of returning to the island becomes a concrete option for dealing with a family problem, particularly one involving sexuality. Thus sending the problem person to Puerto Rico to cool off is a coping mechanism on a short-term basis. Consider the following example:

> Miguel, a 10-year-old boy, was sexually molested by his brother's best friend. After his brother found Miguel's underwear stained with blood, he confronted him and Miguel disclosed the abuse. The brother told their mother, who became very upset and replied that she could not think about the problem. She decided to send Miguel to Puerto Rico to live with her own parents. Miguel never obtained professional help.

A family may also decide to cope with crises such as sexual abuse by moving back to the island or to another Puerto Rican community in the United States, believing this will help the child to forget. In other cases, a family may decide not to report abuse to authorities if the offender agrees to move away.

Delivery of Services

Working with Puerto Rican sexual abuse victims involves using multileveled systemic approaches. These approaches require an empowerment orientation that integrates external and internal perspectives. In addition, the clinician needs to act as a cultural broker for low-income clients, helping them negotiate the tumultuous legal, medical, social, and psychological systems that intersect in the lives of sexual abuse victims. I will be using the term *client* to identify both the individual victim and his or her family.

Psychoeducation and Prevention

An initial step in working with sexual abuse victims is to emphasize psychoeducation. Psychoeducation can offer Puerto Ricans an awareness and understanding of the problem of sexual abuse, both for the victim/survivor and for the offender. This type of intervention is crucial for Puerto Ricans because of the specific ethnocultural values that hinder disclosure of sexual abuse (Fontes, 1993b) and the general taboo against discussing sexuality. Psychoeducation can also address the issue of revictimization and the cycle of abuse prevalent among many sexually abused individuals. As a tertiary prevention, psychoeducation regarding the effects and correlates of sexual abuse can offer help to clients in the form of reframing the experience and attaining some understanding of general oppression (societal powerlessness) and specific oppression (sexual abuse).

Psychoeducation involves providing information regarding the physical, emotional, legal, and systemic components of sexual abuse. It also involves addressing the differential effects of sexual abuse according to clients' sex, age, sexual status, sexual orientation, language preference, transculturation status, religion/spirituality, and support system. Within this context, it is essential that psychoeducation involve the extended self—the family—to help them understand the different psychological stages that the victim/survivor may face.

Psychoeducation as primary prevention is also imperative. The problem of sexual abuse needs to be discussed openly within various sectors of the Puerto Rican community. Schools, churches, neighborhoods, social clubs, mass media, and other structures can be potential outlets for preventive efforts. The psychoeducational materials need to be culturally sensitive and gender informed, taking into consideration variables such as language proficiency, education levels, and socioeconomic class, among others (Marín, 1989).

Assessment

Several dimensions need to be included in the assessment phase. These dimensions include type of sexual abuse, relationship to the offender, demographic characteristics, gender roles, cognitive style, and religious and spiritual beliefs. It is important to keep in mind that victims/survivors may tend to be revictimized. If the abuse was of an incestuous nature, several family members should receive clinical services. It is also crucial to examine demographic characteristics, including the transculturation level of the clients who are confronting the sexual abuse problem. Differences in transculturation between the individual client and the family also need to be noted and addressed.

The assessment of gender roles and the adherence to traditional gender roles can provide important information regarding significant others' reactions to the disclosure of sexual abuse. Family gender roles can also elucidate the areas for therapeutic intervention. For example, if the client's mother displays marianista behavior, the clinician may want to emphasize the nurturing aspect, stating that taking care of her abused offspring is part of her role as a mother. On the other hand, if the client's mother behaves in a hembrista fashion, then the approach could emphasize the modeling behavior of a strong woman who takes stock of her own resources in the face of adversity. Where the victim is a daughter, psychoeducational work around the mother-daughter relationship also can be invaluable.

Similarly, if the father or male parental figure behaves in a macho way, the protective aspects of this gender role can be used therapeutically in the recovery process. The male relatives may need to find a way to "save face" without seeking revenge on the offender.

Assessing the client's cognitive style often provides a blueprint of how he or she will react and cope with sexual abuse. Clients' and families' explanations and understanding of the sexual abuse may also provide a key to their recovery. Interventions need to be tailored to the client's particular coping style. For example, a family that uses escapism may be identified as resourceful at coping with immediate crises but also confronted with the negative consequences of this pattern and the long-term effect on the victim and/or offender of sexual abuse.

The provider also needs to assess the belief systems used to frame the sexual abuse. For example, does the client use medical, psychological, legal, or spiritual models, or a combination of these, for explaining the event? A comprehensive approach involving medical, social, and emotional aspects of sexual abuse is part of mainstream programs. However, the spiritual aspect may be neglected. Although the client may not volunteer a belief in spirits, this information can be assessed indirectly. For instance, the provider may explore this area by indicating that some people believe that sexual abuse may have spiritual causes. Another way of assessing this area is to ask whether there was any sign (including dreams) that suggested the problem. Consider the following vignette:

> Lucia, 38, presented in treatment after going through sexual abuse counseling with her 12-year-old daughter, who was raped by a distant male cousin who was baby-sitting her. Lucia stated that she needed mental health help because she had a dream before the sexual assault in which her daughter was getting married, but she was crying and wearing black. Lucia interpreted this dream as a premonition that her daughter was in danger, but she did not follow through. Consequently, Lucia was experiencing profound guilt because she had not paid attention to the warnings provided in her dream.

The clinician needs to use clinical judgment in assessing spiritual or alternative belief systems. This is a complex area, and many clients may not trust providers enough to disclose these issues. They may fear that clinicians will misjudge them or label them as ignorant and primitive. If the assessment confirms the existence of a belief in spirits, then the provider can explore the usefulness of coordinating professional help with the work of an espiritista, curandero, or santero(a). Comas-Díaz (1981) provides a model of collaborating with espiritistas within a traditional mental health approach.

Trauma Therapy

After the assessment is completed, the clinician needs to identify the stage of trauma. For example, was the client abused recently, or is he or she suffering from PTSD? The clinician also needs to identify the different levels of victimization that the client experiences. For example, the cumulative dose of discrimination for some victims may become so toxic that the processes of denial or suppression are similar to those in PTSD, where emotional flooding and disorganized behavior can be triggered by subtle clues, reminders, or even mini instances of what has been suppressed (Hamilton, 1989). This situation is exacerbated for Puerto Ricans, who confront societal barriers due to their assigned inferior colonized status. Furthermore, the sexual abuse may have a cumulative traumatic effect because of Puerto Ricans' history of political and transgenerational trauma.

People of color in general and women of color in particular may be exposed to what Root (1992) calls insidious trauma. She believes that this type of trauma includes the cumulative effect of racism, sexism, dislocation, and other types of oppression. Moreover, sexual and physical victimization are so prevalent among women in the general population that it has been postulated that they are normative aspects of female development (Hamilton & Jensvold, 1992). Similarly, it can be postulated that multiple types of oppression constitute a normative aspect of Puerto Rican development. The sexually abused client may experience an exponential amount of trauma.

At an internal level, corrective learning experiences may contribute to functional new coping skills. Cognitive behavioral approaches are helpful in challenging a victim mentality and increasing a sense of self-determination. These techniques constitute tools for correcting cognitive errors caused by victimization. This approach is highly relevant for many Puerto Ricans because their cognitive errors reinforce their victim mentality by mirroring the hopelessness, helplessness, sense of betrayal, and low self-esteem resulting from sexual and political trauma. A victim mentality involves (a) intolerance of mistakes in self and others, (b) denial of personal difficulties, (c) dichotomous thinking, and (d) continuation of survival tactics (Matsakis, 1992).

The narration and reconstruction of the victim's life story can be healing and empowering. These techniques need to be balanced with an understanding of the context of the external reality. Similarly, in working with victims, Matsakis (1992) recommends rewriting the trauma story with a different ending as a healing technique. Indeed, the use of fantasy or symbolization is a means of reworking overwhelming painful experiences.

Another narrative tool, testimony, is a first-person account of one's experiences with attention to experiences of loss, trauma, and oppression. Testimony is valuable to women and other oppressed individuals because it validates personal experience as a basis for truth and knowledge in an affirming and empowering manner (Aron, 1992). In my experience, this approach is extremely helpful for Puerto Ricans who have suffered sexual abuse trauma.

Narrative approaches can facilitate the recovery of the self through a life-story construction. The cultural story is another healing narrative approach. As an empowering approach, the cultural story narrates an ethnocultural group's origins, migration, and identity (McGill, 1992). At the family level, the cultural story is used to tell where the ancestors came from, what kind of people they were, what issues are important, and what lessons have been learned from their experiences. These issues are key for Puerto Ricans who experienced sexual abuse in the midst of transgenerational trauma. Discussing family and cultural stories can enhance self-esteem among victims by learning from other Puerto Ricans' struggles, triumphs, and defeats.

Working from a systemic perspective allows the clinician to contextualize the sexual abuse. Within this perspective, the individual is considered part of an interactional context that includes culture, ethnicity, gender, class, and age, as well as other systems such as family, schools, neighborhood, and community. An example of a systemic perspective involves using the multigenerational family context in connection with school, work, and other systems. Family therapy is culturally congruent with the Puerto Rican value of familism (Canino & Canino, 1982), and transgenerational genograms can be useful with Puerto Rican sexually abused clients and their families. As with the family stories, which provide inspiration, warnings, and cherished values (Stone, 1988), genograms can unfold family scripts, coping skills, and reactions to victimization. Even if the family is not available for treatment, I have found that conducting family therapy with one individual and/or with the client and one parent can prove helpful for this population.

Empowerment and Decolonization

It has been argued that oppressed groups need to express their truth, assert their identity, and achieve autonomy (O'Hara, 1989). Similarly, delivering clinical services to oppressed clients requires incorporation of empowerment approaches. A feminist approach is relevant to working with sexually abused Puerto Rican females. The feminist emphasis on the equalization of power can help these clients address their powerlessness and helplessness by recognizing the right to develop egalitarian relationships. The feminist belief that oppressed individuals have had limited choices as a result of their oppression and that internalized negative self-beliefs stem from such oppression can help sexually abused Puerto Rican clients combat pervasive low self-esteem. Moreover, the feminist principle that the personal is political can help Puerto Rican clients cope and work toward the transformation of their oppressive realities, enabling them to achieve more control over their lives. The feminist value of social action follows from the belief that oppression problems are based in a societal as well as a personal context. This aspect of feminist empowerment is relevant to female survivors, many of whom may become active through educating the community about sexual abuse.

Therapeutic Decolonization

The sexually abused Puerto Rican client could benefit from a therapeutic decolonization. The sexual abuse can symbolically represent the enactment of the colonizer-colonized relationship. The decolonization involves a paradox for Puerto Ricans in the United States because their being part of the colonial nation makes their alienation from others and from themselves all-pervasive, resulting in an identity crisis. The dynamics of liberation and decolonization involve a three-stage process: recovery of the self, achievement of autonomous dignity, and action toward fundamental change of self and/or the colonial condition (Memmi, 1965). The therapeutic decolonization approach follows this process by helping Puerto Ricans recover from the abuse and reclaim the self.

Psychotherapeutic decolonization involves *concientization*. According to Freire (1967, 1970), concientization entails an awakening of consciousness; a change of mentality involving a realistic awareness of one's place in nature and society; the capacity to analyze critically its causes and consequences, comparing it with other situations and possibilities; and action aimed at transformation. On an applied level, the process of psychotherapeutic decolonization for Puerto Ricans involves (a) recognizing the systemic and societal context of colonialism and oppression, thus becoming aware of the colonized mentality; (b) correcting cognitive errors that reinforce colonized and victim mentality (e.g., working through dichotomous thinking: superior-inferior; colonized equals good; colonizer equals bad, etc.) and acknowledging ambivalence toward self and others; (c) asserting and reaffirming multiple identities and developing a more integrated identity; (d) increasing self-mastery and achieving autonomous dignity; and (e) working toward transformation of self and/or the colonized condition (e.g., improving the condition of Puerto Rican women, men, and children) (Comas-Díaz, 1994).

According to Comas-Díaz (1994), the psychotherapeutic decolonization also attempts to increase awareness of and differentiation between external and internalized colonization. It facilitates the exploration of options and attempts to empower clients to make informed decisions within their personal spheres, encouraging personal control and mastery. In addition, decolonization addresses the colonized person's need for fundamental change by helping Puerto Ricans become aware of their capacity to shape their reality.

Group Therapy

Group therapy has been used successfully with Puerto Rican clients (Acosta & Yamamoto, 1984; Delgado & Humm-Delgado, 1984; Ramos-McKay et al., 1988). All female participants, all male participants, as well as mixed and specific topic groups have been reported in the literature (Comas-Díaz, 1987; Vasquez, 1994). Although Puerto Ricans tend to be gregarious and group oriented, I have experienced difficulties working in group modalities with Puerto Rican clients who have been abused sexually. Many of the clients have rejected this treatment modality while continuing to attend individual and family sessions. When asked about this behavior, they indicate that they do not feel comfortable talking to others about their intimate problems. The topic of sexual abuse appears to be too much of a taboo for Puerto Rican clients to share with other victims in a group. Feelings of shame, internalization of the victimization, and fear of gossip may prevent Puerto Ricans from obtaining support in a collective format. Furthermore, discussing sexual abuse with nonprofessionals may suggest that the clients' family and friends are being ineffective in providing support. Hopefully, psychoeducational and prevention interventions will stop this type of cultural taboo.

Therapeutic Relationship

Successful clinical work with people of color depends on the therapist's skill in establishing and managing the therapeutic relationship (Jenkins, 1990). It also depends on the therapist's self-awareness and understanding of how ethnocultural and racial factors (Jones, 1985), in addition to gender factors (Bernardez, 1987; L. S. Brown, 1990; Comas-Díaz, 1994), affect both practitioner and client.

Regardless of ethnicity, therapists may have diverse representations of Puerto Ricans. Moreover, the therapist's own group memberships, such as gender, ethnicity, race, culture, class, sexual orientation, and age, as well as other factors, such as attitude toward Puerto Ricans, can significantly affect the therapeutic relationship. Furthermore, clinicians working with sexually abused clients need to be aware of and work through their countertransferential reactions to sexual abuse, violence, trauma, and oppression.

It is important to remember that by virtue of their therapeutic and healing functions, clinicians are perceived as authority figures and, as such, are awarded respeto. This cultural value can be used therapeutically, particularly in the psychoeducational aspect of the clinical work. Although some Puerto Ricans may expect the therapist to be directive and give advice (Comas-Díaz, Geller, Melgoza, & Baker, 1982), the therapist needs to prevent mirroring the colonizer-colonized relationship within the therapeutic dyad. The relationship can exist along any number of polarities, including aggressive-passive, leader-follower, and dominant-submissive (P. Brown, 1974). Furthermore, it can be reified at the expense of the least powerful member of the dyad (P. Brown, 1974). Therefore, it is essential that practitioners who are working with this population use an empowerment orientation within a culturally relevant context. Although therapists with an empowering framework may be cognitively aware of these issues, they may project onto Puerto Ricans their own internalized domination (if they belong to the dominant group), oppression (if they belong to an oppressed group) (L. S. Brown, 1993), or colonization (if they are Puerto Ricans).

Issues for Non-Puerto Rican/Latino Clinicians

The first therapeutic issue for the non-Latino provider is how to gain cultural understanding and sensitivity to Puerto Ricans who have been abused sexually. However, many clinicians may compensate for their lack of training or experience in Puerto Rican culture. These reactions may be counterproductive to the therapeutic work and are usually a dysfunctional compensation for their limitations. Some of these reactions include guilt, pity, and the clinical anthropologist's syndrome (Comas-Díaz & Jacobsen, 1991).

In the countertransference involving the clinical anthropologist's syndrome, the therapist is excessively curious about the client's ethnocultural background and may spend an inordinate amount of time exploring aspects of the client's culture at the expense of the client's needs (Comas-Díaz & Jacobsen, 1991). Similarly, Montalvo and Gutierrez (1983) argue that the non-Latino provider who is attempting to be culturally sensitive may minimize the family dysfunction by allowing the family to hide behind the "mask of culture." They contend that this reaction may result in a subtle and collusive relationship between the clinician and the family to prevent change. The clinician is under the illusion of being culturally sensitive, but in reality, he or she becomes part of the family denial system (Martinez, 1994).

The scenario involving the mask of culture is dangerous, particularly when dealing with incest:

> A Puerto Rican father was accused of incest. The victim, his 8-year-old daughter, drew a picture at school that was suggestive of sexual intercourse. When asked about it by the school counselor, she responded, "This is the game I play with Papi." Medical evaluation of the girl was inconclusive. The parents, both professionals with postgraduate college degrees, entered family therapy. During the treatment, their 12-year-old daughter also accused the father of "doing bad things to her." An Anglo social worker was assigned to investigate the case. After several family meetings, he decided not to remove the daughters from the home in support of the familism value. Nonetheless, the father was requested to attend a psychiatric evaluation with a non-Latino clinician, who also recommended against disrupting the family homeostasis. A month after completion of the psychiatric evaluation, the mother went to protective services and accused her husband of incest. The precipitating event was that she found pornographic photographs that her husband had taken of their 8-year-old daughter.

Regardless of ethnicity, it is crucial that the clinician develop a therapeutic alliance with the client. Given that an individual problem is a family problem (Canino & Canino, 1982), the clinician needs to form an alliance with the family as well. This implies that linguistic differences may become a barrier for the non-Spanish-speaking clinician. The use of interpreters in psychiatric assessment and treatment has been criticized and should be avoided if possible. In my experience, the use of an interpreter for a sexually abused, Spanish-speaking, Puerto Rican client is often oppressive and disempowering and contributes to the client's sense of voicelessness.

Issues for Puerto Rican/Latino Clinicians

Puerto Rican and Latino clinicians usually have the advantage of a better understanding of linguistic and cultural issues. However, they have to deal with special reactions from both client and therapist that emerge from an intraethnic encounter of members of an oppressed group. Puerto Rican families often feel shame in seeking professional services because it means that the family has failed to provide the necessary support to solve problems (Canino & Canino, 1982). With sexual abuse, some clients may feel extra shame when working with a Puerto Rican or Latino therapist. There may be added concern about trust, specifically regarding the clinician's ability to maintain confidentiality about the sexual abuse. As an illustration, a family working with a Puerto Rican provider about the sexual abuse of their 18-year-old daughter complained to the clinic's director when people in the Puerto Rican barrio found out about their daughter's "dishonor." The clients accused the therapist of not maintaining confidentiality and of gossiping about their problems.

Comas-Díaz and Jacobsen (1991) discuss the ethnocultural transferential and countertransferential reactions prevalent in the intraethnic therapeutic dyad. They identify the transference of autoracism as being present among groups that experience racial prejudice accompanied by socioeconomic oppression. In this reaction, the clients do not want to work with a therapist of their own ethnocultural group because they experience strong negative feelings toward themselves and project them onto their ethnically similar therapist. Indeed, in the previous vignette, unfounded concerns about the Puerto Rican therapist's lack of confidentiality may be a reflection of the client's autoracist reaction.

Another reaction that clients may have toward Latino providers is the attribution of the omniscience and omnipotence to the therapist, which involves a complete idealization of the therapist and the fantasy of the reunion with the perfect, all-good parent, facilitated by the ethnic similarity (Comas-Díaz & Jacobsen, 1991). This reaction can complicate treatment because it tends to set up the clinician for predictable failure. Additional issues for Latino practitioners involve their specific reactions to sexual abuse, which sometimes include a desire to suppress information that they believe will reflect negatively on members of their own group.

Clinicians' Reactions to Trauma

Regardless of ethnicity and gender, clinicians may have specific reactions and countertransference to their clients' trauma. Some of these include anxiety, ambivalence, curiosity, rage, revulsion, horror, negative moral judgments, sadistic or primitive voyeuristic impulses, and a shameful pleasure (Fischman,

1991; Ganzarain & Buchele, 1986; Lyon, 1994; Mollica & Lavalle, 1988). Other types of countertransference involve overidentification with the victim, leading to intense feelings of sadness, helplessness, hopelessness, or rage (Comas-Díaz & Padilla, 1990; Lyon, 1994). Moreover, some clinicians experience secondary PTSD, consisting of nightmares, intrusive and repetitive images, and somatic symptoms (Lyon, 1994), a condition leading to a wounded healer syndrome (Comas-Díaz & Padilla, 1990). Clinicians working with clients who have been abused sexually need to have available and make use of specific clinical training and consultation.

CASE STUDIES

Following are two clinical examples illustrating some of the areas discussed in this chapter.

Sofía: I Am Not My Brother's Keeper!

Sofía, a 29-year-old unmarried woman, entered treatment after she read a self-help book on incest. She contacted a sexual assault hotline and was given the name of a Latina therapist with expertise in sexual abuse. While reading the book, Sofía identified the emotional sequelae of incest as part of her problems within her romantic relationships, which tended to be abusive. She developed intense psychological distress in the form of nervousness, worry, difficulty concentrating, and irritability. Sofía reported remembering her brother sexually molesting her but stated that she had believed him when he said that they were "only playing."

Sofía worked as a paralegal. She had aspirations of becoming a lawyer and was supported by her supervisors in these ambitions, but she lacked the financial resources to study further. Her work seemed to enhance her self-esteem by making her feel competent and efficient.

Sofía reported that her brother Juan began to sexually molest her when she was 8 years old and he was 12 years old. The molestation escalated from masturbation in front of her, to touching her genitals, fellatio, and intercourse. The abuse ended when Sofía began her first menstrual period at age 13. In describing the incest, Sofía exhibited psychogenic amnesia in that she could not recall significant aspects of the trauma. She showed signs of dissociating. She stated that she was unsure of her volitional participation in the incest because Juan told her that they were playing games and that they both liked them. When asked about her explanation for the incest, Sofía replied that she once heard her madrina (godmother) saying that Juan had been possessed by spirits.

Sofía was the third child in a family of three daughters and one son. She had an older sister, Milagros, who was the mother's favorite, and a younger sister, Diana, who was her father's favorite. She reported that as the only son, Juan was everyone's favorite. However, Sofía also stated that Juan had the darkest complexion of the family and that he encountered rejection from the extended family due to his skin color. Sofía confided that Juan was an angry person and that she had always been afraid of him.

Both parents were from a small town in Puerto Rico and migrated to the continental United States in search of employment. They worked in factories. Sofía reported that their marital relationship was chaotic because of her father's excessive drinking. She reported family discord, parental neglect, and rejection. She grew up Catholic but then converted to Pentecostalism when she was 5 years old. However, when the clinician followed up on Sofía's explanation for the incest (Juan's spirit possession), she confided that her mother practiced espiritismo.

The initial stages of trauma therapy addressed Sofía's PTSD symptoms. It appeared that in addition to reading the self-help book, Sofía was reacting to Juan's divorce. His wife divorced him because Juan had had a sexual relationship with her 16-year-old sister. The circumstances of Juan's divorce triggered Sofía's feelings regarding her sexual abuse. Additionally, the divorce caused a major crisis in the family.

Cognitive restructuring helped Sofía address dysfunctional thoughts and feelings regarding the incest. Her dysfunctional thinking included believing that she consented to the incest because she and her brother were "playing." Therefore, Sofía believed that she was an easy woman and a bad person. Her feelings ranged from guilt, self-blame, and shame to anger and rage. At this point in the treatment, Sofía was encouraged to narrate her trauma story. Her testimony took several sessions. The themes that emerged during her testimony were self-sacrifice in favor of others, strong loyalty, overresponsibility, and fear of losing control. The clinician also encouraged Sofía to write her recovery process in a journal.

When she completed her testimony, Sofía suddenly announced that she was going to visit her family. She stated a desire to disclose to her mother and to confront Juan. The clinician expressed concern over the timing of the disclosure and recommended that Sofía wait until her next visit. However, Sofía indicated that according to her interpretation of the self-help book material, she was ready to confront her family.

Two weeks after their last session, the clinician received a letter from Sofía. The letter, part of her journal, stated that Sofía had disclosed the incest to her mother, who reacted in a bewildered manner. First she accused Sofía of being disrespectful and then of attempting to destroy the family by lying about Juan. Sofía reacted to these accusations by crying, "I am not my brother's keeper!" As a response, her mother slapped Sofía and refused to continue the conversation.

Sofía did not address her feelings about her mother's reaction. She ended her letter by stating that although it had been painful, she was glad that she entered therapy. Sofía announced that she was terminating therapy and had decided to move to the same town where her family lived.

Jesús: Father, Why Have You Forsaken Me?

Jesús, a 27-year-old single male, presented in treatment ordered by the court, having been convicted of cocaine possession. He was arrested while celebrating with friends the news that he had been admitted to a graduate program in business administration. This event was Jesús's first legal offense, and the judge ordered psychotherapy instead of incarceration. The client selected a Latina clinician out of the yellow pages in the telephone book. Jesús presented in treatment asking for short-term psychotherapy and contracted for 12 sessions.

Jesús reported experiencing feelings of worthlessness, depression, and difficulties with sleeping, eating, concentration, and attention. Labeling these feelings as depression appeared to help Jesús.

The initial assessment revealed that Jesús was an only child who was born in Puerto Rico and moved to the continental United States when he was 5 years old. His father bought a bodega (grocery store), and a year later he was killed there during a robbery. Jesús was sent to live with his maternal grandparents in Puerto Rico, but the following year, he returned to live with his mother, Laura. Being in charge of the bodega, Laura worked 12 to 18 hours each day.

In describing his feelings toward his mother, Jesús stated that it was a love-hate relationship. Although she never remarried, Laura had a long-term boyfriend, Pedro. Jesús indicated that he felt abandoned by her because she divided her time between the bodega and Pedro. He described Laura as a liberated woman at work but traditional and submissive in her relationship with Pedro.

Jesús presented with a pattern of self-destructive behaviors that included alcohol abuse and driving under the influence. He also admitted to having smoked cannabis but denied abusing any other substance. Jesús revealed that he had conflictive interpersonal relationships. His male friendships always ended abruptly, and he usually felt abused and betrayed. Jesús tended to sexualize his relationships with all females. He reported being accused of being a womanizer by his girlfriends. In discussing the types of women that attracted him, he stated that he liked *putitas* (little whores).

The initial stage of treatment involved helping Jesús recognize his dysfunctional behaviors. His alcohol use was interpreted as an attempt to deal with his depression, and he was asked to attend Alcoholics Anonymous. Additionally, the assessment revealed a self-destructive style of coping. Jesús tended to minimize and deny his difficulties. This style proved to be self-defeating. As an illustration, he was failing his university courses, and he responded to this failure with paralyzing anxiety. To cope with this situation, Jesús was taught cognitive behavioral techniques that included deep muscle relaxation and imagery.

Jesús began to feel more proficient at coping with his immediate situation. His depression and anxiety were significantly reduced, but he reported that he still felt inferior to his classmates and that he had difficulties liking himself. His low self-esteem seemed to stem partly from a complicated bereavement due to his father's murder. Grief work was initiated, and it was revealed that Jesús used alcohol as a means of identifying with his father, who had been intoxicated when he was killed.

Grief work also included a cognitive restructuring of Jesús's fears and fantasies about his role in the murder. The family lived in the building where the bodega was located. The evening of his father's murder, Jesús was sleeping on the bodega's second floor. As a result, he had developed a fear of being killed in addition to shame for not helping his father. Jesús appeared to be stuck in rage and was flooded with powerlessness. Cognitive restructuring was used to help him cope with his feelings.

During the bereavement process, Jesús communicated to his therapist that he had a secret that made him feel worthless. He said that because the therapist was female, he had initial apprehension about disclosing this information to her. However, he stated that she had earned his trust and respect and that she might be able to help him. Jesús confided that Pedro had sexually molested him for about a year when he was 12 years old.

Jesús decided to extend his short-term therapeutic contract. Trauma therapy began with identifying Jesús's trauma stage (Matsakis, 1992).

He appeared to be experiencing emotional flooding, disorganized behavior, and lack of control, which are characteristic of PTSD. The triggering event—Pedro's recent death—appeared to have unlocked his suppression and denial of the sexual abuse.

A therapeutic task during this stage was to help Jesús accept his strong ambivalent feelings toward Pedro. He stated that before the sexual abuse, Pedro had been like a father to him, but afterwards he hated him. Jesús explained the sexual abuse as a consequence of Pedro's alcoholism. Although Jesús never disclosed the sexual abuse to his mother, his hatred of Pedro added to their already strained relationship.

Pedro's death also unlocked his grief for his own father's death. Jesús said that he identified with Christ when he said, "Father, why have you forsaken me?" His identification with Christ, grounded in his Catholic background, also emphasized Jesús's martyrdom and victimization. Such identification was both adaptive and dysfunctional.

Jesús's dysfunctional choices in interpersonal relationships appeared to be related to the sexual abuse. With males, he was mistrustful and exhibited a pattern of betrayal and abandonment. Upon exploration, Jesús admitted that his behavior was a form of preventing abuse by his friends. This negative pattern involved a self-fulfilling prophecy. As an illustration, Jesús had sex with a woman who was engaged to his best friend. Consequently, his *pana* (friend) broke off his friendship with Jesús. In relating the incident, Jesús initially identified it as an example of being wronged by others (seduced by the woman, rejected by the friend, and not being invited to the wedding). However, when confronted with his behavior and consequences, Jesús was able to identify the dysfunctionality and accept responsibility for his behavior.

Jesús's choices in romantic relationships also appeared dysfunctional. He chose women mainly for their sexual availability and admitted that he treated them like prostitutes. His girlfriends frequently abandoned him because of his womanizing. He indicated that he terminated relationships due to boredom with those who did not abandon him. Being a womanizer was identified as a resistance strategy against his own sexual abuse trauma. Jesús stated that within romantic relationships, he wanted to make sure that he was the male. Further exploration revealed that, because of his sexual abuse, Jesús was afraid of being a homosexual and therefore was exaggerating his machismo in his sexual encounters with women. His victim mentality was identified, challenged, and cognitively modified. His "fear of homosexuality" was interpreted as a cultural script and as a metaphor for his fear of his own sexuality and difficulties with intimacy with both females and males.

Therapeutic Relationship

The therapeutic relationship provided an anchor to Jesús's treatment. As with many of his relationships with females, Jesús tried to sexualize the therapeutic relationship during its initial stages. The paradigm of paying a woman for her services was congruent with his distorted view of all women as prostitutes. Supportive but firm limit setting helped clarify the therapy boundaries. Jesús was able to recognize the therapist as a credible ally. Within the safety of the therapeutic relationship, he was able to examine his conflicted relationship with his mother. He revealed that he felt sacrificed through the sexual abuse to protect his mother against being abandoned by another man, Pedro.

With an empowering perspective, the therapist helped Jesús make an informed decision about disclosing to his mother. Jesús decided not to disclose the sexual abuse and instead focused on the feelings of abandonment. Laura attended a dyadic session with Jesús in which he communicated his feelings about being sent to Puerto Rico after his father's murder and the consequent abandonment he felt from Laura. A dialogue on these issues was initiated.

The therapist asked Jesús to narrate his trauma story but to develop a different ending. His narration was catalytic and led to further action. Jesús wrote a letter to his father and another to Pedro. He read these letters in therapy and was asked to role play his father's and Pedro's reactions to his letters. Writing these letters and the subsequent working-through process were healing and empowering.

Jesús completed his treatment after 2 years. His depression and anxiety had disappeared. His academic performance improved significantly. Jesús was able to make and maintain friends, and he discontinued his defensive sexualization of his relationships with women. Jesús reported feeling better about himself and had improved his relationship with his mother. He decided to return to church and enjoyed feeling connected to the Catholic community. On a follow-up visit 6 months after treatment termination, Jesús reported that he was in a stable romantic relationship. He said that for the first time in his life he was satisfied with himself.

Discussion

The traumatic experiences of Sofía and Jesús share several common elements. They were both child victims of sexual abuse, with strong incestual repercussions. Although Sofía was a victim of biological incest and Jesús was a victim of non-kin incest, they were both victims of emotional incest. Both clients suffered negative effects in their sexuality, which manifested in a gender-specific manner. Sofía believed that because of the sexual abuse she became an easy woman, whereas Jesús expressed fears of becoming homosexual. Moreover, Sofía had a history of tolerating abusive sexual relationships, whereas Jesús treated his sexual partners like prostitutes.

Sofía's reactions to her trauma involved experiencing strong feelings of guilt, shame, and ambivalence. Additionally, her reactions were characteristic of denial, collusion, and escapism. When her mother rejected her disclosure, Sofía joined her in the denial to continue protecting her brother. This protection appeared to be evident in her explanation of her brother's abusive behavior—he was the innocent victim of misguided spirits. Consequently, she appeared to collude with the family's dysfunctionality. Moreover, Sofía decided to prevent family rejection and even ostracism by leaving therapy and moving back home.

Sofía's case underlines the importance of working with family members in the healing process. Her therapy was abruptly terminated, partly because the clinician allowed Sofía to confront her family without being emotionally ready. By not helping Sofía question the cultural sensitivity of the material presented in the book on incest, the clinician did not properly prepare her for the family confrontation. Moreover, the clinician did not properly assess Sofía's need for security in order to disclose the incest to her mother. In retrospect, perhaps the clinician could have discussed the destabilization in the family created by the brother's divorce, recommending that Sofía wait until her family emerged from the crisis.

Jesús's case illustrates the difficulty of recovery for male victims of sexual assault. Contrary to Sofía, Jesús did not present in treatment with the complaint of sexual abuse. Several sex roles are highlighted in Jesús's vignette. These include his mother's marianista behavior at home and hembrista behavior at work, and Jesús's defensive macho behavior in his romantic relationships. It is tempting to conclude that Jesus's therapy was successful and that Sofía's was not because of her abrupt termination. However, Sofía's own words in her letter indicate that she was glad that she initiated therapy. Although there are several ways of interpreting Sofía's termination, it appears that she obtained what she needed to begin her journey of recovery. Sofía gained knowledge to continue her journey at her own pace.

Conclusion

Sexual abuse among Puerto Ricans involves a complex interaction of multiple factors. Working with Puerto Rican clients who have been abused sexually requires an understanding of the systemic context of this type of victimization (Fontes, 1993a). Complex factors contribute to the problem of sexual abuse among Puerto Ricans—among them sociopolitical context, colonized mentality, and membership in an ethnic minority group. Helpful therapeutic tools include psychoeducation; prevention; treatment of trauma and PTSD; systemic family approaches; and narrative approaches including testimony, empowerment, and therapeutic decolonization.

Puerto Ricans have a long history of resistance and resilience. This history has afforded them incredible flexibility and adaptability. Puerto Ricans' ability to recover from pain, trauma, and oppression is impressive. As an illustration, Nuyorican poets coined a term—*dusmic poetry*—to define the process of transforming aggression into strength (Algarín & Piñero, 1975). The dusmic strength grows out of desperation and a genuine self-affirmation. The dusmic nature of Puerto Ricans gives hope without deceptive illusions. This quality can be used with survivors of sexual abuse.

Asian, Pacific Island, and Filipino Americans and Sexual Child Abuse

AMY OKAMURA
PATRICIA HERAS
LINDA WONG-KERBERG

This chapter will focus on sexual child abuse in American families of Asian, Pacific Island and Filipino ethnic backgrounds. A search of the literature on sexual child abuse among these ethnic groups in the United States reveals a dearth of references (Ima & Hohm, 1991; Korbin, 1981; Rao, Di Clemente, & Ponton, 1992; Wong, 1987). Statistical data on the incidence of sexual child abuse among these groups is also lacking due to data collection decisions on the state and national levels. The National Center of Child Abuse and Neglect, for example, classifies racial/ethnic categories into 3 groups: White (including Hispanic), Black, and other.

Where data are available, the reported incidence of sexual child abuse for Asian/Pacific Island/Filipino populations is relatively low (Vernon, 1994). However, as Korbin (1991) states, "The absence of published or documented cases of child maltreatment does not necessarily mean an absence of the problem" (p. 68). From our own practice, experiences, and anecdotal information, we suspect that the actual incidence of sexual child abuse is much higher in this group than is reported, as in most communities. Cultural factors of shame and denial within the Asian Pacific and Filipino cultural groups reduce reporting. This chapter aims to advance the cultural competency of policy-makers, administrators, judges, attorneys, child advocates, child protection workers, therapists, medical personnel, educators, police, the clergy, child and youth care workers, and volunteers. Guidelines are offered for culturally appropriate assessment and treatment, highlighting the experiences of an effective, community-based model of prevention and intervention.

Overview of the Population

Prior to 1965, there were 1 million Asian Americans in the United States, mostly of Chinese, Japanese, and Filipino origins (Civil Rights Digest, 1967). Immigration laws historically restricted immigration from the Eastern Hemisphere, favoring migrants from Europe and other Western Hemisphere countries. However, the passage of the Immigration Act of 1965, the takeover of Indochina by Communists in 1975, and the political and economic upheavals in Asia in the 1980s caused large numbers of immigrants and refugees from Asia and Southeast Asia to swell the ranks of the newly arrived in this country, making them the fastest growing segment of the U.S. population in that decade. The newcomers have transformed the relatively small existing Asian communities with increased visibility and a diversity of cultures and languages. There are now 7.3 million citizens and residents of Asian, Pacific Island, and Filipino origins in the United States (U.S. Bureau of the Census, 1990). The Bureau of the Census lists 66 different ethnic categories in the Asian Pacific subpopulation in the United States (U.S. Bureau of the Census, 1990), constituting a complex, heterogeneous, and diverse subpopulation of ethnic and national groups with varied cultural backgrounds, languages, lifestyles, socioeconomic status, and migration and settlement experiences in North America. Asian Pacifics and Filipinos cannot be readily described as an aggregate group, despite the tendency to treat them as such. We will begin by highlighting similarities and differences among the groups.

There are three predominant groupings among the Asian Pacific people. Those people who trace their origins to mainland Asiatic cultures share a psychology based on principles of Buddhism, Confucianism, Taoism, and a mixture of animistic beliefs. The first group is made up of the Chinese, Vietnamese, Japanese, and Koreans. The second group is from Southeast Asia, where a Malay influence is evident among the Filipinos, Indonesians, Malaysians, Cambodians, and Laotians. The third group is made up of Hawaiians, Samoans, and Guamanians. They constitute the largest group of Pacific Islanders in the U.S. and are considered "natives" versus "immigrants" because they inhabited their own islands for centuries before American domination (Trask, 1990).

Buddhism spread from India through Southeast Asia and China, and into Korea and Japan, creating similarities in basic worldviews and belief systems among these cultural groups. The far-reaching influence of the Chinese through trade and domination spread Confucianism and the Confucian-based principles of filial piety and preservation of the family lineage throughout most Asian cultures.

The Filipinos and Guamanians are islanders, but their mutual histories of centuries of Spanish influence and Catholicism, followed by wartime Japanese and subsequent U.S. occupations, have reduced their similarities with other Pacific Islanders. Hawaiians and Samoans share histories of native cultures long spoiled and lost after generations of foreign control and the significant influence of Christianity, which viewed much of the native island cultural beliefs and practices as pagan.

Acculturation Levels

Borrowing from the Japanese preference for identifying immigrants by generation, it is helpful to begin with a generational framework and move from a larger ecosystems level to the individual. "Immigrant-descendent families" (Ho, 1992) among Asian Pacifics are those Americans who can trace up to four or more generations in this country. These are primarily Chinese, Japanese, Filipino, East Indian, and Korean Americans who are, in general, highly acculturated to American lifestyles and who speak English. They identify themselves as mainstream Americans or as bicultural, sometimes having less in common with immigrants of the same culture than non-Asian Pacific American cohorts. The members of this group vary in their ethnic associations from having none to having some by choice of friends and food. There is a high rate of out-marriage among Japanese Americans and Chinese Americans in particular, increasing the number of biracial children (America's immigrant challenge, 1993).

The second distinguishable group consists of "immigrant-American families" (Ho, 1992), in which parents are foreign born and children are American born. The primary language in the home is usually the parental native tongue with English fluency outside the home. Child-rearing practices tend to be fairly traditional, with indulgence of the very young and strict discipline at school age. Cultural and generational conflicts are exacerbated by the more rapid acculturation of the young. Not only do acculturation rates vary within the family but so do short-term goals, causing stress and tension. However, immigrant families maintain strong "old country" values and expectations, usually working hard and pooling resources, resulting in high rates of education and economic success (Stevenson, 1992). Although Samoan and Guamanian families cannot technically be considered "immigrants" by virtue of their U.S. status, the description above of "immigrant-American families" is also applicable to those Samoan and Guamanian families who live on the mainland.

The third group in this framework is the "recently arrived immigrant/refugee family" (Ho, 1992), whose energies are focused on adjustment and survival in the new country. Based on our years of human service experience with Asian Pacific communities, we believe that members of this group have the greatest need for social services and are at higher risk for family dysfunction and incidents of child abuse. Korbin (1981) cites increased child maltreatment where migration and social changes have reduced parents' built-in supports for child rearing that otherwise serve a preventive function. Ima and Hohm (1991) found in the Union of Pan Asian Communities' sample of newer Asian and Pacific Islander cases, and in interviews with cultural informants, that patterns of child abuse were connected to cultural differences and adjustment problems. In addition, with a high birthrate, the population of Asian American children under 18 far outranks the general U.S. population (U.S. Bureau of the Census, 1990). Language and cultural differences, poverty, crowded housing in poor neighborhoods, discrimination, violence within and outside the family, low levels of education among parents, and the hostile attitudes of the host society pose significant barriers to adjustment. The newcomers tend to live in urban areas where others from their culture and language live, creating Koreatowns, Japantowns, Chinatowns, and Vietnamesetowns.

When an Asian Pacific or Filipino American family is encountered, it is helpful to determine where they fall in this framework to understand the levels of acculturation. If the family falls into the first group, immigrant-descendent, the acculturation level among this group can be assumed to be high, and it is likely that Western practices would be understood and accepted. For members of the second group, immigrant-American families, there will be a range of acculturation for different family members. Thus the practitioner has more homework to do in terms of learning how to work best with each family member. It is usually most difficult for practitioners working with the recently arrived immigrant family, where language and strong cultural values and behaviors differ significantly from American. It can be difficult for practitioners to establish credibility and encourage these clients to accept help. It can be even more difficult dealing with the taboo topics of sexuality and sexual child abuse.

Culture

Family Structure, Roles, and Responsibilities

The working cultural knowledge base needed for cultural competency requires lifelong learning and interaction on a normative basis with people who are socioculturally different in order to gain appropriate perspectives when an individual and family are in trouble. We recommend that practitioners seek out cultural knowledge in a variety of ways and, in particular, that they develop relationships with healthy members of a particular ethnic group who can serve as appropriate cultural informants and teachers.

The literature describing traditional Asian, Filipino, and Pacific Island cultural values is extensive (S. Chan, 1993; Ho, 1992a; Huang, 1989; Huang & Ying, 1989; Nagata, 1989; Nguyen & Williams, 1989; D. Sue & Sue, 1990; S. Sue & Morishima, 1982) and can provide a framework for understanding shared cultural values and ideals. However, it is important to remember that generalizations about cultural family patterns often minimize the regional, historical, socioeconomic, and class variations found within each group. Thus descriptions and analysis of normative behavior and values at a macro-socio level "need refinement and qualification at the micro-socio level" (Falicov, 1982). We must not simply apply knowledge gained through stereotypes but also sift through individual family patterns to understand the family's life history and adaptation.

The family plays a central organizing role for Asians, Filipinos, and Pacific Islanders. The family is the reference group that provides the individual's source of identity and emotional security throughout life (Nguyen & Williams, 1989). Families reinforce strong interdependent bonds that promote a sense of solidarity. At the same time, family functioning is regulated by clearly defined roles and rules of interpersonal conduct (Ishisaka & Takagi, 1982). Each individual has a role, a place in the family structure and in the social order (Ho, 1987; Ishisaka & Takagi, 1982).

In Asian, Pacific Island, and Filipino societies, the nuclear family is embedded in an extended family network. The boundaries of the nuclear family are flexible with respect to the inclusion of grandparents, uncles, and cousins (Heras, 1985; Huang, 1989; Nagata, 1989; Tran, 1988) and in Vietnamese culture includes deceased relatives (Tran, 1988). The Hawaiian *ohana* (family) and Samoan *aiga* (family) define extended relatives by blood, marriage, or adoption (Mokuau & Tauili'ili, 1992). Within the extended family network, individual and social alliances are maintained by strong family bonds and defined roles. In the Samoan American culture, the village chief (*matai*) and family chief rank higher than the heads of particular households (Mokuau & Tauili'ili, 1992).

Asian, Pacific Island, and Filipino American families are characterized by hierarchical relationships and strong interdependence, both intergenerationally and laterally (S. Sue & Morishima, 1982). Within the extended family, complex patterns of relating and relationships exist (Heras, 1985). The family provides a supportive network of resources that an individual can tap in times of need, as well as an extensive set of obligations. Many family functions are shared, including caretaking, disciplining children, and companionship. At the same time, the family maintains rigid roles and expectations for its members (D. Sue & Sue, 1990). These roles are organized around generational hierarchies based on age and gender.

Although high levels of hierarchical organization and cohesion characterize most Asian, Filipino, and Pacific Island families, there are differences within the kinship systems of these groups. Asian societies maintain a patrilineal family structure, in which males, particularly the oldest males, have the most authority and responsibility (Nagata, 1989; Tran, 1988). Females are expected to obey their fathers, husbands, and eldest sons (Tran, 1988). Older children are taught to care for and be responsible for younger siblings (Huang, 1989). Husbands are expected to maintain the financial welfare of the family and make most major decisions. Wives are expected to manage the finances, maintain the household, and attend to the day-to-day affairs of the children. In traditional Asian culture, the wife became part of the husband's family and had limited rights.

Filipino family structure is characterized by a bilateral kinship system in which descent and lineage are traced from both the mother and father. In such a system, females can inherit property and expect support and protection from their families. Gender hierarchies are less evident, particularly in urban areas (Heras, 1985). A woman's family exerts a powerful influence over the decisions that a couple makes throughout their lifetime. As in Asian families, the father's role is that of family provider and protector. The mother provides nurturance and manages the household. Many Filipino women work and take an interest in augmenting the family's income (Mendez & Jocano, 1974).

With Hawaiian and Samoan families, the primacy of the extended family, the *ohana* and the *aiga,* allows for bilateral kinship structures that are less rigid than that for the Asian family. For Hawaiians, family relationships and bonds are tied to the islands (*aina*) and the ancestral spirits (Mokuau &

Tauili'ili, 1992). Because property belongs to the *aiga* in American Samoa, the inheritance of the authority and title of *matai* is important. Contact with Western cultures and—for Hawaiians in particular, a dissemination of their pure bloodlines—has produced a range of acculturation and lifestyles among Pacific Island Americans.

Predominant Cultural Beliefs and Values

Ho (1992) offers seven predominantly shared cultural values that are traditional in Asian and Filipino cultures. The value of filial piety, meaning respect for and loyalty to parents, grandparents, and other elders, undergirds the importance of maintaining family cohesion for the sake of preserving the family lineage. Children are socialized to give unquestioning loyalty and obedience to their parents (S. Sue & Morishima, 1982). Interpersonal relationships, beginning with the family, are governed by moral and ethical codes of loyalty, obligation, and reciprocity (Ishisaka & Tagaki, 1982), which support the continuity of filial piety.

This hierarchical but cohesive relationship extends to all situations involving interactions with authority figures (Chan, 1993; Serafica, 1990). Spread through Confucianism, this value orientation is manifested in strong interdependence of family members and loyalty to the family, appreciation of the aged and the wisdom of the elder, maintenance of proper hierarchical relationships, and, for children, a sense of their obligation toward their parents for their birth and upbringing (Kim, Okamura, Ozawa, & Forrest, 1981). Heras (1992) cautions therapists about making errors in sexual child abuse assessments when the authoritarian structure and hierarchical imbalance of power are mistaken as red flags for molestation rather than seen as culturally appropriate. Care must be taken when we are unaware of our bias toward the definition of "healthy" families as those conforming to the dominant U.S. idea of democratic, egalitarian relationships and open communications. However, there also can be occasions where culture is used as a screen to hide abuse.

Maintaining harmony to preserve the integrity of the whole, cooperation, and self-sacrifice for the good of the collective are the foundations that balance the complex interdependent roles. Many younger, acculturated children of traditional parents face severe conflicts when their desires for their professions or chosen mates do not meet their parents' expectations. It is fairly common for Asian children to recant stories of child abuse, sacrificing their individual needs for the integrity of the family.

Another factor in the frequency of recanting sexual child abuse and the low disclosure or reported incidence is the value of saving face and avoiding shame. A family can lose face when a member fails to conform to cultural norms. Shame, failure, and inadequacy are felt individually and collectively by the entire family. The words "Hagi," in Japanese, "hiya," in Tagalog, or "changpi," in Korean, describe this shame. If saving face is viewed as an important ego-syntonic behavior for traditional parents, labeling them as "resistant" or "in denial" would serve only to alienate the family further. Heras (1992) suggests that it is better to work with parents along more acceptable paths, asking, "Where do we go from here?" or "How can we make our situation better?" (p. 123).

Ho (1992) describes the fourth important value as "middle-position virtue," which is valued by Asians as being in step with others, neither ahead nor behind. It signifies oneness with the group, belonging, and togetherness (Ho, 1992). In behavioral terms, one finds consensus and avoids confrontations for the sake of group harmony; thus conflict is managed or avoided. Negative expressions and personal complaints are discouraged (S. Sue & Morishima, 1982), and behaviors such as stoicism, patience, tolerance, and maintaining a pleasant disposition are prescribed (Ishisaka & Tagaki, 1982). A child victim of sexual abuse would not want to be viewed differently by the family or be the person to cause disharmony. This relates to another value of being *inconspicuous*. The Japanese describe this value in a saying that translates as, "When a nail sticks out, hammer it down." Contrary to American individualism, the middle-position virtue values humility and being inconspicuous, which contributes to the stereotype of Asian passivity. Thus the victim of sexual abuse is constrained to keep silent or risk emotional estrangement from the family.

To conform in this way, Asians are socialized to have an *awareness of the social milieu* (Ho, 1992), using the situational context to provide cues to appropriate behaviors, thoughts, and feelings. Most Asian languages prescribe specific honorifics for certain relationships depending upon the hierarchy of the individuals involved. Thus contextual awareness is learned through observing nonverbal cues, checking one's behavior in relation to others, maintaining an evenness of emotions, and practicing restraint and moderation in all aspects of life. Nonverbal communication skills become ingrained in cultural behaviors. This is often observed by outsiders as Asians being stoic and having little feelings. A culturally competent therapist would not require these clients to express openly feelings such as anger or grief as evidence of having achieved a healthy level of adaptation (Heras, 1992). In the beginning phases of therapy, the therapist must also display a requisite control of emotions along with respect for the client's restraint. Feelings are expressed in indirect ways and through symbolic behavior and language. Only someone acculturated and socialized in the verbal expression of feelings will engage in Western-style interaction in "talking therapies."

Suffering in silence, persevering against challenges, and accepting fate are values based in Buddhist belief (Kim et al., 1981). The Vietnamese hold ideal a person who combines thrift, industriousness, patience, determination, and endurance, whereas the Japanese say that to complain shows a small spirit, "ki ga chiisai" (Kim et al., 1981). Thus, accepting fate or taking an inactive stance or resigned attitude are common behaviors among Asians that other Americans have difficulty understanding. Asian, Pacific Island, and Filipino American families seldom challenge the interventions of child abuse authority figures. Such a challenge would be unthinkable for traditionally oriented families who have been socialized to behave respectfully toward those in authority. Seeking help from anyone outside the family is unacceptable. This "pragmatic adaptability" may be mistakenly interpreted as resistance to the offers of help by service providers (Ho, 1992).

Child-Raising Practices and Personality Development

In traditional Asian, Filipino, and Pacific Islander cultures, parents claim an inherent right over their children (S. Sue & Morishima, 1982). Loyalty, obedience, and respect are expected. Research indicates that Asian, Filipino, and Pacific Island Americans socialize their children to maintain traditional values of family cohesion, solidarity, filial piety, and a sense of obligation to the family (Huang, 1989; Sluzki, 1979; Wong, 1987). Emphasis is also placed on the character development of the child (Wong-Kerberg, 1993). In traditional Chinese culture, there are two lines of thought regarding this development. One is that a child's character is predetermined and is based on qualities of parents, grandparents, or ancestors. The second belief is that a child's character is formed by his or her parents, who are responsible for guiding and teaching the child to "be" or "become" of good character (Gin, 1978).

A variety of child-rearing strategies are used, including modeling desired behavior (Nguyen & Williams, 1989), didactic teachings (S. Chan, 1993), physical discipline during the earlier years (UPAC, 1982), rewards, and the use of shame (D. Sue & Sue, 1982).

In infancy, children are regarded as gifts and blessings. The relationship between mother and child often takes precedence over the marital relationship (Okamura, 1993; UPAC, 1982). The child is nurtured by all family members and is given continual and close physical contact, rarely left alone (Korbin, 1987). Sleeping arrangements are loosely defined, as are schedules for weaning, toilet training, or bedtime. The Japanese describe a family's sleeping arrangement as depicted in the Japanese word for river (*kawa*), which is one short vertical line between two longer vertical lines. In most traditionally oriented Asian, Filipino, and Pacific Island families, sleeping alone is a punishment rather than a luxury.

As the child moves into the toddler stage, he or she is given great freedom of expression and much attention and affection. Doi (1973) has aptly described the Japanese practice of *amae,* which socializes interdependent behaviors. It is described as a process of asking for indulgence with an expectation of receiving indulgence. This reciprocal behavior reinforces the interdependent bonds.

More demands are placed on the child around the age of 6, often when the child enters school. It is around this age that Filipinos believe that children develop *isip,* or thoughts (Mendez & Jocano, 1974). Parents become more active teachers, fostering correct behavior and using stricter disciplinary measures. Desirable behaviors include respect for elders, obedience to authority, academic diligence and excellence, responsibility toward the family, obligation, and reciprocity (Nguyen & Williams, 1989). The child's entry into school brings about the potential for conflict for immigrant families because traditional cultural values are challenged (Serafica, 1990). Moreover, parents are often disappointed in the school's lack of authority and discipline with their children.

Shaming is part of the socialization in shaping the behavior of children and adults. Negative reinforcements such as scolding, name calling, teasing, and harsh criticism are considered emotionally abusive in Western parenting. However, in Asian cultures, these techniques are used to convey a parent's love for the child through correcting unacceptable behaviors.

American-born children of foreign-born parents become confused when they do not hear direct expressions of love from their parents, as depicted in American media and literature. Therapists may want to translate the immigrant parents' hard work, long hours of sacrifice, often silent and stern resilience as their culturally syntonic expressions of love. The perspective of the cultural context and the intent of the parents have important implications in any child abuse assessment (Korbin, 1979).

When children reach adolescence, they are given greater family responsibilities. They may be responsible for younger siblings and grandparents, as well as responsible for their parents' well-being. Older teens often are expected to contribute financially to the family. Most parent-child conflicts emerge at this time because of intensified cultural and group identification differences.

Sexuality and Gender Roles

For Asians and Filipinos, sexuality is seldom discussed openly. In more traditional families, sexual behavior is a highly sensitive and delicate subject (Huang & Ying, 1989; Nagata, 1989). Open discussion of sexuality varies among groups and is usually limited to same-sex conversations. For example, Vietnamese or Filipino women may tease and joke about sex, whereas Chinese women are less likely to do so (Tsui, 1985). For most Asians and Filipinos, virginity in females is highly valued. Loss of virginity prior to marriage is viewed as a disgrace to both the individual and the family and makes the woman less desirable as a marriage partner (Tsui, 1985). Female sexual behavior is usually limited to the marital relationship.

For males, the expectations around sexual behavior are less rigid. The culture acknowledges male sexuality. Virility and potency are valued in order to maintain family lineage. Sexual liaisons by men outside of marriage with mistresses or "second wives" occur frequently in societies in which there is a relative lack of husband-wife intimacy, such as in the Japanese culture (UPAC, 1982).

Asian and Filipino parents are poorly equipped to manage the sexual conflicts and concerns of their preadolescent and adolescent children. Overt sexual behavior, particularly for girls, such as wearing revealing attire, using makeup, or flirting, is strictly prohibited and criticized. The adolescents' exposure to sexual matters coupled with peer pressure to experiment in sexual behavior creates significant family conflict during this period of the family life cycle (Nagata, 1989).

The literature indicates that women seldom seek counseling for sexual problems, despite the frequency of problems such as dyspareunia (Tsui, 1985). Discussion of sexual matters in treatment is anxiety provoking, particularly with therapists of the other gender (Tsui, 1985). These encounters usually enhance the client's sense of shame and disgrace and can alienate the client from the therapist if the timing, frequency, and presentation are inappropriate.

The Context of Racism and Oppression

Sexual child abuse issues within the Asian Pacific and Filipino American populations in the United States must be viewed within the larger ecological context of American society, which, despite ideals to the contrary, is racist in its beliefs, institutions, and practices. Negative stereotypes, discrimination, and powerlessness are experienced by ethnic minority individuals and families in all sectors of society, from housing and employment to education, services, and recreation. The messages of "you don't belong," "you're different," "you're less than," "you'll never measure up," and "you don't deserve," are conveyed in countless ways that undermine self-worth and dignity. Stereotypic messages abound in the media, which depict Asian men as cartoon characters or despicable torturers and women as sexually mysterious, submissive, and childlike (C. S. Chan, 1987).

When Asian newcomers encounter hostile racist behaviors, they are often initially confused by the minority role assigned to them and accept the discriminatory encounters rather than protest. However, the feelings of anger and powerlessness can be turned inward or expressed within the family, resulting in a higher risk for violence in the home against spouses and children. We believe that incest among immigrant and refugee families occurs more often than community members themselves wish to acknowledge. Wyatt (1990) discusses how ethnic minority children who are victims of sexual abuse are also victims in other ways as members of a racist society that renders their parents powerless in controlling aspects of their lives.

Asian Pacific and Filipino newcomers most often seek communities in North America where social networks exist and where they can more readily maintain a sense of self and ethnic identity within the context of a society that does not accept differences. Particularly in early resettlement years, ethnic enclaves such as Chinatowns and Vietnamesetowns serve as refuges where housing is cheaper and social and language access are available. Because of the low wages earned by immigrants, crowded and poor housing becomes a common environment where children grow up. There is an increased risk of sexual child abuse with relative and nonrelative boarders in the home, and with parents outside the home working long hours and/or pursuing the more immediate stress reducers of alcohol, drugs, or gambling.

In addition, because of unfamiliarity with American ways, recent Asian American arrivals are frequently victimized by those who purport to help them. Unsuspecting parents have allowed their children to be "taken in" by "nice" Americans (e.g., teachers, tutors, neighbors, church workers, landlords, and sponsors) who express interest in helping the children succeed. The families welcome help from the outside when they first enter a new culture and are unsuspecting of anything but the best intentions. We are familiar with cases involving preadolescent and adolescent males who become victims of sexual abuse by adult American "friends of the family" and are unable to extricate themselves after years of dependent relationships.

Pedophiles are known to target Asian children because of their easy access, their physically small bodies and childlike appearance, the lack of body hair, submissive responses, and tendency toward being impressionable (Wong-Kerberg, 1993). Children are then abused sexually and put into a double bind of having to betray their benefactors, whom their parents trust and believe more than the children. Some parents who are dependent upon these Americans choose to maintain their silence for fear of losing what they have gained. Most immigrant and refugee parents do not report sexual child abuse independently, largely due to fear, lack of education about abuse, mistrust of institutions and outsiders, and word-of-mouth stories that abound in the community, many of which are negative. The message is that they risk losing their children forever if they tell.

The code of silence is strengthened by the feelings of shame felt by the family: shame of losing face within their community and shame of their ethnic community losing face within the larger social context. Facing discriminatory messages of "less than," Asian Pacifics and Filipino American minority families struggle to be "more than" and have extreme difficulty exposing such perceived shameful experiences. They prefer to move away from friends and relatives rather than face the social stigma of sexual abuse. Social isolation is an important area of assessment in an Asian Pacific or Filipino American family's risk for sexual child abuse and other social dysfunctions.

When sexual child abuse is reported, these families more often become further victimized by the system that aims to protect. The children are often removed immediately from the home and placed for long periods due to the complications of cross-cultural intervention. Language and/or cultural barriers between parents and child protection system workers and the legal system create multiple areas of differences, miscommunications, misunderstandings, and errors that result in lengthy delays in reunification or permanent placements.

Over many years of work with Asian Pacific and Filipino clients, we have experienced subjective, culturally biased decisions by child protection workers, therapists, and judges that have been destructive to children and their families because of a serious lack of understanding about cultural behaviors. For example, children are not allowed by some child protection workers to speak to their parents in the parents' language when they are placed with foster parents who are monolingual in English for fear of negative influence. In addition, mothers of victims, who often do not communicate as calmly in English as expected, may face punitive reactions from representatives of the criminal, judicial, and child protection systems for their emotional expressions of anguish, anger, and loss (Okamura, 1992). Punitive reactions may include the extension of out-of-home placement or denial of visitation with their children. Children have been placed for permanent adoption in many cases where an immigrant or refugee parent is unable to communicate with the "system" because of cultural and language differences. Child protection systems must assess themselves for cultural competency to ensure that all families have equal opportunities for due process.

Definition, Identification, and Intervention

The following discussion of the complex issues in the definition of sexually abusive practices, identification of cases, and appropriate intervention approaches is based on our clinical work and discussions with other professionals, due to the lack of research in this area.

Korbin's (1979) groundbreaking discussions of cross-cultural perspectives on child abuse and neglect have important implications for American families of Asian Pacific and Filipino backgrounds in this country. Korbin cites the need for viewing and defining child abuse and neglect within the cultural context, using a framework for definition so that the intent of the adults, the interpretation of the child, and the cultural meanings of behaviors are considered. She also discusses the need to make distinctions between culturally acceptable practices and those that are outside the standards of the culture that are "idiosyncratic abuse or neglect" (Korbin, 1991). On a case-by-case basis, however, these issues are not easily teased out. Asian Pacific and Filipino American mental health professionals and paraprofessionals can attest to receiving calls from child protection agencies asking if a certain behavior of an adult with a child is considered an acceptable cultural practice. Examples of this include questions such as the following: (a) Is it true that mothers and fathers use their fingers to wash the genitals of a primary school-aged child? (b) What about a 13-year-old boy sleeping in the same bed as his mother? (c) Do family members kiss and touch a baby boy's genitals as a sign of affection for a boy child? (d) Do fathers of adolescent girls examine their daughter's vaginal area for medical reasons? Cultural informants may disagree with each other about the acceptability of these behaviors in their particular cultural group.

In a survey conducted by Okamura (1992) of 33 Asian, Pacific Island, and Filipino professional and paraprofessional human service providers in a community-based agency, a surprising 15% of the respondents (27% American born, 72% foreign born) agreed that sexual child abuse did not occur in their communities, whereas 24% reported that they did not know if sexual abuse occurred in their communities. The respondents could answer "agree," "disagree," or "don't know" about adult behaviors toward children that are often viewed as questionable by American child protection workers. The small study sample pointed out ethnic differences and intraethnic differences of opinion. For example, on the item, "It is acceptable in my culture for fathers or uncles to check on a girl's body, including the vaginal area, for medical reasons," 15% agreed, 76% disagreed, and 9% did not know. Among the 15% who agreed were Vietnamese, Korean, Chinese, Lao, and Hmong ethnic respondents. None of the Cambodian, Samoan, Filipino, or Japanese respondents agreed to this item. Similarly, on the item, "It is acceptable in my culture or among members of my culture for a baby boy to have his genitals kissed and fondled by family members as expressions of joy that it is a boy child," 35% agreed, 44% disagreed, and 18% did not know. The 35% who agreed included Vietnamese, Korean, Chinese, Lao, Hmong, Cambodian, and Filipino. Among the 44% who disagreed were the same groups plus Samoan and Japanese (Okamura, 1992). This illustrates the difficulty in getting clear answers to questions that arise out of context. When seeking the help of cultural informants, it is important to consult more than one person, as well as others who have considerable experience with immigrant groups in this country.

The silence about sexuality (E. Lee, 1988) in general presents a substantial obstacle in the disclosure, acknowledgment, or treatment of sexual child abuse. Adult Asian women who were sexually abused as children or adolescents have been found to suffer in silence for years about their abuse, telling no one and accepting it as fate (Hicks, 1993). Because loss of virginity brings dishonor to self and family, female victims may deny trauma or reframe the abuse in a more socially acceptable way (E. Cole, Espin, & Rothblom, 1992).

Not only have they been sexually violated, they are not perceived as victims (Rao et al., 1992). Many come from societies where rape is not addressed or acknowledged, or where there is no remedy or avenues of recourse until their migration to a culture that labels and defines it. The legacy of silence and shame are passed from generation to generation (Hu, 1975).

Little is known about male child victims of sexual abuse among Asian, Pacific Island, and Filipino populations. Based on anecdotal information, males are most often victimized by family members, relatives, or friends in the family home, or by someone who has befriended the child as a sponsor, landlord, or neighbor. As with females, boys who report sexual assault to adult caretakers in their families are likely to be disbelieved. Homophobia also plays a part in traditional groups where members fear the contamination of homosexuality if there has been same-sex contact. However, in Pacific Island cultures, homosexuality is more openly accepted and the fear of stigma is less of a factor.

It is rare for an Asian child from a newcomer family to disclose sexual abuse directly. The sexual abuse usually is masked by a myriad of other presenting problems, and when these are unraveled, the sexual abuse may be uncovered. The child's and the family's levels of acculturation have direct bearing on the child's ability to disclose and the family's ability to provide support for disclosure. For children from traditional families, their foremost responsibility is to sacrifice their individual needs and desires for the solidarity of the family. Children are frequently not supported by primary caretakers who disbelieve the children's disclosures. Primary caretakers in the Asian cases in Rao et al.'s (1992) study were less likely to be involved in the initial intake process. Most Southeast Asian parents in Wong's (1987) sexual abuse prevention program revealed that they do not believe sexual abuse to be a problem, that a family member would not sexually abuse a child, and furthermore, if there was sexual abuse in the family, they would keep it a secret.

Shame and Denial

A child may choose not to disclose because of personal shame due to the sexual nature of the abuse. When the child discloses, the family frequently directs anger to the child and the intervening adult. The family perceives the disclosure as putting the entire family's reputation at risk because anything brought to bear outside of the family, especially a complaint from a child against an adult of a sexual transgression, threatens family unity. It cannot be true and parents cannot let it be true. The resulting systematic denial serves to strengthen this resolve.

Because of the sexual nature of the abuse, parents may feel discomfort, embarrassment, and shame to such an extent that they rush to save both the child's and family's reputation by outward and adamant denial. Some parents will firmly maintain that the abuse did not occur. Some parents will contend that the child is lying and pressure the child to recant. In Rao et al.'s (1992) retrospective study comparing Asian sexual child abuse cases with other populations, key Asian family members were found to be least supportive in their responses to the victim. Compared to Blacks, Whites, and Hispanics, Asian mothers or primary caretakers were half as likely to report the abuse to authorities. Ima and Hohm (1991) found that 50% of the Asian Pacific sexual abuse cases reported incest perpetrated by fathers, compared to 36% in a national study.

There are times when the parents will hold to their disbelief and accuse the child of storytelling, furthering emotional damage and trauma to the child, even though the parents truly believe that they are serving the child's interests by protecting the child's reputation and future. The difficulty for the child in remaining in the home after disclosure often leads to removing the child from the home during the initial period of investigation. Rao et al. (1992) state that

> Asian victims were more likely than the other ethnic groups to be living in a shelter at the time of evaluation . . . most often having been sent there by authorities to protect the victims' safety after the discovery of intrafamilial sex abuse. (p. 881)

The dynamics of shame and denial are often followed by blaming and accusations of betrayal. If the parents come to acknowledge the abuse, many will blame the child. Children are held responsible for "being at the wrong place at the wrong time," or for being a "bad child" and somehow responsible for attracting the sexual advances. If the perpetrator is a parent or family member, blaming allows the guilty party to save face. If a child is removed from the home or a parent is ordered out of the home by legal mandate, the child may be blamed for the disruption and breakup of the family. A nonoffending parent often will align with the offending parent against the child in an attempt to preserve the family's respectability in their community.

Parents must also consider the child's respectability. In newcomer ethnic communities, confidentiality is key. There is tremendous fear of the child being stigmatized, resulting in potential ostracism by members of the community. The child becomes "damaged goods" and undesirable for marriage into any family. Rape victims suffer enormously under these cultural taboos, along with widows and divorced women.

Mental Health Risks for Victims

The Asian sexual abuse victim from a traditional family is at high risk for severe anxiety, depression, and suicide. Rao et al. (1992) found that Asian victims, mostly from immigrant households, were more likely to express suicidal ideation. The postreporting trauma often overtakes the effects of the abuse itself with frequent separation from family and friends, isolation from familiar cultural environments, repeated interaction with intrusive strangers, accusations of betrayal from family members, and constant pressures to recant. Many children choose withdrawal as the best defense from what is an overwhelming experience and finally give in and recant, enabling them to return home.

"I made it up," "It didn't happen," and "I lied about it" are retractions that relieve the anxiety, confusion, and unhappiness. Children have much to fear: permanent removal from the home, the perpetrator's reaction, losing parental love and approval, causing the breakup of the family, and responsibility for sending someone to prison. Immigrant children may also fear deportation if they disclose (Agtuca, 1994). In the child's mind, recanting the abuse will make it all go away. For children who recant, or for those who do not disclose, the trauma experience lives on and surfaces in other aspects of their lives, contributing to dysfunctional relationships, depression, and suicidal ideation.

Differential Interventions

Sexual child abuse interventions at all levels need to be assessed for cultural appropriateness. Rao et al.'s (1992) findings that Asian victims, families, and caretakers were significantly distinct in demographic profile and responses to sexual child abuse compared to other ethnic groups points to the need to use such information in designing service delivery. Although child protection services, law enforcement, and judicial systems have standard operating policies and procedures, different approaches can augment existing protocols. Intervention systems also need to assess how regulations and standards can be harmful to culturally distinct individuals and families. The following are a few recommendations that affect victims and families of Asian Pacific and Filipino backgrounds:

1. The child should be interviewed with the trusted adult to whom disclosure was initially made, and not in the presence of the family. In addition, extraordinary measures to ensure confidentiality are necessary. This recommendation is especially appropriate for school settings, where initial reports often originate. Uniformed police should not remove children from the school because it attracts too much attention.

2. Repeated interviews and more than one interviewer inhibit the child's disclosure. The child can be victimized further by those who are unaware of children's intense feelings of isolation from the family and vulnerability to their rejection.

3. The child's ambivalence, resulting from a desire for safety and a desire to remain within the family, should be recognized. An empathic worker or police officer should provide specific explanations about what will happen in the process of disclosure.

4. When out-of-home placement is appropriate, relatives and ethnically matched foster families are preferable. Asian Pacific and Filipino children and adolescents are unaccustomed to relationships with outsiders, probably have little experience being in the homes of different cultural groups, and may experience severe separation anxiety. Infants and toddlers who have been placed in nonethnically matched foster homes where food and language are foreign frequently fail to thrive and appear depressed.

5. Continued contact with nonoffending, accepting family members is crucial during separation. The case manager has a key role in bridging the communication and cultural gap between victim and family, supporting positive and consistent visitations, troubleshooting between foster parent, victim, and nonoffending caretaker, and assisting with acculturation tasks for all concerned.

6. Authority figures such as child protection workers or case managers need to be proactive in their interventions, using outreach and other visible activities that foster communications with all members of an affected family. The imbalance of power, respect for authority, unfamiliarity with the child protection system, and language barriers put Asian Pacific and Filipino American families at a disadvantage. They are confused about what to do, how to act, when to show up, and whom, how, and where to

call. They often wait for the person in charge to inform them of the required actions. When the worker does not take the time to explain or make frequent contact with families, or takes an adversarial approach, difficulties compound.

Assessment and Treatment

Most child protection systems require victims and their families to seek therapy as a means of completing court orders. We turn our discussion to this area; however, therapy alone is not recommended in the healing process nor is it viewed as the cure-all for preventing reoccurrence of abuse. The contextual approach involves multilevel and multisystem interventions with education and family support to mitigate against all forms of child abuse and neglect.

When a child and family are referred to therapy, assessment and treatment begin almost simultaneously. The first session is critical in establishing the therapeutic relationship and engaging the family to stay in the process (D. Sue & Sue, 1990). Revealing family secrets and verbalizing thoughts and feelings to strangers are Western practices that are antithetical to the Asian Pacific and Filipino cultures. Most often, after an initial period of developing trust, the process of psychotherapy must be psychoeducational, with modeling, coaching, and directive activities.

Even if the therapist is aware that sexual abuse has occurred and that a family member is the perpetrator, to confront and focus on the details or dynamics of the abuse after the family has gone through the court system could only further alienate the child and the family. Education about preventing future abuse is necessary, and discussions of how the family members will build a safety net are important. Therapists must demonstrate tangible and practical evidence of their usefulness (Heras, 1992).

Confidentiality is foremost in their minds and must be ensured. The therapist's genuine interest in helping and supporting the family must be communicated through nonjudgmental and nonpunitive messages because the family will be distrustful, suspicious, and distant in many ways. Why should they trust a stranger, especially one who knows little of their cultural values and ways of doing things?

History taking is more productive if conducted informally through engaging the family in conversation that is geared toward building relationships. Gathering data about a family should spread across frequent contacts with a victim and family. As a relationship builds, the information will be provided more readily. Most Asian Pacific and Filipino American clients will not volunteer information about themselves, and therapists must be cognizant of the strong reluctance to self-disclose.

The following guidelines for culturally appropriate assessments are used by most clinicians who work with Asian Pacific and Filipino American families. Primary family data include the following:

1. Ethnicities of family members according to how they define themselves (the father may be Chinese, the mother may be Laotian, and the children would be Chinese-Laotian American)

2. Country or place of birth (if American born, the number of generations in the country gives important information about acculturation; if foreign born, obtain the reasons and history of emigration and relocation along with legal status in this country; premigration and postmigration status and experiences of the family also give clues to status change difficulties and significant past trauma)

3. Languages spoken and comprehended (families sometimes use three different languages within a household, creating complexity and confusion for outsiders)

4. Location of, amount of contact with, and economic support of members of the extended families (most immigrant/refugee families are emotionally and economically connected to overseas family members, which affects their daily lives)

5. Changes in migration including death, separation, new occupations, and loss of homeland, property, and status

6. Effects of culture shock and cultural displacement

7. Family values, beliefs, rituals, and traditional practices for health and illness

8. Acculturation rates and levels, which vary among family members

9. The cultural values, beliefs, and practices that continue to work for the family

10. Sexual values and sexual behaviors

In addition, Sgroi's (1988) recommendations regarding history of sexual abuse of parents and siblings within the family, history of sexual deviance within the family, and histories of mental illness and alcohol and substance abuse are also necessary.

It is important to assess Asian Pacific and Filipino American families for their inherent strengths and their past and current methods of coping with family problems. Consider the following questions: (a) Who makes up the household and to what degree are they connected to members of their physical, social, and spiritual community? "Aunts," "uncles," or "cousins" are not necessarily related by blood and often are adult friends of the family. A "cousin" could be someone who has a similar surname from the same village back home. (b) How is the family structured and organized? The hierarchy and definition of roles clarify boundaries and relationships. Within each extended family, there are built-in safety nets, checks, and balances, which allow family members to reach out to grandparents, aunts, and cousins. The less acculturated a family is to the dominant society, the more authoritarian the relationships between parents and children, and husbands and wives, tend to be. (c) Who is the primary caretaker of the children and what child-rearing practices predominate in the household? Older siblings are often given parental authority over younger siblings. In an effort to bypass the child abuse laws, some Southeast Asian refugee parents ask their older children to beat the younger siblings to discipline them.

Many nonacculturated wives and mothers are expected to take a secondary role behind husbands and sons, which contributes to some mothers' inability to be straightforward about ensuring protection of their children, particularly daughters. Mothers are often torn between protecting their children and protecting their relationships with their husbands. They strive to maintain their husbands' role in the family structure and thereby ensure the integrity of the family unit. Heras (1992) found in her caseload of 60 Asian and Filipino nonoffending mothers of abused children that only 4 separated or divorced their perpetrator-husbands. This is sometimes a difficult area for practitioners to understand because of the inherent belief that women should logically want to protect their daughters. Immigrant Asian Pacific or Filipino women risk losing their economic and emotional means of survival should they lose their spouses or partners, and the women are reluctant to articulate this fear. The therapist must develop appropriate skills to help these women, who are understandably fearful, to be able to learn ways to protect their children without destroying their sense of security. They need support and empathic understanding from a therapist who can patiently assist them to be empowered in a variety of ways that do not threaten their fundamental positions in their families.

Treatment of sexual abuse is often a long-term process. For most Asian Pacific and Filipino American children, disclosure, acknowledgment, and expression of feelings, acceptance, and integration take longer to unfold compared to mainstream American children. Therapists need to adapt "talking" therapies with children and adolescents who are socialized in less verbal cultural environments than their White American counterparts, and to be careful not to pressure a child to express deep, conflictual feelings that they may have toward family members.

Early on, projective techniques are most effective in both assessment and treatment. The nonthreatening and symbolic aspects of projective techniques serve to protect children from their own denial and fear of betraying the family. Some effective modalities include drawing, painting, collage, and clay work (Oaklander, 1988); sand play with appropriate ethnic figures, extended family figures, familiar trees, palms, greenery, a variety of houses, buildings, decorations, and artifacts that reflect Asian Pacific and Filipino cultures (Yoko Fujita, personal communication, 1994); projective, culturally appropriate storytelling cards; and telling and writing stories, fairy tales, and myths, along with puppet and role play with themes of social roles, family life, and experiences of victimization and empowerment. Other themes of overcoming adversity or challenges are also important. When artifacts and stories that are culturally appropriate are not available, therapists have created them to fit the client's culture (Yoko Fujita, personal communication, 1994).

From these play therapy techniques, children may progress to more direct and directive activities that include using body maps, where children draw themselves and where they were violated—including drawing their emotional responses of fear, anger, and helplessness; body tracing, where the child is traced in actual life size and then draws all the above; letter writing, either to the offending parent or the nonoffending parent, or both; and play-acting scenarios to be resolved, such as role playing to prepare for court appearances or to practice confronting the perpetrator, if appropriate.

A bilingual-bicultural therapist was working with five Chinese bilingual and monolingual siblings who ranged in age from 5 years to 10 years. The children had been sexually molested and had contracted gonorrhea from a boarder in the family home. Even after many sessions, the therapist was making no progress with the children either individually or as a group because they did not want to talk about what had happened to them. The children were chaotic and had difficulty settling down and focusing on any play or art activity until the therapist started drawing a man's figure on a large sheet of paper. The children eventually stopped their hyperactivity and "helped" him with the drawing, telling him that "that was the man who was bad." They instructed the therapist to put him behind bars and requested assurance that he would stay there and not come back. As they felt freer to express their fears and anger, they began to pick up crayons and add to the picture, drawing uglier and meaner expressions on the "bad man." He was finally decimated with crayon marks and crushed into a ball and thrown into the wastebasket. The eldest boy ran back into the therapy room after the group left and initially wanted the paper ball back but then changed his mind, saying it belonged there. For many newly immigrated children and their families, therapists must articulate and guide the direction of the therapy by modeling and role playing in this way.

Asian children may disclose after sufficient trust is built, or they may never admit to the abuse even with concrete physical evidence. They may recant a number of times due to fear, ambivalence, and family pressure. If the therapist remains accepting and supportive without pushing for verbal acknowledgment of the abuse, and is consistent in believing the child wherever the child may be between the poles of disclosure and recanting, the child can gain some strength from the relationship. If the therapist offers the child a safe and therapeutic environment with unwavering assurance and understanding, often the child will then finally stand firm in a disclosure.

Evidentiary exams, when timely, can be of great help in relieving the child of the burden of responsibility (Wong-Kerberg, 1993). Tam, a 10-year-old Vietnamese girl who was repeatedly molested by her stepfather, disclosed accounts of her stepfather "touching" and "hurting" her to her Chinese American therapist. However, each time she disclosed a piece of information, she would immediately recant. Symptoms of frequent dissociation, enuresis at home and at school, angry outbursts, somatic complaints, insomnia, nightmares, and tangential thoughts were reported. Her stepfather vehemently denied the accusations to child protective services and claimed Tam was "crazy." Her two elder sisters criticized her and told her to "stop telling lies," and she had no support from her mother. A physical examination was conducted, during which considerable vaginal scarring and inflammation of the labia and surrounding areas were found. The report of the evidence of forced penetration and molestation was shared with Tam by the therapist, who also commended her attempts to disclose while understanding her need to protect her family. She was relieved to have proof, which her mother and sisters could read, that she was indeed hurt by her stepfather. The secret was acknowledged and she was able to begin her therapeutic work.

When physical findings validate and substantiate abuse, parents are less likely to dispute the findings or protest or blame the child or the system. The child is less likely to be perceived as falsifying his or her victimization and usually is relieved and validated by the physical evidence of proof. However, when there is no physical finding, it is essential that therapists help parents understand the emotional harm to the child victim that may still exist.

Asian parents often believe that "if we don't talk about it, the child will forget the abuse" and that if the child "appears to be okay," all will go away and be forgotten. Denial is persistent, and so is the pain.

As parents come to accept that the sexual abuse has occurred, a psychoeducational session can equip parents to help in the child's healing. The importance of believing the child's disclosure should be emphasized. The parents need to be educated sensitively about how harmful it is for the child to be blamed in any way. They must be taught not to belittle incidents where penetration or physical damage did not occur. The parents need to be helped with parenting skills that support emotional health. They must be educated about the extent of the physical and emotional trauma to the child, and what to expect in reactive behaviors that the child may manifest. Parents should be prepared to expect a loss of normalcy in the child's behavior for a time (Sgroi, 1988).

Depending on the acculturation level of the parents and the child, the therapist must be cognizant of the range of "psychological mindedness" among Asian Pacific and Filipino American families, and how emotional needs are expressed or not expressed. When abuse occurs, the value of child protection becomes paramount, which changes the culture of the family. Psychotherapy is the avenue for this change. Therapists must be actively involved in helping the family renegotiate their relationships with each other and learn new ways of expressing themselves and meeting emotional needs. Psychotherapy is an acculturative process, no matter where the family falls on the continuum of acculturation. It does not flow in one direction because the therapist also must be prepared to engage in mutual acculturation by learning with the family some different but equally appropriate and culturally meaningful ways that change can be accomplished.

The major goal in treatment is to stop the abuse and protect the child from further abuse. Treatment objectives include the education of the entire family about abuse; their roles and responsibilities for support and strength; ways to avoid scapegoating the victim; commitment to the process of healing; and for the child, individually, permission to express fears, anger, grief, loss, and hopes for recovery.

Less acculturated families are difficult to engage in the therapy process, and when mandated, many will go through the motions without making changes. Shame plays a part at many levels regarding the abuse, exposure to individuals outside the family, and the inability to resolve the issues on their own. The cultural differences in therapy are significant, and more often than not, Asian, Pacific Island, and Filipino American families are treated by professionals who are not bilingual, bicultural, or minimally knowledgeable about the cultural context. Early termination and other seemingly resistant and avoidant behaviors are common, which result in punitive actions against the family.

CASE HISTORY

Mrs. Machado

Mrs. Machado's case illustrates how the intervention of a culturally competent professional was able to prevent adoption procedures for her daughters, ages 6 and 12, who had been in foster placement for over a year. Mrs. Machado, a Filipina American, was in an emergency homeless shelter, where she happened to talk to a Chinese American volunteer counselor, who gave her the number of the Asian Pacific community-based mental health agency. She hesitantly made the call and was immediately seen and assessed as severely depressed and suicidal, and was referred for a longer term shelter program. Her Japanese American therapist moved quickly and provided immediate concrete assistance based on a vague history provided by the client. She was offered one-way transportation back to the clinic on a regular basis for follow-up treatment. Only after several sessions did she reveal that she had two children in foster care because they had been sexually abused by her boyfriend. She had been jailed for attempting to assault the officer who removed the children, had lost her apartment and all her belongings, and did not know where her children were or who the social worker was. She was distrustful, frightened, and despairing about the loss of her children. She felt powerless against the system, which had reams of, documentation about her inability to parent and follow through with court orders. With aggressive advocacy on one hand, and active support of her motivation to begin a program of rehabilitation on the other, she was able to return to her job after 1 year of therapy, reestablish a residence, and reunite her family. Mrs. Machado participated in therapy, which involved learning about depression and understanding her own history of abuse and victimization. She learned to make responsible choices and consider the safety needs of her children, and at the same time was allowed to express her anger, rage, and grief. She persisted in her goal of improving her English and articulating her needs to her social worker, her lawyer, and the children's therapist.

The immigrant Asian Pacific or Filipino nonoffending parent, usually the mother, requires sensitive and ancillary therapeutic efforts. She often needs to assume the role of head of the family when her perpetrator/spouse is required to leave the home, and she experiences intense ambivalence about her loyalty to the perpetrator/spouse and to the child victim. Supporting and assisting the child may be interpreted as discrediting the husband, thereby invalidating his role, which has negative consequences on the family as a unit. Labeling her as "unable to protect" increases her defensiveness and resistance to engage in treatment. Like the child victim, the mother's ambivalence should not be judged harshly, but rather it becomes a central issue in the therapeutic process. She needs to be educated about the realities of the child protection and legal systems, and given feedback on how the system views her behavior and presentation. Finally, the nonoffending Asian Pacific or Filipino spouse needs guidance and patient encouragement to make a choice if the perpetrator/spouse is unwilling to change.

The therapeutic task for perpetrators who are Asian Pacific or Filipino American, like other perpetrators, is to break the denial and move toward change. Initially, they may make cultural excuses for inappropriate behavior, and this resistance needs to be discussed and reframed. Admissions of guilt and remorse are often subdued, with statements such as, "I think I made a mistake." Perpetrators from these groups may minimize the trauma of sexual abuse, and although minimization is a culturally adaptive response, it becomes a therapeutic issue to work through. The deep feelings of shame, guilt, and loss of face associated with such an admission should be acknowledged by the therapist, with an understanding that the perpetrator will resist repeating the admission of guilt in subsequent sessions. However, accepting responsibility for the molestation is crucial. The therapist who pressures the perpetrator to discuss his or her remorse at every session may increase the shame and destroy the ego resources of the Asian Pacific or Filipino perpetrator. Outward displays or expressions of empathy for the victim also will be subdued, which is culturally syntonic. The perpetrator is often frightened and anxious about losing familial and social standing.

Differences in cultural styles of expression of feelings should be considered in evaluating a client's progress. Therapists who are not cognizant of these cultural differences can make serious errors in evaluating gains in therapy. Similarly, the lack of outward emotional expressiveness can be viewed mistakenly as resistance or poor motivation. Acceptance of responsibility and a focus on the changes necessary for successful reunification are the core treatment issues. These changes should match the values of the perpetrator's family and culture to achieve credibility (S. Sue & Zane, 1987).

In working with Asian Pacific and Filipino Americans, where interdependent relationships and connections have primacy over individual functioning, marital therapy should be initiated early in treatment. The goals of marital therapy will differ based on the family's situation in the sexual child abuse case. Couples need to work with the therapist in setting goals and negotiating role relationships that empower both individuals in a safe family environment.

It is essential to use skilled ethnic professionals and paraprofessionals to reach out to clients using patient and sensitive methods that communicate genuine desire to help. Parents feel extreme shame, anger, and powerlessness that may be expressed in unacceptable behavior vis-à-vis the child protection system. Advocacy, education, and clinical case management are essential in the therapeutic process. Therapists must become generalists in their practice approach, which includes "talking therapy" as just one aspect of helping Asian Pacific and Filipino American families.

Prevention

Prevention strategies that reach culturally different children and their families are extremely important with the multivaried cultural groups in North America. An ecological perspective is key in framing policies and programs. Community organizational factors; leadership structure; social networks; cultural, social, and spiritual resources; and the dynamic interaction within families and in workplaces, schools, and neighborhoods are all essential in planning appropriate prevention programs. In addition, risk factors such as demographic characteristics and responses to sexual child abuse as found by Rao et al. (1992) need to be considered in program design. Immigrant communities are also isolated from access to human service programs and resources, which increases their vulnerability to child sexual assault. A Southeast Asian sexual child abuse prevention program in King County, Washington, used outreach and community support and involvement to develop and test appropriate educational materials that were distributed widely (Wong, 1987). This effort resulted in calls from all of the Southeast Asian communities in which they reported accounts of sexual assault, where, prior to the prevention program, no calls for assistance had been recorded. There is a need for expanded research to understand cultural factors in sexual child abuse in the Asian Pacific and Filipino American subgroups so that prevention and intervention programs can respond more appropriately.

Appropriate outreach, education, and psychosocial supports are key ingredients for successful work in the Asian, Filipino, and Pacific Island communities. The work should be geared toward supporting individuals' and families' adaptation to American culture without significantly removing cultural strengths. The Union of Pan Asian Communities, Inc., in San Diego has used such a model in the past 20 years' work with child abuse victims and families from Asian Pacific and Filipino American communities. Key elements are that (a) the service delivery is community based and sanctioned by the ethnic communities; (b) it offers a range of services including prevention, treatment, advocacy, outreach, and aftercare support; (c) it is physically, psychologically, socially, and culturally accessible, with bilingual-bicultural staff who are trustworthy, professional in their work, and above all, confidential; (d) there is a multidisciplinary team of mental health professionals and paraprofessionals that is culturally competent and trained in child maltreatment; (e) there are collaborative and consultative relationships with other disciplines, such as lawyers, physicians, teachers, and law enforcement; and (f) there is a parallel relationship with the formal authority of the child protection service, where referrals and collaborations enhance service delivery. An ideal program would include a 24-hour hotline available in all ethnic languages and a system that has a trained pool of ethnic foster families for emergency and longer term placements.

Because cases of child abuse in the Asian Pacific and Filipino American communities are usually reported by nonfamily members, a community-based program must be active in its education activities within the ethnic communities and with key informants who work with children. Cultural sensitivity training must be required of the law enforcement, school personnel, health and mental health personnel, clergy, and youth workers who often make the initial reports. Advocacy is an essential element of a community-based program that serves minority populations. Advocacy includes representing, mediating, and consulting with the various systems involved in child protection and adjudication. Advocacy is also an integral part of the therapeutic process with clients who feel powerless in relation to the "system."

Funding for community-based programs as described above should be a high priority in most communities with culturally diverse populations, especially with newcomers to this country. Funding constraints and the small pool of trained bilingual-bicultural professionals, however, have resulted in creative programming where a multidisciplinary team wears many functional "hats." Multidisciplinary teams also have the ability to tailor assessment and treatment services to be culturally syntonic to the individual client and family.

Conclusion

This chapter is an introduction to the topic of sexual child abuse in the Asian, Filipino, and Pacific Island communities. There is a serious lack of data about sexual child abuse intervention in these communities. We know that when sexual child abuse occurs, it is challenging to provide necessary protection for the child and appropriate intervention for the families. Intervention is rendered more difficult because of systemic barriers that do not allow for culturally different approaches and specially trained staff. All of us in the child protection field must work toward increasing our cultural competence and examining the biases we bring into the system that are ultimately harmful to the families we seek to help. There is need for mutual acculturation to accept a differential array of cultural values, lifestyles, and models of how families operate and function. We hope the readers will continue to seek opportunities to enhance, enrich, and expand their cultural competence with American families of Asian, Pacific Island, and Filipino heritage in the area of sexual child abuse.

Cambodians and Sexual Child Abuse

MARY SCULLY
THEANVY KUOCH
RICHARD A. MILLER

When we were asked to write a chapter about sexual abuse and Cambodian children, we responded immediately because we recognized that it is a subject much in need of discussion. We did not expect it to be an easy chapter to write because we knew there were few statistics available and we would have to base our writing on anecdotal records. However, we were not prepared for how difficult it would be to review these stories and place them in a context that is already saturated with trauma.

The Mahantdorai, the Cambodian holocaust, is an unbelievable journey into the heart of human suffering and betrayal. Over the past 13 years, we have been privileged to listen to hundreds of personal accounts of the Mahantdorai. Every time we hear a story, we are amazed at the depth of the evil that caused this destruction and the courage of the people who survived it.

The word *survivor* implies a person who at the very least endured an extraordinary trauma and, as we like to believe, did so with a measure of courage and strength. Rarely does the image of a survivor include an understanding of the terrible price that is paid to stay alive; yet it is this price that is the compelling factor that brings or forces the survivor into treatment. In this chapter, we will attempt to describe the experiences of the survivors of the Mahantdorai and the effects of these experiences on Cambodian life. Understanding this background of trauma is imperative for effective interventions with Cambodians.

Cambodian Flight During the 1970s and 1980s

Cambodians arrived in North America during recent decades not as immigrants seeking a better life but as refugees whose story of death and survival defies human understanding. Cambodians arrived in North America in three stages. Before 1975, there were no large settlements of Cambodians anywhere in North America. Of the thousand or so who were in the United States, the majority were students scattered in colleges and universities across the country.

In April 1975, thousands of people fled from the Khmer Rouge to the Thai border or left Cambodia by sea. These people were placed in makeshift refugee camps, and about 7,000 were resettled in the United States. After arriving in the United States, they again spent time in camps before being resettled primarily by church groups. They had fled their country in great haste and now were forced to rely on the charity of strangers to survive. Cut off from all information about what was happening inside Cambodia, they were plagued by guilt and apprehension. They were also spread out across the country and had few support services available to them.

In 1979, after the Vietnamese invaded Cambodia, thousands of sick and terrorized Cambodians fled over the Thai border, seeking refuge and telling of atrocities that, conservatively estimated, cost the lives of over 1 million people from 1975 to 1979 (Etcheson, 1984). Instead of being given sanctuary, these survivors were pushed back at gunpoint over the mountains. The majority of these were the elderly, women, and children, and it has been estimated that 10,000 died during those hideous months (Greve, 1987).

By November 1979, a wall of "walking skeletons" poured over the Thai border, lured there by the promise of food. Soon the faces of starving Cambodians were on every television set and magazine cover, and the United Nations began the biggest relief operation since World War II. By 1980, half a million Cambodians were in refugee camps inside Thailand or along the border.

For the first time since the country was closed off from the world in 1975, relief workers and historians were able to begin to piece together what had happened during the Khmer Rouge reign. Refugees described a life of terror and atrocities. Their matter-of-fact tone and seeming acceptance of these events led some to suggest that this was a plot to spread propaganda against the Khmer Rouge. No one wanted to believe that what they were telling could be true.

Life in the camps offered safety from the Khmer Rouge, but at an extraordinary price. Not only were many families living alongside their Khmer Rouge torturers, they were also at the mercy of the Thai military. Rape, extortion, and murder occurred regularly, and there was no law or power to protect the refugees once the sun had set and relief workers were forced to leave the camps. With every year that passed, the policies of the Thai became more punitive in an attempt to discourage additional refugees from coming into the camps.

Between 1979 and 1988, 136,300 new Cambodian refugees arrived in the United States (Hamilton, 1988). They came with the baggage of over a decade of trauma. Their idea of normal life was lost, and they faced the additional burden of trying to make sense of life in a new country, a country in which they had no resources except those they carried in blue plastic bags. Cambodian refugees who preceded them were too widely disbursed to establish functioning communities and soon became overwhelmed by the stories of the new refugees who were giving accounts of those who had died.

Life and Culture Before the Mahantdorai

The Mahantdorai saw the dismantling of Cambodian life as it was known before 1970. The massive destruction of Cambodia brought on by civil war and the bombing by the United States disoriented the Cambodian people. The Pol Pot regime preyed on this confusion, systematically destroying institutions and resurrecting icons of Cambodia's past glory, declaring 1975 as "Year Zero" (Ponchaud, 1977).

The "Angkar," a title that means the "high command," brings images of Angkor Wat and the delusional goals of the Khmer Rouge, who wished to return Cambodia's people to that time of perceived greatness by enslaving the population and attempting to rebuild the waterways and irrigation systems associated with their glorious past. Like the Angkor Wat, which reigned from the 6th through 15th centuries, the new empire was to be built with the muscles and bones of slaves.

Before Year Zero, over 80% of the people in Cambodia were peasants living in villages and rural areas (Ebihara, 1985). Although the people of the country were quite attached to their prince and the royal family, most of Cambodian life was ordered by local authorities, and the country was just beginning to move into an era of centralized government. Infrastructure and institutions such as schools and health services were in the early stages of development. The modern world was pushing its way into this small country, and as the war in Vietnam deepened, the pace of Cambodian life also began to speed ahead.

Although standards of behavior may have been different or changing for some urban families, the majority of the people maintained traditional beliefs regarding marriage, family, spirits, and religion. These beliefs and traditions had changed little since the fading away of Angkor Wat in the 13th century, and even the invasion of the French did little to alter or order Cambodian life.

There is no doubt that family life has always been of greatest value to the Cambodian people, and traditions for family were respected and honored. Children were raised as the center of family life and were given extraordinary amounts of attention. As babies, they were rarely allowed to cry and could be found with the mother or on the hip of an older child who was playing outside. They were not considered an inconvenience for their older siblings but almost like toys. Girls and boys alike were keenly sensitive to the babies' needs and took responsibility for their care.

Children were raised to believe that marriage and the creation of a new family was the central goal of their lives. Consequently, the marriage partner was so important to the family that the parents had to be entrusted to decide whom and when a child would marry.

The girl was considered the prize of her family. If she remained virtuous and obedient, she could attract a suitor from a family who could elevate their standard of living or their class status. On the other hand, if she behaved poorly, she could ruin the name of her family.

Although Cambodian women present a public image of being passive or even submissive, there is a great deal of evidence that they shared a status equal to their husbands regarding family issues. Traditionally, it is the wife who manages the money and the mother who disciplines the children. She is the one who passes on the rules of culture and tradition.

As children, Cambodians have little shame about their bodies. Male genitalia is not mystified as it is in the West because boys rarely wear pants before puberty except as part of a school uniform and for social occasions. For the most part, even today, they can be seen running around *au naturel,* skillfully avoiding pinches and tugs inflicted by playmates or teasing adults.

Prior to marriage, the boy must prove his worthiness to his intended bride's family, and this is based on his reputation and the material possessions he brings to the girl. It is expected that these possessions will be passed down to their children. The groom is expected to be as chaste as the bride when he enters marriage, and marriages are often speeded along if the family is concerned that the young people cannot contain their passions.

Cambodians consider sexual urges a powerful force that can be contained only by social structure. Unrelated teenage boys and girls are never left alone together, and they are not allowed to touch each other, even casually. Kissing and holding hands is not considered proper social behavior and is not allowed privately unless there is a plan for marriage. Improper behavior not only threatens the social standing of a family, but also can be a threat to the family's spiritual and physical well-being. Many families believe that such behavior offends the spirits and must be rectified with special prayers.

The boy or man who forces himself sexually on a woman is considered to be that woman's husband from that time on. He must take financial responsibility for her and for any child that results from their union. It is up to the family to protect a girl from situations that might lead to her being attacked, and it is the family's shame when they are not successful in doing so.

In addition to social controls that temper sexual behavior, as Buddhists young men and women are also taught to control their urges by practicing moderation and self-control. Both males and females are taught to admire an even-tempered manner and restraint. Young men in particular bring great honor to the family when they become monks for a time and practice strict self-control. After they have been monks, they are considered to be highly eligible as husbands because they have practiced self-control in every aspect of life.

Cambodians' admiration for self-control is matched by their love of sensuous art and dance. Cambodian girls are taught as much about making themselves beautiful as they are about controlling their behavior. They have never been described as a prudish or restrictive people, and despite the many rules for behavior, the community is generally forgiving of mistakes and excesses (Ebihara, 1985).

Cambodian life is complicated by a class system that is based on bloodlines, education, and economic status. There are rules governing behavior between the classes, and even different languages for talking to the different classes (e.g., there are words that must be used when talking to royal family as well as a distinct set of words for talking to monks). Slavery was common even into the early part of this century, and indentured servants continue to be common today.

Although it was not legal to have more than one wife in Cambodia, polygamy was not rare and seems related to the practice of taking concubines by warlords or provincial governors. The more concubines a man had, the more powerful he was considered; in fact, this practice of being "related to" many families through marriage did give him a measure of power. Today, the practice of taking a second wife marks a man as being wealthy because he is expected to provide a home and support for the second wife.

Although the Cambodian community may condone a man's having two wives, there is ample evidence that this practice brings nothing but shame and regret to the children of this arrangement. It is here that we get the first hints of the sexual abuse of children. Women talk about how easy it is for a man to have two wives. In contrast, when a woman remarries, she must always watch that her husband does not turn his eye to her daughters.

Even though Cambodians have always struggled with violent conflicts with neighboring countries, brutal bandit attacks, and battles between local warlords, they prefer to see themselves as a peaceful and gentle people. The idealized Cambodian is generous and compassionate, someone who does not lose his or her temper and is not controlled by passion. Although physical punishment is used widely to discipline children, it is not considered a sign of a "good family." Likewise, a man who hits his wife is marked as belonging to a lower class.

The Mahantdorai

The Cambodians call the events of the past 2 decades the Mahantdorai, the time of great destruction. The name does not refer to one event or political period but includes all of the acts of destruction that occurred from 1969 to the present time. As time goes by, we begin to realize that the extent of this destruction is greater than anyone could have imagined. It occurred just before the "information explosion" in the West. It occurred just before video cameras began to record everyday family life and world events, and before fax machines provided instant communication across oceans.

No war is so damaging to a country's integrity as civil war. From 1970 to 1975, Cambodia divided itself into two factions: those who supported Prince Sihanouk and the Khmer Rouge and those who favored the American-backed government of Lon Nol. Brother fought brother and the classes became more divided. The upper and middle classes prospered from the surge of dollars that accompanied the American invasion of Cambodia, corruption was rampant, and the poor began to starve long before anyone was even certain of who the Khmer Rouge were and what they would mean to the future of Cambodia.

The political and historical forces that came together to create the Mahantdorai have never been adequately described. Intrigue and betrayal were at the heart of a complex situation that would require long-term study of Cambodian history and sociology to understand. For the therapist who wishes to work with the survivors of the Mahantdorai, it is possible and even preferable to focus on the trauma events themselves rather than the political complexities that precipitated them.

Impact of the Mahantdorai on the Cambodian Family

Over the years, we have attempted to come to terms with the magnitude of human suffering experienced by the survivors of the Mahantdorai by evaluating and respecting the defense mechanisms that this trauma has created. Our focus is always on the family and the resources the family offers for the reconstruction of the individual's story and rebuilding of trust. For this reason, we offer a summary of the trauma not by describing chronological events, but by categorizing these events in terms of the defense mechanisms they produce and how the families learn to cope.

Denial was already a powerful defense mechanism long before Cambodia fell to the Khmer Rouge. In talking with Cambodian survivors in the refugee camps in 1980, and even today, we find that few have memories of the events or have access to the memories of what occurred before the fall of the country.

A historical review of those times tells us that there was a progression of events that monumentally changed Cambodian life within a short period of time. The blanket bombing of Cambodia by American B52s dropped half a million tons of explosives on that small country. That was three times as many bombs as were dropped on Japan during World War II, including the atom bombs. Phnom Penh, a beautiful city of 200,000, swelled to a population of 2,000,000 over a period of 4 years. Thousands and thousands of refugees in Phnom Penh were starving long before the Khmer Rouge was even a threat to the city. By 1974, the only way to get to the provinces was by airplane, and the airports were regularly shelled.

Despite these events, countless refugees recall that period of time as being one of prosperity. Others who experienced the trauma of the times moved that experience to a remote area of their recall because what came next was comparatively more significant in that it threatened their sense of survival as no conflict or disaster ever had before.

The Khmer Rouge added a new dimension to denial by committing atrocities that were so outside the realm of human understanding that, to this day, many Cambodians do not believe what they saw with their own eyes. In the camps in the early 1980s, children often drew pictures of events that they witnessed. A theme that occurred over and over was of a Khmer Rouge cadre cutting open the belly of a pregnant woman and pulling out a baby that he killed either with a knife or by smashing it against a tree. Stories circulated at that time that these pictures represented not actual events but a massive plot of propaganda against the Khmer Rouge. But the stories continued in accounts described to relief workers and in the nightmares of children living in centers for those who were separated from their families.

The evacuation of Phnom Penh itself was a spectacle so dramatic that it is hard to even imagine. Two million people were pushed out of the city over a period of three days. All the roads leading out of the city were filled with miles and miles of human beings carrying belongings and searching frantically for lost family members (Ponchaud, 1977). The panic and terror of that situation is a reality that makes sense objectively, but it is an event that is rarely talked about because it pales in comparison to what occurred afterwards.

The relativity of situations adds a dimension of denial or disbelief to all accounts of the Mahantdorai. How can a person claim to have experienced a bad time when a neighbor's experience was so much worse? The phenomenon of defining reality by comparing one person's experiences with another's occurred constantly in the refugee camps and caused a constant revictimization of survivors. An example of this is the immigration officer who screamed at a relief worker, "These people in the camp are not suffering! You want to see real suffering, go to the border!" The reality of the situation was that 18 people were living in a space that was 10 feet by 25 feet. They had to survive on one bucket of water per person per day and lived in constant fear of being rejected by immigration and pushed back to the border, as had already happened on several occasions.

The process of demanding the truth from a survivor and then labeling it a lie when it did not fit the interrogator's definition of the truth caused another layer of doubt and uncertainty in survivors. The process of interrogation began with the Khmer Rouge, who demanded that all individuals write their life stories. This occurred shortly after the people were pushed out of the cities into the countryside, and it was identified almost instantly as a means of finding "traitors" and marking them for extermination. It soon became clear that the Khmer Rouge identified anyone who was educated as being a traitor. The logic followed that anyone who wore glasses must be educated because people wore glasses to read. These people were marked for death.

Lying was essential to survival, and remaining consistent in the lies was even more essential. Any lapse in memory was a threat. It is no wonder then that a great deal of emotional energy was used not for deciphering the events that were occurring but rather in creating a new identity, an identity that was acceptable to the torturers.

The Khmer Rouge were torturers who applied their skills for creating an environment of complete control in a systematic and efficient manner. Torture, which is defined as the infliction of physical or emotional pain for the purpose of punishment or coercion, was a way of life for all Cambodians living under the Khmer Rouge from 1975 to 1979. Although the degree of torture may have varied from place to place, and from individual to individual, there were commonalities that can be assumed when working with all Cambodian refugees.

Pol Pot and his followers were masters of all the methods of torture. Whether by strategy or coincidence, they began by isolating and totally disorienting their victims. They evacuated them from the cities and placed them in unfamiliar areas of the country. Within days, their victims were more concerned about sick and hungry children than about planning to overcome their captors. They were further disoriented by the manner of their captors, who spoke to them politely and took none of their possessions while forcing them to relocate. This manner belied the physical evidence of cruelty and murder that they saw all around them. (Note the parallels between this process and common dynamics of incestuous abuse.)

Step by step, the Khmer Rouge began depriving their victims of every source of self-esteem and support. Families were split up and children moved into separate living quarters. Older children were placed in youth mobile teams and sent far away from family. Families were not permitted to take care of their sick or elderly. Those who could not work were isolated in hospitals without medicine. People were marched for long distances to work for long hours at jobs that made no sense. Food was rationed to the point of near starvation when there was evidence of plenty all around them.

Isolation and secrecy were primary elements for control. There was no radio from outside Cambodia and no letters from family or friends outside the commune. The country was ruled by the mysterious "Angkar," or "high command," but no one knew who that really was. Community meetings were held for the purpose of communicating the commands of the Angkar, and soon it was evident that anyone who disagreed with these mandates would "disappear."

Everything familiar was destroyed or prohibited. Music that was popular before 1975 was banned. There were no books, and most of all, there was no religion. Pagodas were destroyed and monks were murdered or forced to marry to stay alive. The defrocking of monks broke age-old traditions, and the cadres, who by now had broken many rules and offended the spirits, became paranoid, certain that they were being afflicted by "black magic." Paranoia became the norm, and no one trusted anyone.

During the Khmer Rouge regime, personal life was completely controlled by the Angkar. Families could no longer live together, food was cooked in a communal kitchen, and marriages were arranged by the Communist leaders. Even simple matters of clothing and hygiene were bizarrely controlled. A black uniform was issued, and clothing taken from those killed by the Khmer Rouge was regularly distributed, sometimes offering the only real evidence that the owner had been murdered. Toilet articles such as soap and toothbrushes were considered evidence of belonging to a traitorous group. A whole generation of children grew up with no memory of ever seeing themselves in a mirror.

The Khmer Rouge leaders and cadres had an idealized image of themselves as being noble warriors who lived by a strict code of ethics. They publicly denounced any excesses and regularly offered themselves as open to criticism. Meetings were held regularly that were both brainwashing sessions and theoretical discussions of the Angkar's philosophy. Drinking, gambling, and womanizing were considered cardinal sins, and cadres prided themselves on being different from the corrupt regimes that preceded them (Carney, 1977).

The reality, of course, was quite different, and we have had countless descriptions of Khmer Rouge leaders eating well while others starved, and one can only imagine that the massive amounts of gold and jewelry that were collected over the years did not all find their way to the Angkar.

The Cambodian people as a whole and the world at large slowly came to realize the scale of systematic, unspeakable violence inflicted by the Khmer Rouge during the Mahantdorai. The resulting exaggeration of the use of denial and reaction formation, supplemented by isolation, secrecy, splitting, and suspicion, permeated what was left of the Cambodian family and culture. These ongoing legacies of the Mahantdorai have provided a fertile ground to foster sexual child abuse.

Sexual Victimization

In a strikingly parallel manner, the long, slow, and painful revelations of rape and sexual abuse of children have begun to creep out of the depths of silence. It is not surprising that the process has taken an additional 10 years. Illicit or forced sexuality was disavowed both in traditional Cambodian culture and, at least publicly, by the Khmer Rouge. It has taken Cambodians a decade to overcome the silence about the realities of adult and child sexual abuse and to build trust with the helping professions in their new, physically removed settings, where daily survival is no longer a main focus and where the truth doesn't always lead to death or torture.

Now we are beginning to hear that clandestine rapes were commonplace among the Khmer Rouge. If the incident became known, the victim was usually killed and the Khmer Rouge perpetrator often disappeared. He was assumed to have been killed himself, but possibly he was able to reappear somewhere else to rape again. Another aspect of Khmer Rouge sexuality was forced marriages. Sex by couples outside "sanctioned" relationships was punished by death.

Once in the refugee camps, children were often used by soldiers or others for sex, sometimes with the forcefully obtained "consent" of parents, who thereby obtained something that improved their chances of continued survival or ultimate escape. Both escaping from Cambodia and surviving in the camps required money for payoffs, and if money was exhausted, then sex was substituted. Once in the camps, Khmer, Khmer Rouge, Thai soldiers, and others participated in the sexual abuse of women and children.

In North America, long repressed and feeling totally impotent to deal with the destruction all around them, Khmer male survivors, themselves victims and full of survival guilt, often became obsessed with sexuality. Outnumbered by women and often either without families of their own or separated from their families, some Cambodian men made the sexual rounds of Cambodian women, and often their children. Alcohol, another addiction, often lubricated both the sexuality and violence in the Khmer community in North America.

In writing this article, we have called upon the experiences of other social workers, therapists, and refugee workers in North America to determine if their experiences with sexual abuse in Cambodian communities was similar to ours. What we know from our own practice and from the accounts of these professionals is that knowledge of sexual abuse comes more from knowing the community and from women's programs and clinics rather than from accounts provided in therapy sessions.

Refugee workers who served in the camps in Thailand from 1979 to 1981 were overwhelmed by the litany of abuses described by Cambodians who escaped immediately following the fall of the country to the Vietnamese.

During those early days, the refugees formed their public trauma stories. These stories were the narratives that were presented to immigration, researchers, and later to sponsors as the rationale for their leaving their country. These stories had a beginning, a middle, and an end and were the anchors for people to describe their reality without losing their frame of reference. These were the stories they could relate in great detail without triggering emotional land mines.

Health care providers in the camps had access to different stories. These stories were often based on descriptions of injuries or sicknesses and would invariably lead to graphic accounts of the deaths of family members. These accounts were emotionally wrenching and took the survivor and the listener into a separate reality where life had little value and was constantly lived on the verge of panic.

Despite the cruel hardships of the camps, survivors had the one advantage of having their reality validated by other survivors and witnesses. People did not languish in their suffering but used it as an impetus to get out of the camps. Lying, manipulating, and distorting the truth were survival mechanisms that had been necessary during the Khmer Rouge and were still necessary to escape from the camps. Now, survivors prioritized their trauma stories to meet the perceived needs of the interviewers rather than as a presentation of their personal experience. They told trauma stories based on political correctness, offering stock descriptions of their "fear of persecution" and harboring a belief that the real story, the story that threatened the very foundation of their humanity, would not be considered "awful enough" to entitle them to a safe haven.

In the women's clinics, the stories of rape were presented in a matter-of-fact manner, and women described how they "married" their rapists to have some protection from the predators who roamed the camps after the expatriates left for the day. Babies were born and claimed as the sons or daughters of husbands who had been dead for years. Everyone had a tacit understanding that to talk of rape and abuse might undo the tenuous hold that women had on their existence.

Without question, the face-saving behavior of Cambodian women belies the intensity of the effect of rape on these women and their families. It also demands more than any other abuse that a woman emotionally deny what happened to her, her sisters, her friends, and many times, her children. It is this denial that threatens to perpetuate the cycle of sexual victimization in families of survivors.

The secrets spawned by the rape of Cambodian women hold families in a state of bondage that suffocates the normal process of storytelling and sharing of family values and legacies. Children born of violence become an unexplainable paradox of love and fear. The scene that comes to mind is that of a very old grandmother who carried her 2-year-old grandson on her hip everywhere she went in the camp. She would call over the expatriate staff to see how clever and lovable he was, and then she would try to give him away. She would say, "Take this little Khmer Rouge, you can give him a good life." Her obvious love for the baby and her desire to get him away from the family was made clear when she said, "His father was a Khmer Rouge. He was not a good man and he made a lot of trouble for my daughter. This boy cannot have a good life with us. Take him, he's a good baby."

The need to survive creates a state of denial that permits people to do what they must without becoming overwhelmed with emotion. The need to keep a family safe and fed led many widows with children and single women to marry in the camps. They married men who were available, often making choices that were extremely difficult. Because women outnumbered men in the border camps, many men had more than one "wife"; the conflicts involved with these arrangements led to many episodes of violence. Children lived in dwellings where there were often three families living in a space no larger than 12 feet by 36 feet; they undoubtedly witnessed sexual scenes and scenes of violence. Because the only form of privacy came from the deliberate "act of not seeing," children were not free to question events that were strange or frightening for them.

Women abandoned by their husbands or widowed in the constant border war often had no choice for survival besides prostitution. Thai military and others who had access to the camps made frequent visits to "taxi girls," paying small fees for service that the women would then use to feed their children or bribe their way into another camp where there was some chance of being resettled. Once in a camp where residents were considered refugees instead of displaced persons, they were considered "illegals," a status that made it necessary for them to hide in tunnels dug under the earth. With no food cards and the constant threat of being sent back to a border camp, women and children often had to trade sexual favors for protection.

Secrecy shrouds the rape and exploitation of Cambodian women that occurred as part of a policy of torture and dehumanization. There is little doubt that the abduction of young Cambodian women and, in some cases, young men from the refugee camps and selling them into the sex trade was as political as it was exploitative. It was necessary for relief workers and U.N. authorities to "not see" what was happening or else risk a public embarrassment of the Thai military that could result in retribution for all Cambodians.

From a historical perspective, it can be seen that efforts to deal with sexual abuse in the camps were nonexistent until the late 1980s, when human rights groups began to push for a policy regarding rape and the treatment of the survivors. There were no policies for the protection of single women or widows and children, and certainly no reversal of administrative practices and economic conditions that bred sexual abuse (Wali, 1991).

Refugee workers from the camps and here in the United States can all describe episodes of sexual violence that are so horrifying that they could not be kept secret. An account from a refugee camp in Thailand describes the body of a Cambodian woman found "at the fence." Her tongue had been cut out and a branch from a tree had been used to mutilate her genitals and uterus. This was just one account of many murders of women in and around Site 2 and Khao-I-Dang evidence that the wretchedness of concentration camps did not ward off serial killers and the mutilators of women.

Extreme brutality has accompanied some Cambodians to the United States. We have heard from the neighbors of a young woman who dreaded the sexual advances of her obviously tormented husband. One night, they were all awakened by the sounds of this man beating his wife to death. By the time the police arrived, he had hanged himself near her body. One can only guess at the story of misery behind this couple's death, but the response from the girl's family offered a glimpse of the hopelessness that hung like a black cloud over the marriage. The body of the husband, who had absolutely no surviving relatives, was taken by the girl's family for burial, and they made a ceremony for him as they would for their own son, saying that their daughter and this son had been destroyed long before they even came to the United States.

In the United States, a 5-year-old Cambodian girl was raped and then murdered by a young Cambodian man who said that after he raped the child, he didn't know how to keep her from telling so he had to kill her (Reid, 1992). He described his actions as if he had made reasonable choices. In our work, we have heard adolescent Cambodian gang members matter-of-factly describe how they raped the sisters of rival gang members in retaliation for territorial offenses.

In a bizarre tale of kidnapping and extortion that we encountered in our clinic, a Cambodian woman described how she was kidnapped from her home in a quiet Connecticut suburb. Her Cambodian kidnappers raped her and forced her young children to watch. She told us in terror because she said that the kidnappers were part of an extortion ring and would return to kill her if she told anyone about the incident.

The frequency of rape and sexual abuse does not in any way diminish the intensity of the act or its devastating effects. As we can see so clearly in Bosnia, rape as a method of torture and demoralization of an enemy is highly effective in reducing the self-worth of both the victim and the witnesses. Within weeks of disclosure of the systematic abuse of women and children, the international community teetered between outrage and despair, finally succumbing to a state of futility regarding the whole situation. Bosnia, like Cambodia, has been moved by catastrophic trauma into a realm where reality is the enemy.

When reality is the enemy, what does that mean for the survivor? What does it mean for those who will be called upon to help heal the wounds of this catastrophic trauma? In attempting to write this chapter, we have tried to reconcile what we know, what we suspect, and what we predict in terms of the treatment of survivors of the Mahantdorai.

From the stories of Cambodians, we can generalize that sexual abuse falls into the following categories:

1. Rape as torture, which occurred during the civil war and again in the Pol Pot regime and in the camps in Thailand
2. Sexual abuse as exploitation in the refugee camps and in post-Pol Pot Cambodia, which includes the forced prostitution of women and children for survival of the family
3. Sexual abuse as the acting out of rage and violence in today's communities
4. Sexual abuse as a dysfunctional attempt by survivors to meet sexual needs or deal with psychological symptoms
5. The sexual abuse of Cambodian children and teens in foster homes

Treatment in Context

Khmer Health Advocates, Inc., has the unique position of being a Cambodian organization with the mission of meeting the health and mental health needs of the survivors of the Mahantdorai. Our mental health clinic is part of a community-based program that also provides outreach and supportive services for families and cultural programs for children. Because of this, we have the advantage and disadvantage of knowing the community on several different levels.

Over the years, we have become part of a network of providers that shares a similar relationship to the Cambodian communities, and we rely on shared stories and experiences to provide support and treatment for families of the Mahantdorai. What has become painfully clear to all of us is that the primary reason we receive referrals to our clinic for sexual abuse is for court-ordered evaluations of families where there is suspected physical or sexual abuse of children. Although the evaluation process may turn up evidence of sexual abuse by parents or adult family members, it does so in an atmosphere of legal inquiry that triggers all the fears and terrors of past inquisitions. Again, the focus is on the crimes of the victims rather than the crimes of the perpetrators who created victims.

To protect children from victimization while providing for the needs of family members who are themselves survivors, we base our therapy on the contextual family therapy model of Ivan Boszormenyi-Nagy (Boszormenyi-Nagy & Spark, 1973) and believe that the family is the greatest resource for healing. Although we have modified techniques to meet cross-cultural expectations, we keep as the bases of all of our therapy the goals of rebuilding trust within the family; restoring the give-and-take between family members; addressing individual experiences, needs, and pathologies; and dealing with the ethical issues of relationships.

Telling the Story

Cambodians come into evaluations or therapy with well-developed insights into their own psychological problems. After getting past the initial period of defensive protection, they offer us an understanding of their anguish and the behaviors they use to cope with it. Most adults report that they "haven't been the same since Pol Pot," and describe having trouble concentrating and feeling disconnected to the people in their lives. Among people who rely heavily on intuitive understanding of their family members' needs, episodes of dissociation in one member often precipitate chaos with the family's internal communication system and a chain reaction of withdrawal and anger in other family members. As time goes on, families are becoming more aware of this pattern but are helpless to stop the cycle of emotional reactions.

In seeking help, one of the factors that Cambodians commonly identify as most important in a health care provider or therapist is an understanding of what happened in Cambodia and Thailand. Most survivors have a surreal understanding of their experiences and describe feelings of fatigue or lethargy when they have to present their background in a concise, generalized manner. The therapist must be able to help survivors put a form to their stories by offering a framework or structure.

One of the basic tools of our therapy with Cambodian families is the genogram. The simple procedure of drawing a diagram of who makes up a family is a dramatic testimony to the extraordinary losses of the Cambodian people. The listing of parents, children, grandparents, aunts, and uncles opens the door to trauma stories. As the dates of births and deaths are recorded, family myths and secrets become clearer.

By defining who was in a family, the truth may emerge about a child or children who cannot possibly belong to a man who was claimed as their father as a way to save face in a family or avoid traumatic memories. Siblings are often aware of the circumstances of the birth of a younger brother or sister, and many witnessed the rape of their mother or the forced marriages that were a part of life under the Khmer Rouge. This often becomes a family secret that is talked about only at times of crisis or anger, making it a destructive force in family life.

We recently saw a 14-year-old boy who was referred because of problems in school. He described at length how he "missed his father" and went on to describe his father in heroic terms, saying that he was sure that if his father were still alive, he would make life better for all of them. After he left the room, we asked his sister, who was 14 years his senior, how her father, who had died in 1976, could have had a son born in 1979. She described how her mother had been forced to marry and had escaped from the boy's father at the border. She said that the other four siblings were all aware of what happened and hated the man who was their brother's father. "We never talk about his father, except sometimes when my younger brother gets mad at him, he'll say, 'you're no good, just like your father.' My mother cries and then he stops."

The process of storytelling is easier when the therapist requests basic information about how the family worked together. "How did you help your family during the Pol Pot regime?" and "How do you help them now?" are two extremely powerful questions for exploring the give-and-take in family life. This approach also helps the survivors restructure their memories around events that strengthened their relationships instead of the usual focus on negative events. Without question, the family is the survivor's greatest resource, and the therapist must first "do no harm" to the fragile support system that shelters the victims.

The story of sexual abuse may be the opening crisis for the storytelling, but the context of the abuse has important meaning for the survival of the whole family. For Cambodians, the family is the center of life, and healing must occur within the context of the family. As therapists, we see ourselves as helpers who are very much part of a process that we are striving to understand.

CASE HISTORIES

Neang

Many stories stand out in our memories, but one of the most disturbing involved several generations of a family who had suffered extraordinary terror and hardship during every phase of the Mahantdorai.

We first met Neang, the daughter of the family, when she was referred by Child Protective Services. She was telling her teachers and school friends how her uncle had sexually abused her. When we questioned her about this, she described an incident that had occurred in 1979 when she was in a refugee camp in Thailand. At the time, she was 13 years old and the oldest child of two families who shared a house together.

She lived with her mother, four siblings, her mother's younger sister and husband and three small children. Neang's father had been killed by the Khmer Rouge. One day, Neang's aunt became very sick and was taken to the hospital. Neang's mother accompanied her, leaving Neang to care for the children and cook for her uncle. During the first night that they were together, the uncle slipped into her bed and began to sexually molest her. When she screamed, the neighbors came and took the uncle to stay in another place until his wife came home from the hospital.

Neang was ashamed of what her uncle had done to her. When she told her mother and aunt about what happened, they told her that her uncle was a good man, but he was sick. They never left her alone with him again. The neighbors in the camp talked with him and kept their eyes on him when he was around young girls. They did not blame him because they knew that he was sick.

When Neang contacted us, the aunt was sick and in the hospital again, and Neang was afraid that her mother had forgotten what had happened before and would make her go to take care of the aunt's children. She loved her uncle but did not want to be alone with him again.

We spoke with Neang's mother, who confirmed that her brother-in-law had molested her daughter but said that he was a very good man who had helped her and her family after her husband died. She described how he had risked his life to get food to her children when they were in the Pol Pot regime. She said that they worked together in a place where a lot of people "disappeared" and there was little food.

Neang's mother said she knew that he now had some very strange behavior and that he was "killing my sister with his demands for sex." She was going to bring her sister's children to live with her and would not let her daughter be alone with her brother-in-law again.

Shortly after this conversation, we were called in to see Neang's aunt, who was ill with a serious infection and was also suffering from depression. She is a tiny woman who usually weighs no more than 90 lbs., but she must have been closer to 80 lbs. at that time. She talked openly about her desperation because she always felt so sick and it was hard for her to care for her children. She had come to the United States with three children and had an additional two pregnancies since she arrived. She had miscarried both times and was afraid that she would get pregnant again. She described how her husband demanded sex five or six times a night, never sleeping. This behavior had been happening off and on since they were married, just before 1975.

We asked to see the husband, and he described openly what was troubling him. He raised the subject of sex once we began talking about his sleep problems. He talked openly about his shame and how he did not understand why he could not think about anything but sex. He never experienced satisfaction from sex and did not know why he had to keep repeating the act. He was a practicing Buddhist who valued self-control and hated himself for what he was doing.

He described years of trauma that had begun during the civil war. He had been a soldier who fought many battles and was injured twice. During the Pol Pot regime, he had lied about his military record and knew that it was only a matter of time before someone betrayed him. He came from a large family, but now the rest of the family members were either dead or missing. When he thought about his troubles, he could not sleep and felt that he would die from the anxiety that filled his chest.

We started him on an antidepressant, which greatly reduced his obsessive behavior, and his life seemed to improve dramatically. His wife returned from the hospital and was doing better than she had in years. He had a new job, which gave him the opportunity to make a better life for his family. He continued to see us over the course of several months, but then began skipping appointments and saying that he felt better and did not need to come in.

We did not see any of them for another year, and things seemed better until Neang's mother began to have problems. It seemed that she was making a name for herself in the community because of her many boyfriends. She was drinking and gambling and had had several pregnancies. Her sister was worried about her and brought her to see us in a state of crisis one evening.

Neang's mother was wild-eyed and having trouble breathing when she arrived at our office. When we asked her what was wrong, she described seeing images from her life during the Pol Pot regime. These flashbacks had been a problem mostly at night, but now they were invading her days. In rapid-fire succession, she went from one incident to another, describing atrocities she had witnessed and sexual attacks on her and on others in her group. She said that she did not want to sleep because she could not stop the images.

Using one session of hypnosis, we were able to help her describe the most intrusive images, identify them as memories, and then calm herself. After the session, she was drained but relieved. Because she had responded so well to this approach, we hoped to continue the process with other intrusive thoughts. We started her immediately on an antidepressant and an antianxiety agent, which seemed to calm her. We asked her to come back to see us the next week. She was grateful that we were able to help her relieve her panic and assured us she would return. Week after week, she canceled appointments with seemingly valid excuses: one of the kids was sick, she could not get a ride, and so on. When we arranged for a ride, she again made an excuse, and later we noticed that she would avoid us at community events. Her daughter later told us that her mother did not like to see us because "we made her remember."

Several years later, Neang's mother returned to see us and said that she wanted to try again to get rid of the images that haunted her day and night. Since she had seen us last, she had had two more children by different fathers and had been ill with hepatitis. She had been hospitalized recently and was very thin. We asked to check her medical records before we started treatment, hoping we could help her understand her medical condition. She said that she was through with all of her boyfriends and that she just wanted a peaceful life with her children.

The medical records revealed that she had recently had two blood tests for pregnancy and that she was about 4 months pregnant. She denied this adamantly and said that she was sure she was not pregnant because she had just finished her period. She was sure this was a mistake, so we decided to call her doctor, who assured us that she had indeed been pregnant when he saw her four weeks earlier. Neang's mother stared at us blankly and said she had no idea what we were talking about. We started her again on an antidepressant and again she stopped coming in after a few sessions.

Several months after this incident, we got a call from an emergency room where Neang had been admitted. It seems that Neang had been in an argument with her mother and in a moment of despair had cut her wrists. The ambulance brought her to the hospital, where she was met by her aunt. When the aunt walked in the room, she saw her niece strapped to the stretcher because she had been trying to pull out the sutures. The aunt began screaming and trying to pull off the restraints. One of the children who came with the aunt said that she was screaming, "Don't kill my niece. I won't let you kill my niece." The tiny woman fought off three security guards and several other staff before she was sedated. The next day, there was no sign of any of the behavior of the previous night in Neang or her aunt. Neang had been admitted to the psychiatric unit and the aunt had been allowed to go home when her husband came to get her. We were not able to see Neang because she was in another state, but we called her shortly after this incident. She said that she was fine and that she had just gotten upset because her mother did not want her to marry her boyfriend. It was all worked out now and she was sure she was fine.

From members of the community, we know that the problems continue with all of the family members and have started with the next generation. Drinking and gambling have become a major issue for most of them, and they live from crisis to crisis. When they become too overwhelmed by their circumstances, they attempt a geographical cure by moving to a new community to start over.

The story of this family is heartbreaking because they have given us a glimpse of the terror they have survived and of their desperate desire to make a safe place for their families. They loyally stick together, bailing each other out of one crisis after another, including car accidents, beatings, and gambling debts. They are a classic example of just one family out of thousands, perhaps, who cannot bear to look back at their trauma stories and now are recreating the terror for their own children.

Periodically we hear from a teacher or social worker who is attempting to help Neang's family, and every now and again we get a message from one of them through someone in the community. The message is usually that they were thinking of us and someday they would like to come back to see us.

The casualties list of the Mahantdorai grows every day and includes new victims, the children who witness not only the agony of the survivors but experience their own terror. Cambodians are no longer seen by Americans as victims of a terrible holocaust but have quickly become "those people." Social service providers can be heard saying, "Those people are always fighting," "Those people are always drinking and gambling," and "Those people think they can have a dozen wives."

The story of Neang's family is just one of many that remind us of how difficult it is to ask trauma victims to remember their pasts. Although we as therapists are certain of the necessity of going back and looking at the reality that caused so much pain and terror, we also have no doubt of the terrible price that a person must pay to do so. When people dare to speak of their memories of lost family and their images of inhuman acts of cruelty, they open the Pandora's box of images that belongs to others who are often on the edge of despair.

From a clinical perspective, all the adults in Neang's family are at one time or another suffering from depression, posttraumatic stress disorder, or dissociative episodes. All three adults also have various health problems, including chronic hepatitis with its risk for liver cancer. Financial stressors are a constant problem because none of the adults has the language skills necessary for a well-paying job. In addition to concerns about supporting their children, the Cambodian adults must worry about siblings who are in refugee camps in Thailand or living on the edge of starvation in Cambodia.

A look at the children reveals that at least three of them have learning disabilities, and some have obsessive disorders and phobias. Several have behavior problems and are perfect candidates for gangs. As she grows older, Neang becomes more depressed and anxiety ridden.

The losses experienced by this family and others like it are almost incomprehensible. As survivors, they must always make decisions based on the crisis of the moment. This family, like others, has a need to deny and avoid the past. They protect their families by moving from community to community in an attempt to create a new life. When they are sick, there are few resources to serve them. Language and cultural barriers ensure that they make do with piecemeal services. In Connecticut, the only system that has a plan for translator services is the court system.

As therapists, we are often overwhelmed by the problems that families like this present. But if *we* are overwhelmed, we can only imagine what they face on a day-to-day basis. For this reason, we keep our goals simple. Whenever possible, we alleviate symptoms and find resources to help the family help each other. We always offer hope for the future because we do have hope. These are people who have lived through our worst nightmares.

We hope we will see Neang's family again and that we can offer them some comfort and support as they attempt to survive and make a better life for their children. We continue to be committed to a trust-building approach because it offers hope that families will return to therapy when they feel safe enough to do so. Although this approach is slow and not always easy, it has allowed us to help some families resolve difficult problems.

Boreth

One of the first families we saw back in the early 1980s was a husband and wife who were fighting. The husband, Boreth, could no longer contain his anger because his 45-year-old wife insisted that he allow her to sleep with her young lover in their house. She had met the boy in the camp when he was only about 16 years old. For a long time, she treated him like a son, but once they got to the United States she began having sexual relations with him. She did this in front of her husband, confusing him with her insistence that this was normal because he had allowed it to go on for over a year.

When we asked this man how his wife helped him during the Pol Pot regime, he described her courage and self-sacrifice in trying to save the lives of their children. All but one of their six children died, and he felt such great pity for her that he could not confront her behavior. The pain of dealing with their mutual loss was so great that he could absorb her bizarre behavior. When the community began ridiculing him, he was finally forced to address the issue of his wife's behavior. When he was certain that we could help his wife, he began describing their losses during the Khmer Rouge regime.

People often feel that they are giving something to their injured family member or taking care of them when they ignore bizarre or downright crazy behavior. The ethics of family relationships imply that the injured, the sick, the young, and the elderly are to be taken care of, and like all families where there are handicaps or injuries, deciding how to distribute family resources to do this is often a difficult matter. We always ask families to describe how they took care of their children and their sick before and during the Mahantdorai. Then we ask them if they are now taking care of them as they want to. This opens the communications between family members and usually rekindles a "connectedness" that has been missing for a long time.

Child Protection

Families often excuse the "sick behavior" of one or more of their members because they are acutely aware of how that person became "sick." The traumatized family, like the alcoholic family, often makes excuses for the abuser as much out of denial as out of compassion. They all know that confrontation of behavior will mean facing the real story. Unlike the alcoholic family, however, where the truth has become a victim to organic memory loss, the traumatized family can piece together the important details of survival by listening to how each family member tried to help. The search for the truth about what happened has offered many families precious shards of memories of courage and love that become the legacy for the next generation.

Working with the Cambodian family offers opportunities for interventions that can prevent child abuse and domestic violence. Because of the recentness of the trauma, it is still possible for families to piece together their stories as part of a healing ritual, but time is running out. Already we see families falling apart because of alcohol abuse and other addictive behaviors, such as gambling and sexual addictions. The crises created by these behaviors become the focus of family resources and energy and threaten to create a new story, a story in which the victims become the victimizers.

Although we have seen few cases of documented sexual assault of children, we strongly suspect that it is happening in the community because of several observations. In many families, there is evidence of sexually obsessive behavior in both men and women, trouble with intimacy, dissociative disorders, and social isolation. The confusion and shame associated with these behaviors fuels the denial that already has a stranglehold on the families.

The divorce rate of young Cambodians is often attributed to the sexual unfaithfulness of one or both partners who become involved in obsessive relationships that they often can identify as destructive but that they cannot seem to stop. Intimacy presents a formidable problem because feelings of closeness are deeply attached to memories of lost loved ones and scenes of terror. A young Cambodian man confided that every time he had sex with his wife, he saw the Khmer Rouge cutting his father's throat. He said that he was sure that this was a bad omen and that if he continued to have sex with her, he would die.

Dissociative episodes come and go in survivors. Stress often triggers a numbing response that causes caring people to stop feeling. Parents who are normally attached to their children feel distant and often do not pick up signals of danger in their environment, thereby failing to protect their children adequately. When dissociated from feelings, one can easily make inappropriate behaviors seem normal. We once made a home visit and attempted to talk with the parents of young children over the din of the TV. While parents described their worries about family back in Cambodia, their small children were watching a scene in which two people were having intercourse graphically, and then the man hacked the woman to death with a big knife. When asked about this, the parents shrugged it off, saying, "Oh, they always watch those movies."

When parents can no longer feel, they substitute control for care. The formula for safety involves a greater and greater restriction of the environment, and we are seeing families becoming increasingly isolated. Isolation often has been associated with sexual abuse of family members (Herman, 1992). Dissociative disorders also increase the likelihood that the primary caretaker will "not see" destructive or abusive behaviors and therefore fail to protect children from inappropriate or abusive behavior.

Because we are an organization that is committed to rebuilding trust in families and the community, Khmer Health Advocates, Inc., has established a clear policy of protecting children from abuse. Woven into every aspect of our evaluations and therapy is the understanding that we will not lie in our evaluations or avoid issues of abuse. We rely heavily on the belief that parents do not want to harm their children and that the loyalty of family members makes it not only possible but necessary to confront abuse.

What we see as the important factor in directly dealing with the abuse is that abuse must be put in the context of the original trauma. This in no way justifies the victimization of children because of the trauma of the parents but instead helps the abusers see that they are doing something to the children that is painful. They can identify that pain only when they begin to feel their own pain. In all the years of our practice, we have never had a parent attempt to justify abusive behavior, even though the Cambodian culture sanctions physical discipline, and we have found that presenting the truth to the court system has not jeopardized our relationship with a family.

Treatment Guidelines

We believe that treating sexual abuse in Cambodian survivors and their children is similar to treating other victims of sexual abuse. What differs, perhaps, is the need to put the sexual abuse in the context of the whole trauma story of the Cambodian people. At Khmer Health Advocates, Inc., we have established the following treatment practices:

1. We have created an office environment where patients can feel welcome and safe. We always offer refreshments and often share a meal when a family comes from a long distance or shows up at mealtime. The patient is always the center of attention, and other staff members are often enlisted to help with children. In a sense, we have tried to recreate the atmosphere of the refugee camp, where refugees knew that the relief workers were there for them. Over the years, we have heard countless stories about how important the relief workers were to the survivors because of their willingness to listen to stories and their obvious advocacy for the refugee.

2. We maintain strict rules of confidentiality. We are a small community in which everyone knows each other, and the staff is careful not to discuss any family's problems with anyone outside the family. Although this may seem like a given in any professional practice, the concept of confidentiality is a relatively new one for Cambodians, who often grew up in villages where behavior was controlled or modified by public opinion.

3. We always try to treat patients with their families. Even though we may see a patient individually to work on some trauma issues, we always ask the family to support the patient while he or she is in treatment. We may tell the family member or members who came with the patient that the patient has been talking about difficult memories and is feeling tired. We might ask them to cook special food or "make massage" for the patient.

4. Right now, all of our Khmer-speaking staff are women; it has been suggested that it is best for a woman to deal with both men and women on the issue of sexual abuse (Kanuha, 1990). Although we believe that women are probably more comfortable in dealing with this issue with a female therapist or translator, we think that the most important factor is the maturity and comfort of the staff in dealing with sexual issues and their compassion for the victim.

5. Once it becomes clear that a child is being abused, we always make judgments that support the safety of the child. At the same time, we are sensitive to the reality that separating a child from the parents is a life-and-death issue for Cambodian survivors. Almost every Cambodian family has had a child "taken away by the authorities," and many have never seen that child again. When we are certain a child is being abused, we attempt to enlist the help of extended family to provide a safe haven or to live in the house to ensure the child's safety. Usually, this can be negotiated with the family with the leverage of the courts. Threats of putting the child in foster care often precipitate sudden moves out of state or activate symptoms of PTSD in the parents.

6. No attempt should be made to provide treatment for any trauma issue using a family member or nonprofessional translator. It must be the responsibility of the provider to be certain of the translator's skills and integrity because the patient becomes highly suggestible and compliant when trauma memories are evoked. Therefore, it is not fair to ask the patient, "Is it all right if your son or your neighbor translates for you?" It is also not all right to continue with an interview when it becomes apparent that the translator is not comfortable with the issue.

Unfortunately, we are aware of many instances in which it was easier for a social worker to arrange foster care than to find a translator. The issue of translators is a difficult one because few areas where there is only a small settlement of Cambodians have access to anyone with any training in translation. In Connecticut, there is one part-time translator available for the whole state. Again, for this reason, children are often separated from their parents for a long time because the parents have no idea about how to seek help. The catch-22 is that they are then seen and labeled as negligent or uninterested.

7. Even if we are not certain that abuse is taking place, we are especially concerned when there is drinking in the house. We will ask the nondrinking parent to make a plan of how to keep the children safe when the drinker is intoxicated.

8. Unless a child is in danger, we never push people to face their trauma stories until they are ready. We will ask direct questions about trauma, such as, "How many people in your family died?" "Did you witness the torture or murder of people?" "Was anyone in your family or your group raped?" We often suspect the answer to these questions according to

where the person was and the circumstances, but we will not return to the subject unless the person gives us an opening.

9. During the past year, we have been extremely lucky to have a therapist certified in massage who treats patients after each session. She herself is a survivor of the Mahantdorai and extremely sensitive to their fears. Massage adds an important dimension to our therapy because it is a culturally familiar treatment, and also because torture victims have learned that touch induces pain rather than comfort. Our therapist is often able to distinguish which pain a patient is experiencing is due to psychological factors and which is due to physical problems. This focus on under-standing the patients' experience of pain confirms our commitment to helping them find relief. We also find that having massage after a session allows patients to leave our offices feeling relieved and comforted instead of raw and exposed from telling their story.

10. We often encourage our patients to seek the help of traditional healers or to have family members use traditional healing techniques. We do not base our referral to these methods on the patients' verbally stated belief but on the family's usual use of these methods before the Mahantdorai. There is ample evidence that these resources are helpful, and in our own experience, we have appreciated the help of fortune tellers and of Khrou Khmer, as well as Buddhist monks who bless holy water. Our respect for these methods is important because many people believe that a sick person is in danger if spirits are not consulted or if there is an imbalance or disharmony in treatment methods (Kuoch & Scully, 1984).

The importance of traditional methods also comes from a cultural acceptance of explanations for inappropriate behavior and their face-saving value. An example is a story we heard in the camps of a woman who had become sexually obsessive and bizarrely promiscuous, a not-uncommon story. Her behavior shamed her husband and brought great dishonor to her family. A Khrou Khmer diagnosed her as being under the influence of spirits, a condition brought on by someone seeking revenge from her family.

This proclamation turned a personal condition into a family problem, and the shameful woman became a victim. By removing the spell, the Khrou ensured that the woman could be treated and returned to her family without any shameful aftermath (Hiegel, 1984).

Most often, a family will have knowledge of a Khrou Khmer. We are careful to warn them that they should check out the reputation of the healer before going to him or her because there are many people who are passing themselves off as Khrous only to make money. Experienced Khrous can be a great asset to a treatment program because they are able to frame problems in a manner that removes guilt. We have never had a conflict in working with legitimate Khrous who are aware of the conditions they can and cannot handle.

11. Our treatment team is made up of a Cambodian family therapist who is herself a survivor, a psychiatrist, a psychiatric nurse specialist, a massage therapist, and two outreach workers. Both outreach workers have years of experience with Cambodians and are well known for their creativity in finding solutions to problems. At any given time, one or all of us will be working with a family. We have worked hard to be a team in which all members are seen as being equally important resources for the family. This gives us greater flexibility in working with families because there is not a reliance on just one therapist.

   Our treatment approach relies on the therapeutic process rather than the relationship between the therapist and the patient. We work to restore the give-and-take between family members and to alleviate symptoms. The patient's relationship is with the team, and trust building is the most important factor.

   We know that dealing with the trauma story takes a toll on everyone on the team, and often we are the ones slowing down the story-telling process because we simply cannot absorb anymore that day. We try to spend a period of time with our own debriefing process and usually find ourselves getting irritable and/or depressed when we don't.

12. We expect the treatment of Cambodian survivors to be a long-term process. We intend to be here for the long haul. We create a therapeutic atmosphere that allows patients to start and stop telling their trauma stories as they wish. We do not encourage catharsis but rather a debriefing process in which the goal is to derive new meaning from the trauma event rather than just examine it. No matter what the problem is, we make it clear that our primary goal is to rebuild trust within the family. A solution that stops the problem but does not help to rebuild trust is a bandage and will not provide long-term relief.

13. Finally, we understand that lying was an essential survival mechanism. We do not condone lying and we will not help preserve a lie, but we are also keenly aware that piecing together the truth is a complicated and

painful process for the survivor that can take place only in a nonjudgmental, supportive environment.

Over the past 14 years, we have worked with Cambodian survivors on the mental health issues that are a natural result of catastrophic trauma. Our work has been like a dance with the community, and it is fair to say that the survivors themselves have modeled the treatment approach that we use. When we move too fast in approaching the trauma, they deliberately move away from us. When we do something right, they move closer again.

Today, survivors are faced with new problems that are a clear aftermath of their experiences. In just the past year, we have seen many patients come to us with debilitating physical problems that have been described in trauma literature as concentration camp syndrome or KZ syndrome. Symptoms include extreme fatigue, headaches, heart palpitations, GI distress, and muscle and bone pain. These symptoms are present alongside the symptoms of depression and PTSD. These symptoms confirm that the massive starvation and physical abuse experienced by the survivors has caused permanent, debilitating damage and has added to their already overwhelming needs.

Dealing with issues of sexual abuse in adults and children takes great effort and resources to heal the survivors and to solve the problems that this abuse has caused in families and communities. As we have already seen, Cambodians have few resources available, and, for many reasons, it is not likely that new resources will be funded readily. The Cambodian community itself has become crisis driven, and for all the obvious reasons, dealing with issues of sexuality and abuse are not high on the list of priorities.

Over the next few years, therapists, social workers, police, health care providers, and others will be faced with two categories of Cambodian sexual abuse victims. The first consists of survivors of the Mahantdorai, and the second, of the victims of the survivors. Common sense tells us that if we act now, we can probably prevent a generation of abuse in a group of people that has already had more than its share.

Many important questions remain to be answered. What is the relationship between dissociative disorders and abuse in this population? How prevalent was rape during the Mahantdorai? How prevalent is physical and sexual abuse in Cambodian families today? We already know that there is a correlation between rape and domestic violence in the refugee population (Wali, 1991). Does this violence also include the repeated sexual abuse of women and children? Can families be successfully treated? What are the long-term physical and psychological effects of the Mahantdorai? Will communities be able to heal themselves? What kinds of resources do they need? Where will the money come from for these resources?

In closing, we are hopeful that the information we shared will be helpful to others who are working with the survivors of the Mahantdorai. We invite you to network with us so that we can exchange ideas and resources and advocate for meaningful research and treatment. We are grateful to have the opportunity to work with the Cambodian people and have been enriched by their courage and compassion.

Jews and Sexual Child Abuse

JOAN M. FEATHERMAN

Cultural Context

"How can we describe an ethnic group on the move, with thousands of years of history, yet no single language or country of origin?" (Herz & Rosen, 1982, p. 364). This question suggests why writing about the North American Jewish experience in general is difficult. Within American Judaism, there is an astonishing diversity of culture, race, class, religious observance, degree of assimilation, and identification with historical Jewish concerns and practices.

Some Jewish families of German and other Western European descent have been in North America since the middle of the 19th century. The majority of Jews in North America are second- and third-generation descendants of Yiddish-speaking Eastern European Jews who emigrated in the last century, fleeing persecution and eventual death in the concentration camps. Jews of German and Eastern European descent are called Ashkenazi Jews. About 150,000 Jews in the United States are descended from the Sephardic Jews of Spain, who fled the Inquisition (Arditti, 1991). More recent waves of Jewish immigrants have originated in the former Soviet Union, Israel, and parts of

Author's Note:

Gratefully, the author wishes to acknowledge the assistance of Rhonda Shapiro Rieser and Rabbi Louis Rieser in their reading and discussion of this chapter. Thanks also to Rabbi Bob Gluck, Marcia Cohn Spiegel, Ellen Ledley, Ian Russ, and Etti Hadar, who freely shared their ideas and resources.

Africa. The largest concentration of Jews has tended to be in New York and California, although there are significant Jewish populations in most urban areas. Jewish communities are found in rural America as well, and rural Jews may experience their Jewishness quite differently from their urban counterparts.

In addition to diversity in countries of origin and immigration history, the American Jewish community is also divided into four main branches of religious practice: Orthodox, Conservative, Reconstructionist, and Reform. Although these branches of Judaism differ in the ways they express Jewishness, they are linked by a common history and by the Torah, the traditional collection of Jewish teaching. Jews who are affiliated with organized synagogue communities, regardless of branch, celebrate the same holiday cycle throughout the year, the same Shabbat (sabbath) each Friday evening and Saturday, and recite the same Sh'ma, the ancient prayer that differentiated the biblical Jews from the cultures in which they lived, expressing belief in the oneness of God.

There is a fifth segment of American Jewry, the so-called secular Jew. These are people of Jewish descent who are not affiliated with organized religion or traditional Jewish practice and yet feel a cultural kinship to other Jews, Jewish history, and Jewish concerns, often including allegiance to the State of Israel as a Jewish homeland. The condition of being a secular Jew or a religiously observant Jew is not static; it can change at any time over the life course and, within families, from generation to generation. This reflects the complex interweaving of religion, culture, the pressure to assimilate, and nearly 6,000 years of history. Many Jews are not religiously observant and yet are very Jewish identified.

All North American Jews (and Jews worldwide) share in common a vulnerability to attitudes and acts of anti-Semitism. Anti-Semitism may be expressed covertly and unconsciously or blatantly and violently, but whatever the degree, it always resounds with the ghastly echo of thousands of years of persecution, expulsion, and, in our own era, the annihilation of most of a generation of European Jewry.

For the Jews, both as a religion and as a people, beliefs, values, and codes of behavior are rooted in tradition as articulated by the Torah, in written form, and by the Talmud, a body of oral commentary on the Torah that has evolved over generations. Many phenomena in Jewish families, such as gender relationships, norms of child rearing, and attitudes and myths about physical and sexual violence are influenced by Jewish tradition. This influence is literal and concrete in the most Orthodox sects of Judaism, where daily life is prescribed in great detail by *halacha* (rules and norms of Jewish law) and interpreted and enforced by the rabbi, who has a place of prominence in the Jewish community and in each family within the community. In non-Orthodox Jewish communities, where there is more contact with and assimilation to the dominant gentile (non-Jewish) culture, strands of traditional Jewish values and dynamics are interwoven with attitudes and norms of behavior from the dominant culture.

In providing therapeutic services to Jewish families where sexual abuse has occurred, the clinician must be sensitive to the religious roots of certain family values, the effects of assimilation and anti-Semitism, and also to widespread myths and stereotypes about Jews. Searching for the meaning of sexual abuse in a certain family or for a certain individual involves a complex process that may be likened to an archaeological dig, where fragile fragments must be unearthed with patience and delicacy.

Characteristics of Jewish Families

There is much emphasis in Jewish tradition on the family as central to the survival of Judaism and for passing customs and values from generation to generation. Jewish adults experience pressure to form stable Jewish marriages and to procreate Jewish children in order to ensure Jewish survival in the face of assimilation and the Holocaust, where whole families, with their shared history and knowledge, were forever lost. Jewish adults often come to their primary relationships expecting the same quality of caring and commitment as they received in their family of origin. Emotional and geographic closeness between and within generations is positively valued, and conflicts that threaten this closeness are not easily tolerated. Jewish families tend to break off contact with family members who are perceived to have breached their commitment to the family harmony. These perceived breaches of commitment range from not attending a family event or moving far away from the parents, to divorce, intermarriage, coming out as gay or lesbian, or disclosing sexual abuse.

Jewish parents tend to rear their children to be extensions of themselves. Paradoxically, however, Jewish parents also tend to encourage their children to be independent thinkers and to express their thoughts and feelings freely. Through the ages, Jews have valued learning above all else. Because Jews were always prepared to flee their homes, wealth or material possessions had to be easily transportable (e.g., money or jewelry) as opposed to land, large houses, or many books. Therefore, the most typical style of learning was verbal skill developed through argument. There is an old Yiddish saying: "Wherever there are two Jews, you'll find three opinions" (Herz & Rosen, 1982). Loud and emotionally expressive arguments among Jews are not necessarily conflictual but rather in the tradition of intellectual development. In the same spirit, Jewish children are encouraged to express their opinions and expected to become successful intellectually and financially. There is such pressure on Jewish children to be successful and to reflect positively on their families and on Jews in general that few Jewish children ever feel "successful enough." Because of this emphasis on family togetherness and success, and the expectation that lifestyle choices will be similar to those of the parents, Jewish children often leave their homes as young adults with some turmoil, particularly when they veer from well-entrenched paths toward heterosexual marriage and procreation. For example, when gay and lesbian Jews come out to their families, they are frequently cut off emotionally and financially. A loss of family connection and support, for whatever reason, may be experienced by the young adult as a loss of access to membership in the larger Jewish community and, therefore, a loss of access to a positive Jewish identity. Because young adulthood is an age where a history of sexual abuse is often explored directly for the first time, therapists must be prepared to assist Jewish clients in untangling abuse-related issues from issues related to leaving the family of origin to launch into adulthood.

Jewish families have other characteristics that can influence the course of therapy. Within Jewish families, there is a high tolerance for emotionality and an ability to laugh at oneself and at life. Giving and receiving is important in Jewish culture, and generosity to charities and to family is common. However, embedded within this generosity may be the assumption of certain obligations and privileges owed to the giver.

The importance of family, combined with respect for and willingness to rely on experts, makes Jewish families generally positively motivated for treatment. Family members may challenge credentials and be most prepared to engage with therapists who are highly educated and credentialed. They may look for a Jewish therapist who can understand their experience and thus keep the shameful knowledge of family dysfunction and abuse within the Jewish community. Or they may seek a non-Jewish therapist to ensure privacy or to pursue solutions from the non-Jewish dominant culture. Jews are most responsive to a therapist who is bright, open, and sensitive to Jewish values and beliefs. Jewish clients are usually expressive and insight oriented, preferring complex explanations with many levels of meaning. In fact, it may be easier for Jewish clients to express intense affect than to change behaviors.

Shalom Bayit

Shalom Bayit, or "peace within the home," is a central organizing concept in Jewish families. It fosters an ideal of tranquillity, family harmony, and the kind of emotional nurturance needed by children and adults to grow to their fullest potential. Paradoxically, violation of Shalom Bayit carries such stigma that this idealized concept itself contributes to massive denial within the Jewish community about the existence of domestic violence and sexual abuse. The belief that Jewish families are nonviolent fosters positive regard for Jews by non-Jews. Thus Jews may be reluctant to seek help for abuse-related problems, fearing "A shanda for the Goyim" (bringing shame to Jews if non-Jews should know).

It should be noted that the first study of domestic violence in the Jewish community was conducted in 1980 (Giller & Goldsmith, 1980). This survey of Jews in Los Angeles found that rates of domestic violence in the Jewish community were comparable to rates in the non-Jewish community. Sexual abuse in Jewish families still remains shrouded in secrecy and denial. There is no published research on it except in the many accounts of such abuse by adult survivors, who tell their stories in therapists' offices or in anecdotal writings. In searching the literature for this chapter, I found no professional articles or references to incest or sexual abuse in the Jewish community. The few recent sources that mention sexual abuse within the Jewish community were suggested to me in conversations with Jewish therapists, rabbis, and scholars from across the country. These people freely shared their resources with me, Jew to Jew. The process of bringing this information to the non-Jewish community, in the form of this chapter, has felt surprisingly risky for me at a deeply personal level.

That domestic violence, including sexual abuse, existed in biblical times is indisputable because there is much conflicting commentary and discussion in rabbinic writings about whether or not a man has the right to beat his wife or to force sexual relations upon her.

It should be noted that biblical sources prohibiting wife abuse and marital rape refer only to married women. Single, unbetrothed women are in a different category, presumed to belong only to their fathers. Rush (1980) points out that biblical rape was often indistinguishable from marriage:

> If a man took an unbetrothed girl's virginity without her father's permission, the culprit had infringed upon another man's property, committed a civil crime which could be erased by payment to the father. And if the father insisted, the rapist had to marry his dishonored daughter. Rape was a crime of theft, legitimized by payment and marriage. (p. 21)

According to the Talmud, the ideal age to marry off a daughter was 12 to 12½ years of age (Rush, 1980, p. 19). This young age reflects both the shorter life expectancy more than 5,000 years ago when the Talmud was written and the prevailing custom among desert peoples of that time of marrying off their daughters at a very young age.

In contrast, modern rabbinic sources (Dratch, 1992) state categorically that any sort of sexual contact between adults and children is prohibited by the Torah. The biblical source for the prohibition of incest is not a detailed specific list of laws and practices but instead a brief but powerful injunction against "uncovering nakedness" (*gilui arayot*). Gold (1992) describes this injunction against gilui arayot as "unethical sex, . . . defined as any sexual act that hurts another by taking advantage of his or her vulnerability. We can hurt another human being profoundly with our sexual organs. This is why Jewish law prohibits gilui arayot" (pp. 41-42). Because incest exists in Jewish families despite this strong prohibition, further exploration is needed to understand other factors, such as gender roles and anti-Semitism, which may interact to create an environment that supports or condones sexually abusive behaviors.

Gender Roles

Jewish men are often extolled as good husbands, good fathers, and good providers, and they enjoy power and privilege in the Jewish community. As Pogrebin (1991) notes, religious tradition is unambivalent about the male role: In New Square, New York, a village largely inhabited by Orthodox Jews, there is a sign advertising a Talmud course:

TALMUD FOR EVERYONE—MEN ONLY.

Pogrebin comments, "I have a perverse fondness for this sentence. Absurd as it is, it strips away all of religious Judaism's polite rationalization and puts the truth out in the open: Men are 'everyone,' women are not" (p. 49).

Historically, a Jewish man's identity was directly linked to his study of the Torah. In the *shtetls* (villages) of Eastern Europe, the highest honor for a man was to be found in study and scholastic pursuit. In shtetl life, therefore, it was the women who ran not only the homes but also the businesses. This arrangement created a paradox in the development of male identity: Men achieved prestige and position outside the home through study but at the same time were often peripheral to and distant from the family. When such Jewish families immigrated to the United States, they found that accepted norms for male and female roles demanded a shift in their usual gender arrangements. To "become American" meant that men had to take over the role of breadwin-ner; success for American men was measured in great part by financial success.

The pressure on Jewish men to accumulate wealth and professional prestige has been exacerbated by cultural differences in gender socialization and by anti-Semitism. Because Jews tend to seek verbally aggressive rather than physically aggressive solutions to conflicts, Jewish boys may experience isolation and even assault from peers, especially in areas where there are few other Jews. Gluck (1988) identifies this as a source of rage and potential violence for Jewish men as they struggle against stereotypes that denigrate their masculinity. Gluck suggests that this rage becomes directed against Jewish women because of the underlying negative and sexist attitudes toward women in the broader society and in Jewish tradition.

In Judaism, where religious and cultural tradition ensure male power, and where male helplessness and rage are generated by external oppression and internal conflict, conditions are ripe for abuse of that male power over those who are vulnerable and accessible. In Orthodox communities, male power is absolute and concrete. The female voice is considered lascivious—an impedi-ment to men's prayers—and therefore women may pray in synagogues only behind a curtain. It is a challenge for the therapist working with incest in Orthodox families to intervene successfully in the sexually abusive dynamic without invalidating the family's belief system, which may seem to undergird that abusive dynamic.

This challenge is not limited to work with Orthodox families, however. Even in the least obviously religious Jews, traditional gender roles are deeply embedded. "Traditional Jewish views of women and men have persisted with greater tenacity than classical religious beliefs in God, revelation, and observance of the commandments" (Heschel, 1991, p. 31).

When the capable, worldly woman of the shtetl immigrated to America, she learned to restrict her public life in order to "fit in" with American norms of womanhood. Thus her prodigious energies and talents were redirected into her family. Traditionally, the Jewish woman has been responsible for the transmission of Jewish culture and ritual to her children. The power of this maternal role conflicts profoundly with the marginal role of women in religious tradition and practice, and this conflict creates a terrible ambivalence in attitudes about Jewish women and Jewish female identity.

Jewish women are exhorted to be patient, hardworking, self-sacrificing, submissive to God and their husbands, and devoted to their children (Zborowski & Herzog, 1952, p. 138). At the same time, they are stereotyped as bossy, tough, and aggressive; able to handle any challenge; and as dangerous provocateurs, especially when single. "Jewish men are the ones traditionally and popularly perceived as the victims in gender relations" (Gluck, 1988, p. 168).

Traditionally, a Jewish woman's only legitimate sphere of power is within the family. The Jewish mother is deemed to be the mother to the whole family, including her husband. The endless caretaking and boundless self-sacrifice that are prescribed as the best and only creative outlet for women provide fertile ground for the stereotypes of the Jewish mother, who demonstrates her love by "constant overfeeding and by unremitting solicitude about every aspect" of her children's and husband's welfare (Herz & Rosen, 1982, p. 379). Cantor (1992) has called the Jewish mother an "altruistic assertive enabler." Despite the important and life-sustaining aspects of this role, the "Jewish mother" stereotype conveys scorn and contempt for Jewish women. Jewish men demean their mothers, perhaps feeling infantilized or emasculated by them. Jewish daughters may become targets for misdirected male rage and abuse of power. Jewish women are split from their own mothers, struggling with ambivalence about female power, intrusion, and submission, and with the competing values of success and caretaking.

The "Jewish American Princess," or JAP, stereotype also compromises female identity. Although this stereotype can be understood as a form of anti-Semitism (with racist undertones), it is also deeply misogynist. "JAP jokes" are intended to hurt Jewish women by exposing sexual practices or vulnerabilities, or by reinforcing anti-Semitic stereotypes about money, class, and power. The emergence of the JAP as a venomous stereotype over the past 2 decades has supplanted the negativity expressed toward the "Jewish mother" in previous decades. Beck (1991) encourages us to examine more closely the way in which the Jewish daughter is transformed from the "little princess" who sits on Daddy's lap, even when she is grown, into

> the monstrous figure of the "J.A.P." who manipulates men. Could there be some reverse projection at work here? . . . There is something about the family configuration embedded in the stereotype (the daughter compliant in early years, the doting father who later turns against his daughter, and the silent mother) that suggests sexual abuse or incest, or at the very least incestuous desire. (p. 27)

Spiegel (1988) elaborates on the risk of being raised as a "princess," "a 'woman-child' whose sense of approval comes from daddy, a girl who cannot turn away from daddy's love, for with it comes daddy's approval" (p. 11). If the father sexualizes this relationship, this "daughter who has been so much at the mercy of her father for her self-esteem will not have the assertiveness skills and sense of autonomy needed to protect herself from violence even as an adult" (Spiegel, 1988, p. 12).

A further complication in the identity development of Jewish women, particularly women who have been abused sexually, concerns body image and sexuality. The exhortation to "be fruitful and multiply" is a powerful reinforcer of heterosexuality, marriage, and childbearing, particularly for a people who lost 6 million in the concentration camps. Yet Jewish tradition is shaming and judgmental about female sexuality, both overtly, as in the requirement that Orthodox women cover their hair outside their home, and covertly. Furthermore, the dominant American standard of beauty, blonde and slender, suggests to the many Jewish women who have rounder bodies and darker coloring that they are undesirable and unattractive. When a girl is abused sexually by an adult, whether this abuse is perceived as a violent attack or a confusing act of love, it confounds the already difficult task of building positive physical and sexual self-esteem.

The conflicts in identity for Jewish women are frequently expressed in a quest for perfection: perfect children, perfect home, perfect appearance, and perfect performance at every level. L. Brown (1991) suggests that this "expectation of perfection is a defense against shame, and that this expectation embodies the notion that the 'other,' be it Jew or woman, is evil unless sinless" (p. 50). Perfection is impossible for the woman sexually abused in childhood, for whom even the illusion of perfection has been forever destroyed.

Anti-Semitism

"I believe that most Jews, even the most assimilated, walk around with a subliminal fear of anti-Semitism the way most women walk around with a subliminal fear of rape" (Beck, 1991, p. 22). The belief that family together-ness provides a safe haven from inevitable persecution is bolstered by a sense of pride and reassurance at being God's "chosen people," and having survived despite great suffering. Domestic violence and sexual abuse are seen as "the way of the gentiles." The myth of the happy (and never sexually abusive) Jewish family burdens abused Jewish women in particular, who feel invisible because of the strength of this myth. "The anguish felt by many women about revealing family secrets is exacerbated by a sense that Jewish families in particular need protection. That we need to be better than the goyim [non-Jews]. That by telling the truth, we're validating anti-semitism" (Kaye/Kantrowitz, 1991, p. 11).

Anti-Semitism is the oppression of Jews, which takes many forms. Violent and overt anti-Semitism, which arises unpredictably, is expressed in the form of synagogue and cemetery desecrations, Nazi graffiti, death threats to elected officials, the rise of vocal White supremacist groups, and, occasionally, assaults and murders of visible Jews. Covert anti-Semitism, which is the kind most frequently experienced by Jews in the United States, arises from igno-rance and faulty assumptions about what it means to be Jewish. For example, Jews are assumed to be upper middle class or wealthy, when, in reality, most Jews fled to the United States with little wealth and few possessions. Where material success has been achieved in successive generations, it has been through dedication, creativity, and hard work. Even today, many working- and middle-class Jewish families struggle along with non-Jewish Americans to sustain their families through economic downturns.

The assumptions that Jews are rich and are knowledgeable about accruing money are translated into anti-Semitic stereotypes such as the "Shylock," the greedy, selfish Jew, and the JAP, anti-Semitic language that has found its way into common usage: The price can be "jewed down." Beck (1991) describes how openly expressed anti-Semitism became unacceptable after the Holo-caust, and therefore anti-Jewish feeling "went underground" into discrimina-tory language:

The Jew becomes singled out as the symbol of upward mobility, as if the "American Dream" were not legitimate for Jews, who (as a group) have moved from working class to middle class status. Class and gender come together here, marked by the sharp increase in the number of women entering the work force, especially the professions. And it is the Jewish woman on whom this anger is focussed in the form of jokes and public humiliation, for the Jew as "J.A.P." is blamed for the excesses of the American consumer society. Yet there is widespread denial that the "J" in "J.A.P." has anything to do with Jews. (pp. 21-22)

Ignorance about Jews and insensitivity to the experience of being Jewish in a Christian culture can create a hostile, invalidating environment for Jews. Jews who live in rural America or in the Midwest report feeling isolated from the dominant culture, from the Jewish community, or both. In communities with few Jews, ignorance of the important aspects of Jewish life, including the cycle of Jewish holidays, is common and renders Jews invisible. For example, schools still schedule tests on Rosh Hashanah (the Jewish New Year) and penalize children for being absent on that day. Chanukah may be called "the Jewish Christmas," and the one Jewish child in the class may be asked to speak for all Jews to explain this holiday. Jewish children in such situations feel like the "Other," isolated and shamed by their differentness, and invisible as Jews. However, because anti-Semitism makes being visible as a Jew dangerous, being rendered invisible may paradoxically feel safer than being visibly and proudly Jewish.

This paradox is manifested in the striving of many Jews toward assimilation into the dominant culture. Assimilation has been called a form of "depressive compliance" (Engelen-Eigles, 1992). That is, in the face of hostility, suspicion, and threat of harm, one minimizes the aspects of one's identity that most mark one as part of the stigmatized group:

My mother, raised in England during World War II, taught me by example the techniques of Jewish invisibility: never say the word "Jewish" out loud in public; lower your voice when asking if someone is Jewish; do not list Jewish activities on your resume; do not speak about Jewish issues in front of non-Jews; do not carry Jewish objects unwrapped. (Burstyn, 1990, p. 1)

Jews may have nose jobs, bleach and straighten their hair, change their names from Stein to Stone, from Greenberg to Green, and attempt to disguise and eradicate those characteristics that identify them as Jewish. Non-Jews often think they are being complementary when they say, "But you don't look Jewish."

The Holocaust stands as the ultimate expression of anti-Semitism. Almost every American Jew has either lived through the concentration camps, lost family members and friends, or knows other Jews who have. The threat of the Holocaust lives on for Jews in many forms. For some whose lives have been personally and profoundly changed by the Holocaust, the violence they experienced may live on in hopelessness, depression, or in their own rage and violence toward themselves or others. For the incest survivor, perpetrator, or passive witness, the similarities between the torture and helplessness of incest and that of the concentration camps are evocative and inescapable:

> Imagine yourself on a train, your bag is packed with a few belongings, enough for a short stay in the country. Your family is around you; a novel is tucked half-finished into your lap. You know that you are being transported but you don't know where, and the soldiers laughing among themselves in the aisle do not speak your language. Because the landscape is familiar, because your family is there, because nothing in your experience could have prepared you for such a radical awakening, you do not see that you have crossed over an unmarked border. (Matousek, 1991, p. 16)

Some Jews who strive to heal from the trauma of the Holocaust may seek a feeling of relative safety in assimilation and invisibility, but this choice involves loss of ethnic rootedness and tradition, and frequently of family and community. The conflict between Jewish identification and assimilation often gives birth to internalized anti-Semitism. Internalized anti-Semitism repudiates anything remotely Jewish, in the self or in others, and may exacerbate the loss of identity with the terror of being unmasked as a Jew. This terror may prevent even secular Jewish families from seeking help from non-Jewish social services and law enforcement agencies when sexual abuse or other problems emerge.

Jewish Renewal

Contrary to patterns of assimilation of other ethnic groups, many adult Jews are renewing their Jewish identity in a marked "third generation return." All over the United States, Jews in their middle years are returning to traditional Jewish practice and transforming that practice, creating a new branch of Judaism, the Reconstructionist movement. Prayers are being rewritten to be inclusive of women and the female aspects of God. There are groups that join in prayer regularly, or form new synagogues, as in the gay and lesbian synagogues in New York and other large cities. There is an emerging body of feminist Jewish writing—sociological, psychological, and theological. And, increasingly, both rabbis and lay people are speaking and writing about domestic violence and sexual abuse in the Jewish community. These newly articulated voices in the Jewish community are not readily heard or accepted by all Jews, particularly by the Conservative and ultra-Orthodox movements, even though they resound with a renewal of commitment to Judaism.

For families and individuals suffering from sexual abuse, there is hope for healing in both ancient and modern forms of Jewish spirituality. Even after effective therapy designed specifically for recovery from sexual abuse, many Jewish clients still hunger to heal the Jewish self, to come to terms with their Jewishness and to be connected to the Jewish community. This makes sense not only according to Jewish tradition but also in terms of one of the most difficult sequelae of childhood sexual abuse for both victims and perpetrators: the loss of belonging to a trusted and trustworthy human community, the loss of faith.

> Traumatized people feel utterly abandoned, utterly alone, cast out of the human and divine systems of care and protection that sustain life. Thereafter, a sense of alienation, of disconnection, pervades every relationship, from the most intimate familial bonds to the most abstract affiliations of community and religion. (Herman, 1992, pp. 53-54)

Therapeutic Considerations

The central task for the therapist working with any client affected by sexual abuse is to form a safe, empowering, and empathic relational connection. Within this relationship, the therapist must understand and help the client understand the literal and metaphoric meaning of the experience of being abused sexually or perpetrating abuse. In relationships characterized by authenticity, mutuality, empathy, and empowerment, there is the safety necessary to allow disclosure, the experience of strong but previously split-off affect, and the risk of letting go of old behaviors in order to try out new ones.

In working with Jewish clients, therapists must understand the meaning of Jewishness specific to that client and the role that Jewishness will play in the therapeutic relationship, because it is at the juncture where therapist and client connect where the most deeply enduring and healing change occurs.

Sexual abuse in childhood is inherently traumatizing precisely because it is the antithesis of this positive quality of connection. Sexual abuse is disconnection that masquerades as connection, a double bind that is literally "crazy-making" for the victimized child. Sexual abuse violates the implicit trust of children in adults, and violates their sense of who they are and what they are worth. The myth that Jewish families are peaceful and safe convinces Jewish children that they must be the only ones treated this way, and therefore the abuse must be their fault.

However, children naturally strive for health and growth and continue to try to make sense even out of experiences that make no sense. This effort usually leaves them feeling hopeless, powerless, and deeply damaged. The way children make meaning of their experience of sexual abuse, within their own family and cultural context, becomes a metaphor that organizes their development, behavior, symptomatology, and sense of self.

Together, therapist and client must seek to understand the various aspects and permutations of this abuse metaphor and how these meanings are reenacted and injected into relationships, work, emotional and physical functioning, and self-concept. The framework for such explorations must be grounded solidly in the interaction of the effects of sexual abuse with the client's Jewish identity, the role of Judaism in the family of origin, and effects of anti-Semitism and internalized anti-Semitism. For example, consider the child who is routinely abused by an uncle after Shabbat dinner, and whose secrecy and compliance is ensured through affection or gifts of money, clothes, or toys. In this case, the meaning of observing Shabbat with the family and of receiving in a relational connection is contaminated by the original expectation of silent self-sacrifice; repudiation or denial of authentic feelings; and physical, emotional, and spiritual violation. This relational metaphor of being hurt and diminished when receiving affection or gifts may be reenacted in friendships, sexual relationships, and in the therapeutic relationship. The spiritual hunger for lost safety and comfort in familiar Shabbat rituals may be experienced as loneliness, hopelessness, and despair.

The way children "make meaning," as described above, is determined by internal and external resources. These include temperament; cognitive capacity; coping style; and supportive relationships with peers, family members, and other adults. Some coping strategies continue to serve the original coping function well into adulthood. Achieving academic excellence, for example, may have helped an abused child escape a chaotic home life while at the same time preserving a positive sense of self-worth.

Coping strategies of childhood may become what are called "symptoms" in adolescence and adulthood. Reframing symptoms as coping strategies that have outlasted their usefulness, becoming problems themselves, is empowering for survivors of sexual abuse. The challenge for the therapeutic relationship is to support the development of new, more effective coping strategies, enabling the client to let go of those that have become dysfunctional. For the Jewish client, clarifying the connection to Judaism and reclaiming lost aspects of Jewish identity can present powerful new sources of growth and development.

In the following excerpts from a fictional piece, the reader witnesses a young Jew's attempts to seek therapeutic help in rural New Hampshire:

> Last week, Sheila Rebecca Greenblatt unplugged her phone. She had been in severe psychic pain for weeks. . . . Sheila had swallowed hard before telling her new therapist that she was a lesbian. She had coughed and couldn't get the words out when she tried to tell the woman that she was a Jew. . . . The door in the waiting room opened. A pale white woman with graying blond hair walked in. A WASP, Sheila choked. . . . Sheila Rebecca Greenblatt had not adequately prepared herself for talking to a gentile. . . . Sheila followed Alice into her office. "I can't sit too close to you. I'm just getting over a cold," Alice said, as she pushed her chair what seemed to be yards away from Sheila. Alice didn't want to sit close to her clients, Sheila thought, because she was afraid of catching depression. To Sheila, the distance was more WASPy than anything else. When the Jews had a cold they all sat around blowing each other's noses. In fact, Sheila had seen her own parents share the same square white handkerchief. . . . "You're Jewish?" Alice said the word Jewish very loud. Sheila sensed she didn't say the word often. . . . "Do you think being a Jew has made you unable to have fun?" "What does being Jewish have to do with not being able to have fun?" "In T.A. we like to go back to the beginning . . . you know . . . Genesis. We feel it's important to understand our roots." "I already know where I come from. This is absolutely not helping me." "I'm sorry you feel that way. I think you are

resisting. . . . I have seen this kind of reaction before. Your kind always think you're right." (Felman, 1992, pp. 15-27)

In this story, Rebecca successfully navigates the clash of styles and cultural ignorance and insensitivity of her non-Jewish therapist by being fully aware of her own Jewishness. The cure for her depression comes from within her when she repudiates being treated as the "Other" with Jewish humor and pride. In reality, such dynamics between clients and their therapists (both non-Jewish and Jewish) can be destructive and debilitating, especially if these relationships reenact aspects of the client's sexual abuse. Beck (1991) cautions therapists about the need to understand the way that different minority groups exist in relation to the dominant culture, and warns that "A general understanding of outsider status is not enough" (p. 28). She urges that all therapists, Jewish and non-Jewish, take the issues of Jewish identity seriously; familiarize themselves with Jewish history, customs, and the effects of anti-Semitism; and understand how gender role expectations differentially affect Jewish men and women.

CASE HISTORIES

Sarah

Sarah is a 40-year-old, single, white, Jewish woman. She grew up in a rural area on the family farm and was the youngest of four children. Her birth was unexpected, occurring 9 years after the birth of her next older brother; her sister was 10 years older than she, and her eldest brother, 12 years older. The family was religiously observant and kept a kosher home. Although Sarah was serious about Judaism as a child, often going to services on Friday evenings, neither she nor her sister were Bat Mitzvah'd, unlike their brothers. They were told that the family could not afford this rite of passage for the daughters.

Both of Sarah's parents were refugees from Eastern Europe during World War II. Her maternal grandmother, having heard Hitler speak early in the war, fled with her daughter to the United States. Her father, however, had been one of the first men in his community to be taken to the concentration camps. By the end of the war, he had been in Dachau and several other camps. He had hoped to be reunited with his family in America but found that his mother, twin brother, and four other siblings had been killed in the camps. Sarah reports that the trauma of his experience and of the loss of most of his family were perpetuated in his bitterness and in his treatment of his family. He continuously demeaned, humiliated, and disempowered his wife, and he physically abused his sons. He was particularly hard on Sarah when she was the only child at home. She reports several examples of her father abruptly depriving her of beloved pets, without explanation, apparently in an attempt to "toughen her up." His shame, fear, and devastation about the Holocaust isolated the family from Jews and non-Jews alike and infected family members with a sense of hopelessness.

When Sarah was about 4 or 5 years old, her next older brother abused her sexually on one occasion. This sexual abuse occurred in the context of frequent verbal and physical abuse that continued throughout Sarah's childhood. Sarah believes that the sexual abuse happened only once because she told her mother that her brother had "hit" her. However, this sexual abuse was "very frightening and left a very deep impression about power, my place, and trust." Although her parents explicitly and repeatedly told her, "You can't trust anyone who's not Jewish; we did, and look what happened to us," Sarah says, "The main thing that I saw was that you couldn't trust anyone in the family." When Sarah was 13 years old, the same brother, now of college age, physically attacked her. The ensuing fight was so severe that it broke a window. Sarah's mother walked in on this fight but left the room without intervening. Sarah relates this story as an example of how the denial in her family exacerbated her suffering and sense of betrayal. Even into her adulthood, her brother has continued to verbally abuse and demean her, calling her names.

Immediately following the sexual abuse, Sarah developed sleep disturbances, including chronic nightmares that have persisted into adulthood. Her frequent nighttime wakings, when she would crawl into the safety of her parents' bed, were a source of great shame for not being "brave" enough. This sort of invalidation and shame about her own fear is a common reaction of children of Holocaust survivors: that "no discomfort, disappointment, or difficulty seemed worthy of my parents' attention, considering their own experience in the war" (Herz & Rosen, 1982, p. 367). Sarah also has been troubled throughout her adult life with severe depression; low self-confidence, especially in her professional life; and difficult and unsatisfying sexual relationships. In fact, she reports that all the men she has been involved with have been alcoholics. Through her beneficial involvement with Alanon, Sarah now understands how this has allowed her to feel more in control, "the more together one" in the relationships.

Sarah sought therapy at the age of 21, when she first remembered the sexual abuse by her brother. Becoming sexually active was the trigger for the return of these memories. For the first time, she labeled her brother's ongoing demeaning treatment of her as abusive and saw that he treated her the way her father treated her mother. She worked with a Jewish therapist, and after termination of the therapy, the relationship became sexual. Years later, when Sarah began the therapy that was to help her through meaningful recovery from sexual abuse, the first therapeutic task was to hold the prior therapist accountable for violation of boundaries between client and therapist. This foreshadowed a major therapeutic event that happened years later: the powerful and transforming experience of Sarah's confrontation with her brother.

Sarah reports that her major therapeutic goal has been to get her brother's demeaning voice "out of her head." In the past 5 years, in addition to Alanon, Sarah has seen the same therapist intermittently and has participated in an incest survivors' group. She chose the therapist based on her reputation for expertise in sexual abuse. She did not realize that the therapist was Jewish until they met, and then felt "it really opened up a new arena." Sarah's therapist has helped her to understand her role in the family; parallels between the Holocaust's effect on the family and abusiveness in the family; her own relationship to Jewishness, especially with regard to the role of women; and her need to stop her brother's continued abusive treatment of her.

Sarah used both the resources of her incest survivors' group and her individual therapy to help her prepare to confront her brother. In exploring an incident at work where she felt shamed, she realized that this shame recapitulated the family-based shame in her life. This occurred after her father had died, and when she had financial difficulties due to the breakup of a relationship. The therapist supported Sarah in confronting her brother and asking him for financial assistance. Sarah says that the timing of this event was crucial. Had the therapist urged confrontation before Sarah felt emotionally empowered, or before her father had died, she would have risked either revictimization or the irretrievable breakdown of the family. As it was, the therapist joined with Sarah's sense of family loyalty and longing for safe connection with family members in selecting certain family members for disclosure and in deciding how to confront her brother. In preparation for talking to her brother, Sarah disclosed to her sister, who minimized the importance of the abuse. She decided not to disclose to her mother, believing that denial was her mother's primary defense mechanism and fearing that such a disclosure would jeopardize her mother's important connection with the brother, her favorite child.

After much preparation for a variety of responses from her brother, Sarah telephoned him when she knew he would be alone. She recounted her experience and the effects of having been sexually, physically, and emotionally abused by him. Because of her systemic understanding of her abuse, she was able to frame her disclosure as an example of the intergenerational transmission of abuse and victimization. Although she had hated her father, she saw that he, too, had been a victim. Her father had transmitted this violence and betrayal to her brother, and he had transmitted it to her. She was able to join with her brother as a member of a family "shell-shocked" by neglect and violence, while at the same time naming his mistreatment of her.

Sarah's brother apologized for the pain and suffering he had inflicted. He also responded to Sarah's request for financial assistance with generosity and support, further demonstrating his commitment to Sarah and to their relationship. She thinks that the confrontation was healing for both of them, in part because her perspective on the abuse was nonblaming.

This confrontation led to many positive changes in her life. She feels more meaningfully connected to her family, especially her brother. She has revitalized her connection to her Jewishness, especially because she has come to adopt a feminist perspective on how her family's presentation of Judaism was isolating and invalidating. Through the confrontation with her brother, she has taken back her sense of power and wholeness, resulting in more self-confidence and positive self-esteem.

Rachel

Rachel is a 39-year-old Jewish lesbian in a long-term committed relationship. She specifically sought therapy with a Jewish therapist with expertise in sexual abuse treatment. Jewish identity has been important to Rachel since early childhood. She grew up in a home rich in Jewish culture, in an environment that cultivated an appreciation for the aesthetics as well as the spirituality of Judaism.

Rachel is the youngest of three daughters and grew up in a small midwestern city with a well-established Jewish community. Her father was a clerk who obtained a degree in business at age 50. Her mother taught in the local Jewish day school, but her role as a Jewish wife and mother was always primary. Rachel remembers the lavish Shabbat and other holiday meals prepared lovingly by her mother for her family and frequent guests. Rachel's grandparents had been refugees from the pogroms of Eastern Europe in the early 1900s and played an important role in the family.

Rachel was an intelligent, articulate, creative, and expressive child. She excelled in school and in many forms of artistic endeavor, including writing, dance, theater, and sculpture. Despite encouragement from her parents for her academic success, Rachel remembers sensing quite early that she was "too much": too loud, too intense, too visible, too expressive, and that she overwhelmed people. In other words, she was too powerful for a woman and a Jew. Despite these covert silencing messages, and despite many different experiences of sexual abuse that occurred sporadically throughout her childhood and adolescence, starting around the age of 11, Rachel continued to find sustenance and focus in her Jewish education, Jewish youth activities, and in the yearly cycle of Jewish holidays.

Rachel was sexually abused for the first time by a baby-sitter, the 14-year-old son of her mother's best friend. When she disclosed this abuse to her mother, she was warned not to tell his mother because it would be too upsetting for her. This lack of appropriate response to Rachel's pain was repeated many times. She understands this as consistent with the strong but clearly inaccurate messages she received that Jews don't get sexually abused, don't beat their children, don't steal (she knew that her father had whipped her older sister for shoplifting), and particularly don't ask outsiders for help. When Rachel was hospitalized for extreme anxiety at the age of 14, she convinced her parents to send her to Florida instead of the psychiatric ward; this was an acceptable solution that maintained the myths. Over the next 5 years, Rachel experienced several "breakdowns" and had two brief hospitalizations, but each time she convinced her parents that a change of scenery was the way to solve her problems, thus sparing her family the shame of acknowledging her emotional difficulties to outsiders.

At 14, Rachel was accepted into a special school for integrated art training. It seemed to her that at last she would be able to express her creative nature without the limits she felt from her parents. One of her teachers was a charismatic, brilliant painter in his mid-30s, by whom she felt recognized and validated in her talent: "He saw something no one else did." He began to sexually abuse her in his office, in the art gallery, and in his car. This abuse occurred regularly for at least a year. She did not disclose this abuse because she was aware that it was commonly thought that Jewish girls don't get abused. Also, she remembers wondering why her parents did not pick up the obvious clues as to what was going on and intervene. Rachel finally stopped this abuse herself by leaving the art school, a tremendous loss and further silencing of her creativity.

During her adolescence, Rachel was also abused sexually by camp counselors at the Jewish summer camps she attended. In her first year of college, she was abused sexually by her oldest sister's father-in-law, an Orthodox Jew and prominent member of his community who, when confronted, assured her that he was a devout man who needed to fulfill his passions. Years later, when Rachel was confronting this history of sexual abuse, she realized that the theme of being inappropriately sexualized by older men had, in fact, begun in her family, with the dreaded but frequent wet sexualized kisses of her grandfather.

Rachel became increasingly symptomatic as an adolescent and young adult as she felt more and more silenced and cut off from the power of her creative voice. In high school, her increasing depression was exacerbated by the development of an eating disorder, where she would alternate between bingeing and starving herself using diet pills. After she finished high school a year early, which she accomplished without informing her parents of her plan, she went to Israel. Here, faced with the difficult developmental challenges of living independently and becoming sexually active, she overdosed on aspirin and was sent home. Rachel began therapy with an older Jewish woman who became a friend of the family, attending family events, discussing Rachel with her mother, and overtly taking her parents' side in conflicts that Rachel discussed in therapy. In this way, the "shame" of Rachel's emotional difficulties was, indeed, kept within the family.

When Rachel went to college, she continued sporadic phone contact with this therapist. Nevertheless, she became increasingly depressed and immobilized. She decided to pursue writing, and her early stories express the pain of her sexual abuse and her parents' emotional distance and invalidation. Her first story was about a prostitute, going door to door disguised as a beggar. She shared this story with her father, who responded, "I can't believe this is all you can think of to write about." Her father had no comment about the next story he was shown, and with the third story, a fictionalized portrait of his father and the family, he stopped speaking to her for a year.

This form of cutoff, the refusal to speak to and thus acknowledge another's existence, was common in Rachel's family. She reports that any time one of his daughters became sexual before marriage, her father stopped speaking to her for a long time. Her paternal grandfather had stopped talking to her mother as a young bride, for no identifiable reason, until one day he asked her to pass the butter.

Rachel internalized the family tendency to cutoffs by becoming blocked as a writer, cut off from her own voice. In graduate school, she finished stories only during a few periods of release from her deepening depression. Otherwise, she was blocked, gaining weight, fearful of the continued silence between herself and both parents, and grieving the loss of her own voice.

A pivotal event in Rachel's life was her coming out as a lesbian. She describes this period as the beginning of taking back her voice. Here was one aspect of her life that her father could not control, even though, again, he stopped speaking to her. Her mother's collusion with her father's cutoff was a source of great pain and disappointment for Rachel.

Although successfully teaching in a college setting and having her first intimate relationship, Rachel's own writing continued to be blocked. She says now with humor, "I was so blocked, I went to business school." Business school was emotionally unbearable for her, and although she graduated, she has never used this degree. She now sees her pursuit of a business degree as a way to make it impossible for her father to disconnect with her, despite his silence. In his response to Rachel's coming out, her father stressed her obligation to her parents for having fed and clothed her, and gave her 3 years to "grow out of" this stage and return to heterosexuality. The various physical changes that occurred for her outraged him: Her unshaven legs were an affront ("Those legs belong to the Jewish people"), her short hair reminded him of the concentration camps, and her embracing of her female identity was an embarrassment to him. For several years, Rachel rarely visited her parents and they never visited her. It was through her maternal aunt that Rachel's parents learned about her year-long primary relationship and that Rachel learned that her mother had developed Parkinson's disease. A turning point in the cutoff came when Rachel's mother learned that her partner, Leah, was Jewish and that the couple was sitting shiva (ritualized mourning) for Leah's father. Acknowledging that Rachel and her partner were observant Jews, carrying on Jewish traditions, enabled her mother to reestablish a tentative contact. Over a period of 10 years, there has been a gradual process of improved communication.

Through 6 years of individual therapy, Rachel has worked hard to understand the meaning of her history of sexual abuse, the dynamics of her family, and the depression and self-loathing in her life. She has struggled to regain her voice, has committed herself to writing as a profession, and has succeeded in both publishing a book of short stories and lecturing and reading her work widely. She has come to realize that, for many years, she and her oldest sister have alternated being the symptom bearers in the family. With Rachel's successful work, both in therapy and professionally, her sister's role of symptom bearer has become more pronounced. Rachel continues to witness the family's denial about the serious and life-threatening nature of her sister's mental illness.

When Rachel talks about the elements of her therapy that have enabled her to reconnect with her voice by working through her terror and self-loathing, she identifies the importance of working with a therapist who understands the role of Jewishness in her life. Just as Jews have had to be flexible, adapting to the constraints of their environment, Rachel needed a therapist who could be flexible in terms of her need for safety. The therapy began in Rachel's living room and then moved to a clinic setting, where the therapist advocated for Rachel regarding fee and payment: "I saw my own cultural survival mirrored back to me." When Rachel's sensitivity to noise meant that office chatter disrupted sessions, the therapist closed doors and asked people to be quieter. And, most important for Rachel, the therapist invited her writing in as part of the therapy, serving as witness, audience, and enthusiastic recipient of her deepest and most painful truths.

Suggestions for Prevention and Treatment of Sexual Abuse

Traditional therapy focuses on an individual's exploration and healing; its very bias runs counter to the bias of Jewish culture, which is towards the collectivity. Not that the individual should be sacrificed to the community, but that the individual is profoundly connected to the community, so profoundly that separation is not truly possible without extreme loss. . . . Fuzzy boundaries between the self, family, and community can be a sign of Jewish health. (Kaye/Kantrowitz, 1991, p. 13)

As Kaye/Kantrowitz suggests, the importance of the larger Jewish community cannot be underestimated even for the most secular Jews. However, for those Jews who have been sexually abused, fuzzy boundaries have meant violated boundaries, which complicates both the process of recovery from abuse and the healing of Jewish identity. This is particularly true in families of Holocaust survivors. A daughter of Holocaust survivors who was sexually abused by her older brother for 8 years writes:

Because of the Holocaust, people's sense of boundaries were so broken down that other dysfunction could sneak in without any problem. . . . I

> think that my brother learned he could be abusive because he learned he
> could have no boundaries because my parents had all their boundaries
> stripped away from them. (Round table discussion, *Bridges,* 1991, pp. 30-31)

Whether the risk factor is the trauma of the Holocaust or simply the trauma
of belonging to a stigmatized and oppressed minority, Jewish families can be
fertile environments for the intergenerational transmission of abuse.

Prevention of sexual abuse must take place at several levels. The first step
must be to name publicly the sexual abuse that occurs in Jewish families and
hurts not only individuals but the entire community as well. In recent history,
shock waves from the well-publicized death of Lisa Steinberg led to many
articles about domestic violence and some about child abuse in the Jewish
press. Such writing needs to continue, even in the absence of sensational
headlines, to chip away at the extraordinary denial that continues to exist in
the Jewish community. Lay and rabbinical communities have issued adapta-
tions of traditional Jewish liturgy, including prayers for healing of the spirit
for both victims and perpetrators of domestic violence. Such efforts must be
extended to the specific naming of sexual child abuse. It is particularly
important to enlist the leadership of the rabbis in ultra-Orthodox communities,
for in these communities, the rabbi is literally part of each family, and no steps
toward prevention, disclosure, or treatment of abuse may occur without his
approval and cooperation.

Research must be conducted to understand better the prevalence and risk
factors associated with sexual abuse among Jews. Currently, no large-scale
studies of incest in Jewish families exist. Etti Hadar, a psychologist who has
worked with Jewish incest survivors in Los Angeles, has recently submitted
a research proposal to Jewish funding sources for a binational study "to
remove the veil from the problem of molestation and incest of children in
Jewish families" in both the United States and Israel (Hadar, 1993, p. 1).

Another level of prevention effort regarding incest must address the
interpersonal power dynamics that are risk factors for incest. Bart (1986)
describes how the socialization of Jewish girls undermines the development
of effective rape avoidance strategies. Strong predictors of a woman's ability
to avoid rape successfully include picking up on internal danger signals early
and having the ability to express outrage that someone would dare to rape her.
Although the socialization of Jews does encourage the early identification of
the danger of anti-Semitism, the myths surrounding the existence of sexual
abuse in the Jewish community leave children, male and female, unprepared

to identify early warning signals related to abuse. Furthermore, Jewish children are not socialized to express their rage but rather to channel it into productive activity. Jewish children must receive prevention education that encourages them to refuse inappropriate touch from *anyone,* not just strangers, and to disclose sexual abuse when it occurs. Jewish girls must be allowed to be powerful and successful directly and in their own right, not simply through their choice of an appropriate husband. Jewish boys must learn that "no means no" and that their male identity is not dependent on feeling powerful in comparison to the women in their lives. In ultra-Orthodox communities, where role restrictions for women and men may appear inflexible and the pervasive power of men a risk factor for abuse, the concept of "unethical sex" (Gold, 1992) is a useful and theologically sound avenue for prevention.

Jewish boys who are abused sexually suffer similar developmental and psychological consequences as their female counterparts, tempered by the particular influences of their cultural and gender role expectations. Male victims are also burdened by the lack of information and silence about the sexual abuse of boys. Homophobia in Jewish culture may further confuse boys who have been abused by men. As more research is conducted on male victims, the prevalence estimates consistently rise, suggesting that all children, regardless of gender, are at risk for sexual abuse and its damaging effects.

At the forefront of prevention and treatment efforts addressing all forms of abuse and gender inequity in the Jewish community are Jewish feminists, who work in many professional disciplines, communities, and families. The 1992 conference on Judaism, Feminism, and Psychology, sponsored by the Jewish Women's Caucus of the Association of Women in Psychology, gathered together an extraordinarily diverse group of 350 Jewish women who presented their research, writing, thinking, and spiritual beliefs. Several presenters spoke specifically on sexual and physical abuse in the Jewish community. These women and other Jews are beginning to speak out about what has been previously unspeakable, thus changing the face of American Judaism.

For law enforcement and social service agencies to meet the needs of Jewish families where incest has been disclosed, Jewish and non-Jewish professionals must be sensitized to specifically Jewish concerns. Cultural sensitivity must be manifested concretely by collaborating with religious leaders and providing kosher foods in shelters for Orthodox and observant women; by not scheduling support groups and workshops on Shabbat; and by monitoring the environment and professional interactions for Christian symbols, language, or assumptions. A recognition, understanding, and interruption of anti-Semitism, both external and internal, will enhance the potential for a working therapeutic alliance.

To facilitate disclosures of abuse by Jewish children, professionals must understand how the Jewish traditions of *lashon hara* and *hillul hashem* may mitigate against disclosures of sexual abuse, particularly in the Orthodox community. *Lashon hara* (Leviticus 19:16) refers to the biblical injunction against harming a person's reputation by talebearing. *Hillul hashem* (Leviticus 22:32) prohibits the adjudication of Jews in non-Jewish courts. In a position paper on the physical, sexual, and emotional abuse of children, Dratch (1992) uses biblical sources to dispute that these traditions prevent disclosures of abuse, proposing instead "that it is a mitzvah [blessing] to report a child abuser to the civil authorities" (p. 11).

In the treatment of a Jewish family where incest has been disclosed, or of a Jewish adult attempting to work through a history of incest, therapeutic decisions about modality, technique, and interpretation must be firmly grounded in Jewish historical, sociological, and psychological reality. Schwartz (1992) reminds us that "symptoms are the path to consciousness." Many symptoms manifested by survivors of sexual abuse are intensified when those survivors are Jewish. Self-hate may manifest as eating disorders or body image disturbances; feeling contaminated; hating other Jewish women, especially one's mother; and exaggerated self-improvement efforts. An emphasis on suffering and persecution may be manifested as somatic symptoms that may hold together a family threatened with dissolution because of intergenerational conflict or lead to the disclosure of sexual abuse. Terror may be expressed through anxiety, tics, obsessive/compulsive behavior, perfectionism, low sexual desire, compulsive overeating, hypervigilance, chronic self-criticism, and taking refuge in invisibility. Jews may experience a "cultural depression" (Kaschak, 1992), with a sense of lowered expectations of life as the only reliable antidepressant. The pull of assimilation can be experienced as a loss of self, isolation, and a feeling that one does not exist, without being able to identify the source. Grief at a history of extermination and loss of identity through assimilation can prevent clients from leaving home, from differentiating from parents, or, conversely, from maintaining any family connection. Even in individual therapy with adult survivors of sexual abuse, the therapist must invite the meaning of the family and community context into the therapy room, either symbolically or literally. Groups for adult survivors offer powerful settings for clients to rework their relationships to their family and community; self-help networks for Jewish survivors of sexual abuse are also forming.

As survivors of sexual abuse attempt to clarify and reclaim a Jewish identity that is not compromised by betrayal and violation, they may be drawn to healing variations of traditional Jewish ideas and forms. Examples of the efforts of Jews to reclaim their Jewishness in the process of healing are offered here in the hope that these may be useful tools for others.

In the traditional practice of sitting shiva, where Jews gather to mourn a death and provide comfort for the living, Jewish survivors of sexual abuse have found meaningful release for their grief about betrayal and violation at the hands of loved ones.

> I returned to my inner work of therapy and healing for a number of years. . . . Sadly, it became clear that I would not ever have parents who could be caring of me or who could behave in a loving or even decent manner to me. . . . Sitting shiva for one's abusive parents is indeed a holy and spiritual process. . . . The mourner is taken care of by her community for a period of time, cooked for, cared for; one cries and tells one's story and feelings so often and with so many supportive mirrorings being reflected back, that it transforms one's memories from painful stones in one's shoes to threads lining the back of one's coat. In other words, what one has suffered no longer is a source of new original fresh pain, but part of what is behind you and magically transformed into something that protects and keeps you warm. (M. Wolf, 1991, pp. 7-8. Reprinted by permission of the *Valley Women's Voice*.)

Survivors of childhood sexual abuse often report persistent feelings of physical and spiritual contamination. Klem (1992) describes the use of the Mikvah, or ritual bath, to provide an experience of spiritual cleansing and purification for clients who struggle with these feelings of contamination.

Other healing rituals for survivors of sexual abuse can be integrated into daily routine as prayers or affirmations:

> Holy One, bring me comfort,
> For I have seen terror;
> Cradle me and I will feel safe,
> Heal me and I will become strong,
> Nurture me and I will grow.

You have taught me that to do righteousness and justice
Is more acceptable to You than sacrifice.
You have taught me that, with You beside me,
Fear is not eternal.
Help me to live by Your teachings.
Blessed are You, Holy One, Source of Life,
Who guides, who protects us, who sustains us. Amen.

(Rogow, 1991/1995, pp. 77-78;
reprinted by permission)

For the secular Jewish survivor, examples of such rituals may provide access to a nurturing spirituality that was previously unexperienced. For others, a sense of spiritual and emotional healing may be found in political or social activism. There is a long history of such Jewish involvement in the labor union, civil rights, and feminist movements, among others.

Successful therapy with Jewish survivors of incest most often involves assisting the survivor in reconnecting to some safe element of Jewish history and family. This may involve the reworking of the mother/daughter or the father/son relationship, or facilitating communication among siblings. It may involve validating a family of choice when the birth family has been unable to acknowledge the abuse or grow with the survivor. It must always involve the therapist joining with Jewish clients in their cultural, historical, and spiritual context.

Anglo Americans
and Sexual Child Abuse

MARIAN SCHMIDT

A young WASP couple was calmly informed by their 8-year-old daughter that a teenage boy in the neighborhood had stood in his window, exposing himself to her and a friend. The couple deliberated extensively about what they ought to do, debating their obligations to their child, the best treatment for the teenager, the need to inform an authority for the safety of the neighborhood, and ways to avert further incidents of a similar nature. Finally, they decided to consult with the mother of their daughter's friend, who was Italian. When this woman finally was made to understand by the WASPs that her daughter had viewed someone's penis, her course of action was immediate. She hung up the phone, marched to the boy's window, and screamed at him for several minutes. Following this, the WASPs, who were surprised, withdrew; the Italian woman returned to her family, satisfied because she had expressed her outrage. No more was said on either side; the family with the offending son soon moved away.

The heterogeneous ethnic makeup of American culture gives rise to a variety of responses in families to aberrant behavior. The purpose of this chapter is to consider, speculatively, the ways in which responses by Anglo American families may be influenced by their ethnic background. Following a description of stereotypic Anglo American traits, the interaction of these traits with the problem of sexual abuse will be considered, with illustrative examples.

Overview of Culture

White Anglo-Saxon Protestants often ignore their origins, considering themselves rooted in North America. They have no annual parade, but they are intensely loyal to that which is called "American." They believe that every person should have a voice in the political destiny of the country, which is still seen as a "melting pot," with citizens of equal political, if not social, status. The term *WASP* is a pejorative to some. I use it here simply as an acronym without value judgment and with appreciation for the strengths of WASP culture, which is my culture. WASPs may feel defensive about the label and may deny that they have ties to other countries prior to immigration.

Perhaps because of their lack of ethnic identification, WASPs tend to underappreciate group differences, which can sometimes give members of other groups the feeling that they are invisible to WASPs. WASPs do not seem to be aware that being a WASP is not recognized and valued by all. Partly owing to their lack of cultural identity, WASPs do not step outside of themselves, which is a prerequisite for understanding or explaining oneself. Instead, they assume responsibility for the "dominant culture" in America. "By the end of the 19th century, the American standards of ethnicity accepted Anglo-Saxons as the norm, placed other whites on what might be called 'ethnic probation,' and excluded subcultures from serious consideration" (Franklin, cited in Locke, 1991, p. 4).

WASPs subdivided themselves into "upper," "middle," and "lower middle" classes. (It has never been acknowledged that a WASP could be "low class," regardless of dirt farm lifestyles in areas such as Appalachia or rural Maine.) Upper-class WASPs may be listed in the "Social Register" of major cities; such a listing is influenced by high income but even more by family history dating back to the American Revolution and before. Accessories that help determine status may include size and cost of housing, brand of car, private school education, attendance at Ivy League colleges, "coming out" at debutante balls, vacations in distant places, and clothes by fashion designers.

Middle-class WASPdom encompasses those families depicted in television shows not otherwise ethnically described, from *Married With Children* to *Thirtysomething.* Families considered lower middle class are generally those in which the father holds a blue-collar job, even if his job offers a high income. A major WASP trait is the valuing of independence, and this influences the thinking and emotional relationships between generations in WASP families. WASP children receive the message that they should be self-sufficient and have their own individual goals, which the family will support. There are repercussions from this: WASPs are apt to be self-centered and intolerant of those who are dependent. They try to control situations and tend to deny those that cannot be controlled.

The pioneer figures in any movie called a "Western" are, in fact, WASPs. The frontier life featured social isolation, arbitrary parental authority, and patriarchal values; these factors are said to contribute to sexual abuse (Finkelhor, 1984). Many societies have these characteristics; for example, the Irish treasure privacy and tend to sweep conflictual issues "under the rug" in a somewhat arbitrary, isolating manner. But the Irish live in expectation that a storm will break over their heads; from the Irish viewpoint, hell is for this life and heaven is for later. WASPs do not have a history of potato famine and subjugation by another nation. Unlike the Irish, they are vulnerable to catastrophe because they have no adaptive fatalism. It is either "Nothing bad ever happens in our family," or else they are overwhelmed, like the mother in the film *Ordinary People* who denies her son's depression and, when forced to accept it, cannot maintain her relationship with her son or husband. WASPs work hard to maintain the veneer of a happy family, making it difficult to recognize and challenge the sources of unhappiness that arise in all families.

A certain emotional and physical isolation comes with this great emphasis on individual independence. Distancing is a commonly used defense. There is apt to be a lack of overt emotional intensity and a corresponding weight on the intellectual side. This can cloud a WASP's awareness of a very real emotional attachment and give an "educational" aspect to parenting that bypasses a feeling of closeness. The grandparents in WASP families may not be involved with childbirth and child rearing because, once launched, the next generation is on its own. Family dinners are social occasions that join the family in communication; the factor of appetite is ignored or repressed. This structure may lead to family rigidity, which is a frequently reported characteristic of incestuous families (Allen & Lee, 1992).

Emphases on work, achievement, success, and progress are also characteristic of WASP culture. In their independence and self-responsibility, WASPs are future oriented and task oriented. High motivation and steady work toward goals are typical. Where there is difficulty expressing and experiencing strong emotion directly, work becomes an outlet for both intimacy and aggression. WASPs are optimistically convinced that human nature can be perfected by work. Material comfort is evidence of the good life, respectability, and even salvation because of Calvinist-Puritan influences.

Some human relations, such as marriage and therapy, are seen as contracts, with problems occurring when someone's performance does not seem to fulfill the contract. The nuclear family is a WASP idea. The ideal of independence creates a contradiction in which a female must be financially dependent on a husband and at the same time raise children to be independent. Achievement and success are expected of WASP children. Some male WASPs who feel isolated at home are rewarded only in their work situations, where their disciplined, productive activity is seen as a worthy end in itself (R. M. Williams, 1970). Elderly WASPs struggle with the WASP emphasis on youth and the future. Their nonmaterial assets are likely to be ignored. Their growing incapacity equals, in the WASP mind, giving up, which in turn equals death. Stoicism is a virtue in the WASP view; a high value is placed on self-control, whereas suffering is to be born in silence (McGoldrick & Rohrbaugh, 1987).[1]

Interaction of Traits and Problems of Sexual Abuse

Secrecy and Isolation

"Isolation is the major variable associated with the evolution of incestuous relationships" (Lutier, cited in Barnard, 1984, p. 8). It is a curious paradox that WASPs feel representative of dominant North American culture and yet are prey to feelings of isolation, inadequacy, and emotional distance. Perhaps because they are trained in individual independence and self-responsibility, they also receive training in isolation and inadequacy. One might expect the Anglo American, "all-American" family to meet the world confidently because their assumption is that the WASP way is the "right way," but features of denial, isolation, and secrecy are often present in WASP families. These characteristics are described by Barnard (1984) as also common to both incestuous and alcoholic families. Barnard explains that such families use much psychic energy to maintain secrets that deprive them of the potential for greater emotional expression and relatedness.

Not all WASPs are isolated or secretive, and many have satisfyingly close relationships. When in conflict, WASPs tend to withdraw and seal themselves off from others in a way that increases the rigidity of their family boundaries and inhibits easy and appropriate emotional contact. In one WASP family where incest was strongly suspected, it was customary for the family to dine together and then separate, each to their own room, with a closed door until they slept. This behavior suggests rigid boundaries with an overemphasis on privacy, preventing open communication. Why were the doors closed—to hide or protect against sexual abuse, or simply to fend off tension? When questions were raised, the family, true to form, withdrew from counseling.

Loyalty and Denial

In place of emotional expressiveness, WASPs demonstrate loyalty to their traditions, whether through treasuring family antiques or maintaining family myths. These are unique, individual antiques and myths, not cultural ones. Writing of his own background, Phipps (1991) says,

> The great emphasis is on the idea of tradition, the tidal repetitions of inherited form and their patterns of sameness. The tribe *is* the world and has no need to change or assimilate. Naturally xenophobic and insulated, the WASP has the moated psychology of an islander. (p. 27)

Because we lack clear emotional outlets available to those in other cultures, WASPs sometimes have to be taught to express our pent-up feelings (Schmidt, 1991). WASP parenting tends to be more educational than demonstrative of affection, and WASP children learn to manifest self-control and cool reactions at all costs. Feelings of emotional distance can ensue, with repressed feelings finding outlet in uncomfortable ways. A southern WASP expressed frustration with her two brothers for refusing to discuss her upset feelings over sexual advances made to all three by an uncle when they were children. One brother had suffered from night terrors and the other was experiencing relationship problems with women, yet their family pattern was such that they preferred denial over working through the anger. In a notable example of both denial of problems and the high value placed on work, the uncle's wife retained her job in his business, even after divorcing him following the revelation of his abusive behavior.

Typically, as in this case, the secret molestation is buried for years, possibly because the victim is made to feel responsible for her own life and cannot express her feelings overtly across the generational boundary, or perhaps because it would be disloyal to have something so "wrong" happen to her and would reflect on the family standards of normalcy. In some rigid, unemotional families, a victim may tolerate or even encourage whatever kind of attention or affection that is available, even though it crosses sexual boundaries (Finkelhor, 1979).

A WASP mother will attempt to ensure that her children grow up to stand on their own two feet and be reliably hardworking and emotionally stable. She will model these attributes for her children, keeping secret any discord with her husband that would undermine her efforts financially or emotionally. The resulting strain may prevent her from attending to all but the most negative attention-getting behavior of her children. The sadness on her daughter's face may seem like dependent sulkiness to be ignored; she may deny depression on the part of a son by finding him more activities to engage in, or changing his school. If both parents have inherited Victorian myths and traditions, they may confine their discussion of sexual issues with their children to forbidding masturbation. This reticence may stem from their own childhood experience of silence on sexual subjects from emotionally distant parents.

The unavailability of one or both parents has been linked to risk of sexual abuse (Finkelhor, 1993). It would be interesting to compare the availability of WASP mothers and fathers with those of other ethnic groups. Because the work ethic is strong with WASPs, they are apt to spend many hours working, and WASP mothers are relatively free in their culture to engage in work away from their children (Schmidt, 1990). In the Anglo American-dominated business world, it is expected that WASP fathers will work late in the evenings and put their family's needs last. Emotional closeness is a kind of availability that may be lacking in authoritarian, Puritan homes.

A group of British authors has speculated that some families cannot tolerate closeness and use violence to achieve distance, thus stabilizing their family systems (Asen, George, Piper, & Stevens, 1989). These authors theorize that previous abuse, when the parent was a child, is transferred into the present by a trigger that awakens past associations. Therapists know that a parent in a counseling session will often exclaim that they had sworn not to do to their child what was done to them, and yet old anger had its way and spilled out on the closest vulnerable being—usually the youngest. In a midwestern WASP family, the father, as a child, had been told constantly by his mother, "You'll never be the man your father was." He became an aggressive teenager and then a physically and emotionally abusive parent, often hitting his son and throwing him across the room. When his son became a parent, the son succumbed to the temptation of showering with his daughter and masturbating himself and her. When the abuse was reported, he resolved his guilt by an immediate full confession, which also served to distance him from his wife and child. The WASP wife's greatest anger was reserved for the therapist who reported the family, and for the Black caseworker who wore her identifying badge while accompanying the wife and daughter in a public setting. The mother could not tolerate the loss of secrecy nor admit that her family needed help. Her husband's background served to excuse him in her eyes, and she saw herself as the victim of state violence when her family was disbanded.

Individuality and Patriarchy

One Anglo-Saxon theme identified by R. M. Williams (1970) as reflecting the influence of WASPs on North American culture is individual personality: Every individual should be independent, responsible, and self-respecting, and the group should not take precedence over the individual (Locke, 1991). This outlook has been termed "ideocentric," in contrast to group-oriented cultures, which are "allocentric" (Marin & Triandis, 1985). In an interesting study, Hosch, Chanez, Bothwell, and Muñoz (1991) compared Anglo American and Mexican American jurors' judgments of mothers who fail to protect their children from abuse. The Anglo Americans were described as belonging to an ideocentric, individualist culture in which behavior is regulated by personal likes and dislikes and by cost/benefit analysis, suggesting that attitudes, rather than norms, would mainly determine behavior. An allocentric culture, such as that of Mexican American families, would be characterized by warmth, openness, community dependence, and sensitivity to the feelings and needs of others. The ideocentric culture would feature emotional detachment from groups other than one's family and friends, whereas the allocentric culture would be ruled by community norms. Hosch et al. (1991) found in two experiments that Mexican American jurors were harsher in recommending sentencing of the neglectful mothers than the Anglo American jurors:

> The strong identification with community, family, and traditional sex roles found in the traditional Mexican American ethnic group provides a readily useful, culturally based standard against which to judge the behavior of persons who violate role expectations and norms. (Hosch et al., 1991, p. 1696)

These powerful group norms may be lacking in WASP families. One sees the emphasis on individual decisions, regardless of community norms, in the case of the WASP who abused his daughter in the shower and whose wife could not blame him.

In a sample of college students, sexual abuse was found to occur more often in the families of rural Yankee stock than among other White ethnic groups (Finkelhor, 1979). Supporting this finding, a Canadian study found that female victims were more likely to come from English-speaking, Protestant, small-town, or rural backgrounds (Bagley, 1991). The motto "Don't tread on me" stems from Yankee Revolutionary pride in the ability of the free American soldier to hold his ground and, so to speak, his boundaries. Why, then, are so many cases of incest found in the memories of Yankee daughters? The answer may lie partly in the tremendous need to control others exhibited by the competitive, capitalist entrepreneur, whether businessman or farmer. The ruthless decrying of the needs of others, and the overriding of the group norms, accords with the emphasis placed by WASP males on individual rights and needs. Satisfying one's own needs at the expense of others becomes a moral right, and a definition of "freedom," when one is fighting one's way up in the world; stepping on the faces of others is part of the game of winning, and winning is morally good.

To a WASP, freedom may mean a clear path to acquiring and maintaining socioeconomic status. WASPs may value external conformity in dress, housing, recreation, manners, and even political ideas, but in private, individual freedom takes on an almost religious connotation (R. M. Williams, 1970). A man may be king in his own house in many cultures, but the WASP male has a sense of sovereign power, tradition, wealth, and privilege that is daunting to both daughters and sons. Sexual domination may be another manifestation of that power. According to Phipps (1991), some WASP males feel a need to be perceived as lady-killers for a sense of masculinity and power, whereas young WASP women are often viewed as "trophies." Self-esteem based on sexual control of women may carry over to father-daughter relationships, where a man's moral responsibility to satisfy his needs extends to his daughter's body.

Even in the public domain, the religious righteousness with which the Puritan ethic rules historically has taken a toll. The mass abuse of women that comes to mind in WASP history is the physical stripping and inspection of women by Puritan men to detect tiny flaws by which they could be "proved" to be witches. This sexual abuse was falsely justified on religious grounds by what we may suppose to be a salacious group of dominant WASP males and is typical in its projection of guilt onto the victim.

Ever since Freud, some therapists have discounted reports of women who were incest survivors, blaming incest on the child's desire for the adult rather than on the predatory adult (Birns & Meyer, 1993; Finkelhor, 1979; Kalichman, 1992). The WASP female is especially vulnerable to professional opinion that she is to blame for her own suffering because of her tendency to be self-responsible and to suffer silently.

CASE HISTORIES

Mary

A 50-year-old Anglo American woman, Mary, called for an appointment but was unwilling to give her address or home phone number for fear her husband would find out she was seeking therapy. She was referred by a coworker because of signs of depression and in fact was hardly eating or sleeping, but she denied any depression. She was still so filled with anger at her parents that she could hardly speak. Typically, WASPs speak in a loud, controlling voice, with a quick, responsive style, while maintaining eye contact (Sue & Sue, 1990), but this woman gave brief, whispered answers after long pauses. Eye contact was finally attained when the therapist distracted her with a dessert recipe, having found that her hobby was cooking.

Therapy was made conditional on eating, and Mary began to gain weight. She was functioning normally at her job as a secretary. Her relationship with her children was a comfortable one for her, but her marital relationship suffered from emotional distance and her resentment at her husband's failure to acknowledge her pain promptly when she had been hospitalized for an emergency appendectomy.

At times during sessions, Mary showed a tendency to withdraw; she would draw up her knees and turn sideways in her seat, or stride about the room behind the therapist, or become nearly silent, uttering brief words through clenched teeth. She wished to discuss her childhood abuse, but the memory made her inarticulate. She was given a human figure drawing with no clothes or genitals shown. She was asked to show what part of the figure bothered her, and nonverbally indicated her distress by placing crosses on the hands of the figure. On the reverse side, she was able to draw a figure and label it a man. When asked her feelings about the figure, she wrote, "sad, mad," and then, across the body, she wrote, "hate." On her self-drawing she wrote, "unattractive, lonely, depressed, abused, mad, stupid, unhappy, evil."

When Mary was given clay to work in her hands, it seemed to loosen her tongue. While pinching the clay into a fragile fan shape, she began telling the saga of misery that had begun when she was 10 years old, when her older brother fondled her and made her perform oral sex on him. Reporting this to her father had the effect of making her his victim too, and soon she was servicing her father, her four brothers, and many of their friends. Her mother ignored all communication from her daughter concerning the abuse. A woman of terrible rages, she often beat Mary for real or imagined misbehavior. At school, Mary had a reputation for acting out; her grades were poor, but she managed to graduate high school and got out of her home by means of an early marriage. She was unable to tell her husband of her abuse and thought she would forget about it when her parents died. She was crushed to realize that she could not forgive them or forget their abuse.

Mary's family drawing depicted her husband and three sons, all identical in size and without hands or feet, but with enormous shoulders. The figures had long necks and appeared powerful, even without appendages. Her omission of herself from the drawing was significant. She later reported that during her episodes of abuse, she would lapse into a daze and think, "I'm not really here." She had tried to hide from her brother, and later from her father, but a combination of threats and kindness had kept her from refusing sexual favors until she was 16 years old.

A year prior to therapy, she had made a suicide attempt by taking an overdose of medicine; Mary referred to it as "when I was bad." The doctor she had seen at the time had made Mary feel guilty over her past behavior. Her silences, thinness, and insomnia suggested a major depression; however, she was now frightened of doctors and resisted discussing medication or even a physical checkup. She had learned early a lesson that today's professionals are starting to acknowledge: that "child sexual abuse is about power, control and connection" (Barrett, 1993, p. 141), and she recognized the same conditions in a doctor's office that had existed in her parents' house. Her sense of guilt over her own past and present behaviors was already disproportionate. This was more than the natural shame of the victim—her greatest pain was expressed over the fact that she had come to enjoy oral sex with her relatives. Enjoyment of sex or any bodily appetite is antithetical to Puritan WASP values (e.g., Phipps, 1970). Mary felt herself to be evil in some way; this may be why she kept herself covered by a jacket or coat during early sessions, although the weather was hot.

This client exhibited many WASP traits: She shared the Protestant work ethic and expected to earn a salary, and she was an emotionally distant wife and undemonstrative mother. Her difficulty in speaking when emotionally aroused is typical of her culture; Phipps (1970) has referred to a clipped style of speech known as "WASP Lockjaw." Mary's jaw was nearly locked as she attempted to share her pain. WASPs place great value on the spoken word; "My word is my bond" is a byword for WASPs, whose utterances may be thought of as engraved in steel. It was easier for Mary to write down her emotions or express them in drawings than to state them. Possibly she felt ambivalent about using her mouth because of the oral nature of her sexual abuse.

Mary also had a considerable medical history apart from the appendectomy, with multiple incidents of internal distress. This somatization of stress is again typical of WASP repression of emotion, which is internalized until it calls attention to itself by a medical emergency.

This client was clearly at risk, but her manipulative ways prevented the straightforward, task-oriented counseling usually favored by WASPs. (They like to make use of their money and achieve objectives in therapy.) At times, Mary would attempt to touch the therapist physically; other times, she would use silence in true WASP, nonexpressive style to pull speech from the therapist. When able to converse, Mary began to respond to a style of therapy that affirmed her feelings while putting her intellect in charge of them. She read a prescribed book, Black's (1982) *It Will Never Happen to Me,* and discussed the vignettes of the children in it and the small section on abuse. This led her to bring in a magazine article she found that detailed an experience of child abuse. By highlighting statements in the article, she communicated her history of abuse without actually verbalizing it. Gentle sex education was also undertaken that assisted her in replacing guilt with knowledge and understanding of her bodily responses.

When Mary reported a scene in which one of her sons threw an object at someone, she was helped to see that her own refusal to eat was a type of acting out of anger, similar to her son's, but inflicted on herself. In subsequent sessions, Mary reported improved eating habits and seemed more responsible in this regard. Her depression waxed and waned while a medical checkup was urged. A female gynecologist was found for Mary, but prior to her appointment, she again overdosed on medicine and was hospitalized. A letter followed, full of gratitude, but terminating therapy; it showed her strongly attached to a doctor who had attended her in the hospital and who was continuing to counsel her.

Joan

Joan was a 14-year-old girl brought for counseling by her parents because of poor school grades and defiance of home rules. Her father had returned home the year before, following a 6-year absence, during which he had joined Alcoholics Anonymous and practiced abstinence from alcohol. Her mother was a compulsively neat housekeeper who turned to religion for support when her husband had first become unfaithful and left the household. Joan was their only child. She complained to the therapist that she had always been able to get her father to side with her against her mother, but now the two were teaming up against her. She confessed an earlier suicide attempt with pills, which passed unnoticed when she slept off the effects. She detailed a history of inappropriate punishment at the hands of her father and a failure to win her mother's approval.

Before the parents could be informed of the suicidal gesture, Joan ran away, taking money from her parents' desk. The theft enraged her father. Her mother was more concerned with locating Joan, and she especially wondered if Joan had left with an older man with whom her friends had seen her. Three weeks passed; the interstate runaway system was used, and Joan was found in a runaway shelter in a distant state. She had been raped by a stranger while hitchhiking. In an individual session, her mother was informed of the medical tests that would follow. Her mother escorted her home, and Joan returned to therapy. The mother and daughter never discussed the rape, but Joan sadly told the therapist how she had been tied down, penetrated, and abandoned on a country road. She had not been a virgin; in fact, the older man with whom she had been keeping company had first seduced her, an experience she underwent voluntarily but without pleasure.

Postcrisis work was begun on restoring Joan's self-esteem as a person who would become independent, achieving (good WASP values), and sexually satisfied. The last characteristic, although not representing anything she had been taught, was meaningful to Joan. She brightened considerably at the thought that she might one day have "good sex" on her own terms. She brought in the expressive poetry she wrote and seemed once again focused on teenage pursuits. Soon she became attached to a boy slightly older than herself and spent more and more time at his home with his family.

Gradually the work of therapy began to address Joan's use of alcohol. She admitted to hiding liquor in her room, where she would get high and sleep off the effects. Her mother frequently grounded her for rude remarks and the failure to be neat or do housekeeping duties, so Joan had plenty of opportunity to retire quietly to her room and drink. Her father brought her to Alateen meetings while he attended AA meetings; there she could observe his tendency to make overly close connections with younger women.

At length, Joan was persuaded to enter a rehabilitation program. Here, for the first time, she acknowledged her prior use of many drugs, and she also revealed a history of incestuous abuse by her father when she was 7 years old, before he left the home. When an investigation was made, she recanted. Her mother had been extremely angry when her daughter was referred to a rehabilitation program. Emotionally distant and concerned with appearances, this mother reacted more strongly to the discovery that her daughter might be following in her father's footsteps vis-à-vis alcohol, and that this would be publicly known, than she did to the information about incest or Joan's running away. As with the rape, sexual misbehavior was to be ignored and "swept under the rug." Joan's mother subsequently decided that the problems in her marriage could not be tolerated and moved out, leaving Joan in her father's custody. He terminated therapy.

In this case, all the red flags were flying from the start that suggested a history of sexual abuse. An alcoholic parent, marital discord, authoritarian parenting, underachievement at school, defiance and running away by the child, the child's use of alcohol and/or drugs as a buffer, and the child's promiscuity without pleasure—these factors contribute to a standard profile of the incestuous family. Parker and Parker (1986) found fathers' absence from early child care and nurturance to be a major factor for subsequent sexual child abuse. In this family, the father had been absent during Joan's early years because of substance abuse and physically absent during her early school years. Joan experienced an utter lack of warmth and acceptance by her parents, owing to their emphasis on satisfying their individual needs.

A study by P. M. Cole and Woolger (1989) demonstrated that incest survivors have more negative perceptions of their parents than do nonincest sexual child abuse survivors as a reflection of their perception of their parents' control techniques. In the group studied, the incest survivors viewed their parents as lacking in positive involvement. This study found a history of incest to be associated with endorsement of autonomy promotion attitudes, such as a preference for early weaning, toilet training, and independence on the part of the child. Such attitudes are the hallmark of WASP parenting. A rigid approach to family tasks is a characteristic listed as descriptive of families with sexually abused children (Glaser, 1991). Both of Joan's parents shared such rigidity: her father in rating the money he earned, which she stole, as more immediately important than her safety, and her mother in her perfectionist housecleaning.

Treatment Issues

Like any survivor of incest or other sexual child abuse, the WASP client, male or female, needs to gain detachment from painful memory, a clear understanding of the exploitation involved in the abuse, and, if possible, acceptance of the perpetrator as a faulty human. Throughout this process, there must be a steady building of self-esteem. For the WASP, there are special aspects to the progress toward these goals in treatment.

Detachment is a natural emotional stance for WASPs, but once it is lost in the overwhelming flood of pain and anger, it is not easily regained. For this reason, art therapy was used in Mary's case. A nonverbal medium, especially the feel of clay, can loosen tightly repressed feelings so that they can be expressed. It should be noted that therapy did not begin with clay but with pencil drawings. Pencil is the "tightest" medium, with the most control over the product, which, in Mary's first response, was merely crosses placed on a drawing the therapist had made. In subsequent steps, she was able to draw a figure, write words, and finally talk while working the clay. No materials were introduced involving color until she began speaking. She made a few drawings in color but lost interest in art media as words became available to her. Everything she made and said was affirmed, but not with praise, which is difficult for WASPs to accept. The therapist can say, "I like what you made," and a WASP will usually accept this individual judgment, but saying "You did that well" may only entangle the WASP in expectations and denial.

Poetry and music were used with Joan. She wrote songs and was encouraged to bring her music to sessions. In the ups and downs of her adolescent life, with its battles and truces with peers and parents, detachment was seldom a wholly achieved objective. Alcohol use stood in the way, as well as the discord in her parents' marriage, which pulled her in two directions. Joan's dysthymic mood variations were exacerbated by her beer drinking. Once she abstained from alcohol, she did, in fact, gain some detachment regarding her own feelings and her peer relationships. When she left therapy, she was making careful overtures to her mother, who had moved out. Joan behaved as a typical WASP when she took an overdose without telling anyone. It is important to ask about previous suicidal gestures when working with WASPs.

It is especially hard for WASP women to understand the incest experience because they have been raised to feel responsible for everything that happens to them. They must learn that their fathers and brothers were raised the same way. Given the competitive role of successfully mastering the world that WASP men are expected to achieve, they often feel quite inadequate and insecure. If the male child's needs were never responded to in a satisfactory manner by his parents, he may not develop the required sense of mastery or competence; instead he may be highly anxious, with poor interpersonal relations, low self-esteem, and little sense of personal mastery (Parker & Parker, 1986). Thus for the female WASP child, there may be a conflict between the all-powerful, autocratic manner of the father or older brother and the actual weak nature of the abusive male figure. Dependence is forbidden for WASPs, but the male relative appears to be dependent on the girl's physical services, her importance underscored by his alternating threats and pleas. The secrecy and two-sided nature of reality often leads to dissociative thinking, gaps in memory, and behavioral acting out.

The psychological effects of sexual child abuse are detailed by Gardner (1990), who explains dissociation as detachment that serves as a survival technique. The child learns to fear an assault that cannot be controlled. Denial and emotional avoidance of the memory may last for days or years, after which the memory may emerge, accompanied by dreams or feelings of guilt. Because the molestation is often at the hands of a trusted relative or family friend, the child is faced with an unbearable "good object/bad behavior" dilemma and may suffer from impaired reality testing and unconscious reenactment of the abusive relationship (Gardner, 1990). One way to reconcile the opposites is to become bad oneself, as Mary did, both in her acting out in school and in her view of herself as evil. If she deserved to be abused by her father and brothers, her life would make sense and she could let herself enjoy their abuse and their occasional kindnesses.

Mary's second overdose might have been a response to a reenactment of the old abusive relationship; it reduced her temporarily to unconsciousness, removing her from a conflict she could not resolve. She had been available in therapy to learn detachment from her feelings by talking about them and to understand the guiltless role she played as a child, but the first building blocks of self-esteem were hardly laid when she again chose oblivion. Mountains of self-esteem would have to be heaped up before she would be able to see her youth clearly and reach peace with her brothers and the memory of her father. From the height of full self-confidence, she might assess these males as WASPs whose identity is built on denial of emotion and for whom "sex becomes limited to an activity of the penis . . . tied up with competition, separation and power to bolster a man's sense of masculinity" (Mann, 1989,

p. 144). Had she come to realize that her parents could neither give nor get intimacy, Mary might have used her WASP tendency to distance in a useful way—to separate from her pain—and might have used her good intellect to pity her father and brothers. Eventually, an apology session might have been prepared for and attempted (e.g., Trepper & Barrett, 1989).

Summary of WASP Incest Treatment of Girls and Women[2]

Memories of sexual child abuse are often triggered for WASP incest survivors by coverage in the media. A WASP in her 30s told me that she recognized what had happened to her only when she watched a woman describe incest on television. For the first time in her adult life, she felt anger about it and entered counseling. Hearing someone else affirm the experience we have known may well be the "kindest" trigger there is for activating buried feelings of rage. For this reason, incest survivor groups are indicated for WASPs, as well as for people from other ethnic categories.

I would hesitate to use hypnotherapy to trigger such feelings through age regression with WASPs unless the therapist is highly experienced. Being responsibly in control of oneself is a personality trait for many WASPs; once the floodgate of emotion is breached, by hypnosis or other means, there may be a fragile ego structure too brittle to handle the deluge of feelings. The hypnotherapist may use "anchoring" to hold the person in the present and create an imaginary "safe place" with the survivor for shelter when feeling threatened. Needless to say, such treatment presupposes that many sessions of trust-building therapy have occurred.

A WASP may internalize stress of which he or she is not consciously aware as an emotional pressure and suffer headaches, stomach pains, or other discomforts. Attending to the emotional stress often relieves the physical symptom. Many WASP survivors also suffer panic attacks with shakiness, difficulty breathing, sweating, and rapid heartbeat. When suffering from panic, the loss of control may be especially frightening to WASPs. Someone who has always felt she had to be responsible for everything (typically the "superwoman mom") now undergoes a conscious loss of control. Phrases are used such as "washed away" and "it broke over me like a wave." Although medication is available for extreme cases, the role of the therapist is to bring enlightenment regarding the control issues, past and present. Identifying the trigger is a first step, followed by dealing with abuse issues, such as who is responsible and powerful (now and in the past).

Many survivors use self-harm as a defense against painful emotion. It has not been my experience that WASP women tend to cut or pound themselves in order to get a painkilling "rush." Their more usual manner of harming themselves is to abuse alcohol and/or drugs (like Joan) or medicine (like Mary). Oral self-medication by these means can act as a buffer against memories and feelings about sexual abuse. Quiet consumption of toxic materials suits the WASP style of suffering in silence; an array of substances is available, with and without medical assistance, to help the survivor calm down and feel better about her life, or end it, if, as in Mary's case, self-destruction is the intent. Where hospitalization is not required, substance abuse counseling may dissuade the survivor from believing that self-medication is self-preservation.

Control issues are nearly always foremost in treating survivors because after being abused, a survivor often feels unsafe in any situation in which she doesn't have power and control. With early training in independence and self-control, the WASP survivor may tend to become controlling in her relationships and may have difficulty letting go of habits such as lying, covering up, seducing, inviting dependence or sympathy, withholding information, instilling guilt, or otherwise manipulating others to manifest her control. These behaviors are paid for in nervousness and stress, which in turn increase the appetite for control. The wise therapist will avoid enmeshment with survivors while understanding that they don't want to admit that sometimes they have no control and can be hurt.

WASPs have no system in their religion for absolution of sin; many of them subscribe to the Methodist doctrine that "by their fruits ye shall know them." If things go well, it is evidence of future salvation, but if they go wrong, he or she must bear the responsibility for being less than blessed. Sometimes a WASP finds the relief of confession only in the therapist's office, where guilt and self-blame can become major issues. The survivor repeats, like a broken record, "I shouldn't feel upset, it was my fault." The therapist can alternate between standing amazed at this self-punishing attitude and confronting it. In Mary's case, the self-blame balanced the hate toward her father; she felt guilty for hating him but could hate herself without feeling guilty because she finally convinced herself she enjoyed the abuse and deserved to be "damaged goods." During therapy, she came to stand outside this vicious circle for a time, recognizing it in other cases and then in her own. It is not easy for WASPs to release their assumptions and adopt a new stance toward their own behavior. They find it easier to withdraw by running away or blurring their awareness through self-starvation, abuse of substances, or other means.

The strong feelings that accompany memories of sexual abuse are difficult for WASPs to handle because the message from their undemonstrative WASP parents has been not to express strong emotion. WASP parents say to their children, "Don't raise your voice; we don't talk like that!" The lesson that feelings must be "stuffed" begins early in many families; prying these feelings out at a later stage is like cracking eggs—the fragile pretense that all is well may be shattered by an unfamiliar sense of sadness, shame, fear, and hurt. To continue the metaphor, it works better to hard-boil the eggs before peeling them slowly in layers; "hard-boiling" is done by gradual desensitization to painful subjects in an atmosphere of trust.

Building trust in WASP survivors may appear easy: The new arrivals in counseling respond to specific objectives, will probably perform assignments such as writing or reading prescribed material, and give an impression of openness. They will share family information forthrightly once they are comfortable. However, typical WASPs keep a large area of themselves hidden, both consciously and unconsciously. In response to what they may perceive as failure to understand their needs, they may consider the therapeutic contract dishonored and withdraw from it. They are less likely to flare up in a session than to recede into silent suspicion, even while smiling and nodding. Survivors have learned not to trust others and not to trust their own thoughts and feelings. They have been treated as objects by the offender(s) and are sensitive to this attitude in the professional setting. Praise is frighteningly unfamiliar for them, but gentle affirmation of their rights and points of view can be received in most cases.

Supporting improvement in a WASP's self-image depends on how she views herself. Taking a human figure drawing may assist the therapist if the WASP shows the ability to participate this way in the therapy. How feminine or sexual is the drawing? If the woman or girl is "sleeping around," is it because she thinks being a sexual "trophy" is the only thing that makes her worthwhile? Does she feel that her body is dirty? Does she have names for her genital organs and understand their functions? (WASP parents seldom undertake this kind of education for their children.) Has she been taught never to say "no" to sex, or learned that she cannot enjoy sex of her own choice because of its association with violence? Does her body seem to be a bargaining item to her, to gain power or attention?

Self-image encompasses much more than one's appearance and the right to control one's body. Other factors enter into self-appraisal; one is money. This is an important subject for WASPs, relating as it does to independence. WASPs like to talk about money, wills, salaries, and personal estates, although they may be vague about specific sums. One way to boost WASPs' self-image is to detail exactly how much they are worth and what they can expect to have in the future. Such an exact accounting also registers trust in the therapist in a different way and, for this reason, should be postponed to a later session.

Another factor is role fulfillment, such as motherhood or daughterhood. Being a good (or "good enough") mother is a satisfying self-image, partly because it involves safe touching (except where mothers have been perpetrators) and negates the role of the offending parent, thus breaking the family cycle of abuse. The mother-daughter relationship must be considered, with due attention to the gradual approach needed to address a WASP survivor's mother. Does she know? Should she know? Did she protect? Did she participate in sexually abusive behavior? Family-of-origin work is indicated in a later stage of therapy, following resolution of the more immediate issues that impede functioning, and should stress a definition of appropriate relations between parent and child.

Other factors that may be addressed in long-term counseling with a WASP survivor include sibling position and possible support from sisters, career planning, a 5-year plan for the future, and how to have a satisfactory love life. Journal keeping should be started after the first session so that a client may compare her status, as time passes, with her initial condition in therapy.

Summary and Conclusions

WASP traits were described as they relate to a lack of ethnic identification, the valuing of independence and success, and the assumption that their culture is dominant and therefore correct. Relationships among WASPs are characterized by emotional distance, the importance of individual decision making and responsibility, and an educational approach to child rearing. Cases were described that illustrate therapeutic issues with WASP survivors. These issues were further clarified by explanations of problems relating to triggers, panic attacks, self-harm, substance abuse, power and control, guilt and self-blame, expression of strong emotion, establishment of trust, and improvement of self-image.

WASPs suffer as an ethnic group from the narrowness of their own assumptions; this chapter has considered only a tiny segment of the overriding problem.[3] For example, the cases cited have not dealt with the problems of WASP boys who have suffered abuse. These young victims, some of whom are far from home at boarding schools, need help establishing a positive self-image and not falling prey to fears of homosexuality if they have been molested by men. Among their problems are culturally based obligations to be hardworking success stories, like their fathers, with stiff upper lips and no need for tenderness. If the one man who is tender with a young boy is the man who molests him, the boy may limit his emotions in future to sadness and anger and become, in turn, a distant father for a son.

Notes

1. Descriptive material of WASP traits was partly derived from a draft of a chapter from McGoldrick, Pearce, and Giordano (1982).

2. For this section, extensive use was made of material from S. A. Lee, 1995.

3. On first encountering critical descriptions of some of their cultural traits, Anglo American readers may be taken aback. Like the author, they may need time to reexamine their assumptions about the dominant American culture.

Seventh Day Adventists
and Sexual Child Abuse

CATHERINE TAYLOR
LISA ARONSON FONTES

In this chapter, I will discuss some of the reasons I believe that Seventh Day Adventists (and by inference, other evangelical religions) have high rates of sexual child abuse. I will also describe some of the factors that maintain secrecy around sexual abuse in our community, treatment issues, and ways of strengthening the community for prevention and healing. Background information about the church and Adventist culture will be followed by suggestions for prevention and treatment, as well as case histories that shed light on relevant issues.

Adventist History and Culture

I am a Seventh Day Adventist Christian, a convert. I have chosen to belong to a church that believes in the divinity of Jesus and an active Satan who leads the forces of evil. We celebrate the seventh day Sabbath, await the imminent return of Jesus to the earth, and abide by a long list of suggestions for physical

Authors' Note:

This chapter results from a collaboration between Catherine Taylor, L.I.C.S.W., and Lisa A. Fontes, Ph.D. The first person "I" used here refers to Catherine Taylor, and most of the victim stories and clinical anecdotes are hers.

health and well-being. The church has a modern-day woman prophet, Ellen White, and a world organizational structure. The church was founded in the early 1840s as part of the Millerite Movement, preaching about and waiting for the return of Christ to the earth.

We have a larger Protestant parochial school system and give more offerings per capita than any other denomination in the world. We are not officially fundamentalists. Fundamentalists believe that God dictated each and every word of scripture. Our church believes that, with specific quoted exceptions, God gave women and men prophets concepts to share with His people, and these prophets did the best they could in conveying these to others.

The Seventh Day Adventist church is international and houses a great deal of variety in terms of race, social class, and degree of orthodoxy. When working with Adventists, it is important to inquire about their observance. Some sectors of the Adventist church follow a literal adherence to the writings of the Bible and Ellen White, which leads to highly prescribed lifestyles where even the smallest action must follow church teachings. Others have a more flexible interpretation of church teachings. Inside the Adventist church, there are people who eat meat and those who are vegan. There are women who will not speak aloud in the sanctuary, believing it is not their place, and some who are pastors. There are people who use only natural remedies, and those who use modern Western medicine. Some Adventist women will wear only skirts and dresses, but most wear a range of modern clothing. Some households are completely patriarchal, and some gender equal, but most are in the middle.

According to anecdotal research by Wilma Hepker of Walla Walla University and a study presented by Bayley Gillespe of La Sierra College, Andrews University, Berrien Springs, Michigan, Seventh Day Adventist students report a higher rate of sexual child abuse than the general population of the United States.

I am a family therapist specializing in multigenerational sexual child abuse, and I work in a public nonprofit agency. For many years, most of my work with families who had experienced sexual child abuse had nothing to do with my church. Six years ago, the regional church organization asked me to do a series of workshops on self-esteem during the annual retreat called "campmeeting." In those campmeeting sessions, I began to hear stories about the abuse that church members had experienced as children and had never been able to discuss. I also had an opportunity to talk with Seventh Day Adventists who run a national drug and alcohol treatment center. The stories of their clients, many of whom were children of officials in the national and international organization, reminded me of the stories shared by sexual abuse survivors. The program directors confirmed my suspicions.

In recent years, I have spoken with hundreds of Seventh Day Adventists about sexual abuse both as a workshop leader and as a therapist. Most have been women, but many have been men. I have spoken in individual churches, weekend intensive workshops for survivors, campmeeting retreats, daylong classes and seminars, women's retreats, and "town meeting" discussion groups. I helped design the sexual abuse reporting policies for the Southern New England Conference, and I have served as consultant to pastors, teachers, and other church members who encountered sexual abuse in their communities. Clients have been referred to me by pastors, Bible workers, church members, teachers, and friends. I have encountered the continuum of abuse among church members, from voyeurism to ritual and cult abuse.

Writing this chapter is both a professional and personal challenge. When I talk about the responses of the church to sexual child abuse, I am frequently talking about my own experiences. As I present these issues and stories to the public, I personally face the loyalty binds I describe. I have felt the grief and the denial. I have struggled with many of the reasons other Adventists give for not disclosing their abuse. I understand why many people will avoid therapy or drive 3 hours each way to see a Christian or Seventh Day Adventist therapist. In this chapter, I am both a Seventh Day Adventist and a professional who is dealing with an organization that profoundly affects my own life.

I am a clinician, not a researcher. My stories emerge from my experience. When I use the term *spiritual,* I am referring to a person's relationship with God. When I use the term *religion,* I am referring to an organized church structure.

Cultural Issues in Disclosure

Forgiveness and Denial

Several themes common to Seventh Day Adventists affect how individuals, families, and the organization handle sexual child abuse and other kinds of relational trauma. Children are taught from infancy that their relationship with God depends on their ability to forgive those who have hurt them. Stories of Jesus saying, "Father, forgive them, for they do not understand what they are doing" as He was being nailed to the cross, David weeping for his traitorous son Absolom, and the phrase in the Lord's Prayer, "Forgive us our debts as we forgive our debtors," are taught regularly in Sabbath school classes. Many people who have experienced sexual abuse report to me that the first thing their pastors said to them when they came for counsel was, "Remember the importance of forgiving those who have hurt you." When I talk about the need to separate adjudicated offenders from responsibilities involving children, I have been told, with all good intentions, that our job as Christians is to forgive those who have done wrong and let them go on with their lives.

The focus on forgiveness and letting "bygones be bygones" helps create situations that leave children vulnerable to sexual abuse. Seventh Day Adventists have their own scouting organization, Pathfinders. Several members of one church approached me because a man who served time in prison for sexually abusing children was to be elected Pathfinder leader for that year. When I talked to the pastor, he told me the man had served time before his conversion, he had been baptized, and he had asked God's forgiveness for his sins. Why shouldn't he be allowed to work for God in this position? I used the alcohol disease model and said that even after conversion, I didn't think it was a good idea for an alcoholic to tend bar or for someone addicted to narcotics to be responsible for a pharmacy. I emphasized the responsibility of the church to protect its most vulnerable members.

Another woman told me she had been abused by a foster child whom her family had raised. As an adult, she disclosed this abuse to her parents. They apologized and told her they had thought the teen would be a safe person to have around because of his conversion when they became his foster parents. Other parents have told me that the person who abused their children was kind, caring, spiritual, preached, was a member of the world conference, or came from a good home. They had trouble discerning that outside appearances can mask a propensity to abuse power.

Seventh Day Adventists see themselves as examples to a world in trouble, and so they are concerned about their public image. Many of my Adventist clients and workshop participants describe difficulty in talking to non-Adventist therapists because of their concern that those clinicians will think poorly of the church and of its mission to help less enlightened people.

High value is placed on loyalty to the Adventist world community. Observations and feelings about hurtful events that happen inside our community and might be heard by the outside world are often considered with trepidation. Exposure of failings is considered a betrayal of a trust. As I write this chapter, I find myself worrying about the damage I may do to my church by sharing my observations.

Church as Family

Adventists focus on family and on church community as family. We have often heard that those who have lost father, mother, or siblings because of their belief in God will be rewarded a hundredfold family members in the church. The need for the comfort of the church family is powerful, as is the fear of losing that support.

Church members often have concerns about using "outsiders" to address issues exposing personal or corporate vulnerabilities, preferring to employ Adventist lawyers, dentists, doctors, insurance offices, schools, hospitals, and therapists. This gives us both the strength of self-sufficiency and the danger of insularity. We believe that our idiosyncratic beliefs and lifestyle make it difficult for others to respond to our needs and make us vulnerable to their ridicule or judgment. Some of us think that non-Adventists do not have as easy access to our health message, our values, or the throne of God where we leave our petitions.

We rarely encourage children or women to talk to people outside the family or the church if they are scared or confused by behavior directed toward them. Recently, three students at an Adventist boarding academy were having their breasts and genital areas fondled by one of their teachers. They reported these events to their houseparents. Nothing was done to confront or dismiss the teacher. The girls were given my name and called me, even though I was out of state, because they were concerned that no one in the school or local church community would take action to protect them. These high school students weren't even sure if this kind of touching constituted abuse. They were afraid that by calling me, they were betraying their school, their house parents, and their church. I had some of the same concerns about betraying the church as I dialed protective services. These were overridden by my desire to protect the children.

Seventh Day Adventists can be insular. Many families school their children at home. More send their children to church school to protect them from outside influences. After-school activities and weekend events often center around the church. Adults and especially children have difficulty separating family from church. We develop a closed family and community system, the perfect environment for sexual abuse to develop and be contained. At camp-meetings, workshop participants often tell me I am the first person they've heard speak about the issue, about dysfunctional families, self-protection, and boundaries.

Patriarchy, Sexuality, and Church Teachings

The church is a patriarchal organization. Currently, most pastors are men, and women pastors are not ordained. Most organizational positions are filled by men. Most of the articles in the periodicals for adults are written by men. Most of the professors who train seminarians are men. In some adult Sabbath school lessons, emphasis is placed on the subjugation of woman and children to the man of the house. This is an apparent paradox; our church has an acknowledged woman prophet who encouraged women to become doctors and fill other positions that service women.

Our historical tendency to emphasize the subjugation of women to men and children to adults has set up an unhealthy power dynamic. It is common to hear a children's sermon emphasize unquestioning obedience to the commands or wishes of parents because parents and other adults want only to protect them. Survivors of sexual abuse and their therapists have hypothesized that valuing children's unquestioning obedience to authority both increases the likelihood of compliant behavior to sexual abuse and reduces the likelihood of disclosure (Fontes, 1993b). Cross-cultural research is needed to determine the applicability to Adventists of assertions that patriarchal family structures and paternal dominance contribute to father-daughter incest and increased damage to women from sexual abuse (Edwards & Alexander, 1992; Herman, 1981).

Our church originated in the Victorian era, and we usually do not talk about sex openly in religious or educational forums. Seventh Day Adventists believe sex, sexuality, and sex education belong in the home. If a healthy sexual climate is not established at home, we often have no other venue in which to educate children. Survivors of sexual abuse have often told me that their perpetrators were "just teaching me about sex" or "teaching me what kinds of things I shouldn't do." Children and young women have been told by nonoffending church members that they were abused because their dress was immodest.

In the church, we have only recently begun to talk about the difference between marital privileges and marital rape. We do not discuss reproductive choice. Historically, as an organization, we have not acknowledged the possibility of abuse or talked about ways that children can protect themselves. We have not educated children and adults about appropriate body boundaries.

Adventists and Mental Health

Seventh Day Adventists comprise a literate organization focusing on education, science, health, family development, and Bible study. This educational orientation offers great promise for preventive interventions in a variety of spheres, including sexual abuse.

Currently, the church structure provides little information about emotional health, the psychological processes of grief or trauma, or constructive outlets for troubling feelings such as anger, fear, and confusion. Many Adventists have shared with me their guilt at having emotions that are not sanctioned or understood by other church members. There is little support for addressing deep-seated anguish, confusion, shame, rage, fear, or ambivalence. The medical focus is on physical, not emotional, health.

A strength in the church is our real love for children and our commitment to their welfare. Good touch/bad touch education has been added recently to some curricula. We are beginning to talk about the difference between an abuse of power and appropriate sexual behavior.

Sexual abuse affects individuals, families, and communities. I also believe that the stages of grief touch those individuals, families, and communities. Denial, bargaining, anger, and confusion all contribute to the church's response to sexual abuse.

Church Doctrine and Offending Behaviors

Church doctrine in no way supports sexually offending behavior. However, sexual offenders sometimes use alleged jailhouse conversions as "proof" of their rebirth as nonoffenders. Some of these conversions are genuine and heartfelt, and some are undoubtedly a smoke screen meant to help the offenders regain legitimacy. (A local therapist who works at an agency with an offenders' program said she could always spot the offenders in the waiting room because they had a Bible in one hand and a rosary in the other.) Because evangelical Christian groups, including Adventists, proselytize in jails, some of these offenders will inevitably present themselves as members of our church. When faced with people who have offended sexually and who are Adventists, it may be worth asking the history of their beliefs.

A recent study (Elliot, 1994) concludes:

> Parents' endorsement of conservative Christian beliefs, without the integration of these beliefs into family life, appears to increase the risk for sexual abuse. Without further research, the reason for this is not clear. One hypothesis, however, is that conservative Christians who do not integrate their beliefs into their lifestyle may use their religious beliefs to control family members, setting up a rigid authoritarian stance to child rearing. In such families, children may be less likely to question authority and therefore less able to protect themselves from potential perpetrators of sexual abuse. (p. 105)

I work with church members to develop a dynamic philosophy of child rearing that integrates the protection of children with our family values. I suggest that sermons avoid telling children to obey adults unquestioningly. I mention our patriarchal tendencies and our insularity. I encourage us to learn to look out for behaviors that might be signs of a child or adult in need of help—not a slide from spiritual progress.

Firm church beliefs regarding proper sexual behavior can lead to a puritanical home environment. In some families, watching soap operas and reading popular magazines are prohibited because of their lascivious content. In such a climate, children may not even know names for their body parts and may feel they have no language or context to discuss sexually abusive events. In one study (Fontes, 1992), a Puerto Rican woman who grew up in an Adventist family realized that what her father did to her was sexual abuse only upon seeing diagrams in a health class in high school. She said she could not have disclosed the abuse to her family—all words pertaining to sexuality were considered smut.

In an exploratory study of 68 child molesters in therapy (Simkins, 1993), those who were labeled sexually repressed (as defined by delayed psychosexual development and sexually conservative attitudes) showed the slowest and poorest progress toward goals and the poorest attitudes toward therapy, and were rated as most likely to recommit abuse after a year of treatment. They also had significantly less sex information and more cognitive distortions than other offenders, and admitted to fewer sexual interests and activities than the "normal" (presumably nonoffending) heterosexuals studied. Eighty percent of those offenders who were considered sexually repressed were classified as treatment failures.

Although the religious background of this sample is unknown, it is important to note that our church currently fosters an environment where sexual repression is likely. This may contribute to sexual offending, to decreased likelihood of disclosure, and, if Simkins's research holds true for Seventh Day Adventists, lowered rates of treatment success for offenders who are members of our church. Perhaps offender treatment programs that in some way both acknowledge our church's teachings around sexuality and at the same time provide accurate sex education and reduce cognitive distortions would contribute to offender work with church members.

Our shame and judgment of "immoral" behaviors also make it difficult for men and women who act in unacceptable ways to seek treatment. A Seventh Day Adventist schoolteacher who had sexually abused one of my clients recently committed suicide. The local church community has had difficulty admitting that his death was self-inflicted or that he was capable of sexually abusing any of his students. Upon disclosure, there is always a chance that offenders will be suicidal. I think our rigid moral structures make that choice more likely.

I have never spoken to a group of Seventh Day Adventists about sexual abuse in our church without hearing someone plead a version of "Why us? We are supposed to have a special message and special blessings." I tell them I have clinical, political, and spiritual answers, and they usually ask to hear the spiritual context first. I tell them I believe spirituality is about relationships: our relationship with God and our relationship to each other. If the Evil Ones were to plan to destroy spirituality, what better way could they find than to create an environment where there is an abuse that can disintegrate a person's ability to trust, to be intimate, or to live without some form of substance dependence; an abuse that will give many of its victims suicidal ideation and coping mechanisms that are disparaged or condemned by their church? In this way, sexual abuse can be understood as a weapon in the war that Seventh Day Adventists call "the Great Controversy Between Christ and Satan."

Responses to Disclosures

A participant in one of my weekend intensive workshops for survivors of sexual abuse recently told her family she had been raped by her brother for several years. Her parents told her she should ask God's forgiveness for trying to ruin her brother's life and questioned her relationship with God. They told her she should pray about her issues and quit talking to therapists. According to members of the family, therapists only cause trouble and keep their clients from the true healing: prayer to God.

Seventh Day Adventists take pride in their high moral values and ethical codes. Members who indulge in substance abuse, promiscuity, stealing, adultery, or gambling are subject to having their names removed from the official church books. There is little understanding of mental illness, suicide, disassociation, or chaotic lifestyles, which are some of the common ways in which people cope with the experience of sexual abuse. People who engage in coping mechanisms that are eschewed by the church are especially likely to face rejection and disbelief:

> An adolescent client who had been sexually abused by a teacher while in elementary school disclosed his abuse to his parents. They believed him and reported the abuse to the school to protect other children. The school officials said they had heard no reports from other children of abuse by this teacher, and therefore the report must not be true. Other members of the church community asserted that because this adolescent had shown undesirable behaviors since elementary school, he was not believable, failing to recognize that these behaviors might stem from the abuse itself! He had been abusing alcohol and drugs, had run away, had been angry at the church, and had even been known to steal to obtain drugs. They did not think such a disreputable source should be allowed to tarnish the career of a respected teacher. This young man has since been placed in an out-of-state drug treatment center and has been suicidal. His parents, who had been central figures in the local Adventist medical community, are being shunned by their compatriots for "spreading rumors that are ruining the reputation and family of this good church school teacher."

Once, when I spoke at an Adventist town meeting about organizational responses to sexual abuse, some older church members said that these abuses must have been "committed by converts" or against "women who don't dress according to our standard."

As a whole, the church tends to be homophobic. Boys and men who have been abused sexually by men are afraid to disclose because they believe people will think they are gay. The church supports "change" programs designed to turn gay men and lesbians into heterosexuals. Several young gay men who were sexually abused by the director of such a "change" program were afraid to disclose because they believed the church would denigrate their validity, fail to protect them, and dismiss their allegations. After they disclosed, the church closed that center. However, the director never publicly addressed his part in the abuse of his clients. Several years later, individual members of the church are supporting this same director as he opens a new center for "change."

Many families respond to disclosures of sexual abuse with denial, hinging on the notions that we are Christians and therefore protected from relational abuses. The occurrence of events is denied, and their severity is minimized. One client heard the response, "None of us is perfect and we all have these little hurts now and then."

Responses may focus on protecting the family and the smooth corporate operations, not the victim or future victims. God is portrayed as a punishing parent who does not understand the plight of the abused. Victims are told, "You had better ask God's forgiveness for this."

Some Seventh Day Adventists had an early market on the false memory movement. I have heard many workshop participants and clients tell me stories of being questioned about the possibility that Satan may have made up their memories and placed them in their mind as a plot to ruin the good name of the church. Severe dissociative conditions such as multiple personality disorder have been used as additional proof that a client is demon possessed. Although this is not a universal church response, it undoubtedly silences many victims. The stories of disbelief and denial have made some clients reticent to confront members of their Adventist family or church.

"Who am I going to tell?" "Who will believe me?" "Who will protect me if I tell?" The close Adventist community can be extremely supportive, but members may find themselves isolated and alone when family and church fail to protect them.

Although I have heard few reports of abuse in Seventh Day Adventist home school settings, there are no structures in place to ascertain if home schools are treating the students appropriately. In this context, children's isolation from outsiders is total, the silence is complete.

Integrating Interventions With Church Beliefs

In this discussion of interventions with members of the Seventh Day Adventist community, I will discuss the issues that prevent church members from engaging in therapy or protective services, ways of developing contexts for effective intervention, styles of treatment I have seen used by Adventists, and some of the ways that being a member of the community affects my work as a therapist.

Any clinician or protective worker interacting with a Seventh Day Adventist client would find it helpful to understand some of the unique beliefs and aspects of the culture that leave Adventists feeling vulnerable to "outsiders" and to each other. One client is afraid her therapist will think she is crazy if she discusses the amount of money she donates to the church. Other clients have shared their fear that protective workers will take their children from their homes if the children are on a vegetarian diet. Wariness of a professional "not of the faith" or hesitancy to acquiesce to the placement of children in a non-Adventist foster home is not necessarily a way of being defensive or resisting help. These are best seen as reflecting a cultural value, not a means of interfering with the service plan.

Clinicians are often suspect, seen as humanists who have no qualms about destroying the family. In a church known for its far-flung medical facilities and internationally acknowledged research on health, many members are chastised for seeking psychological help. They are told they should take their troubles to the Lord in prayer and lean on His healing arm. This stance requires victims to make a difficult choice between being isolated from therapeutic supports or from their church community.

The Bible says there is wisdom in a multitude of counselors (Proverbs 11:14, 15:22, 24:6). Our church prophet, Ellen White, has written "Oh, for generals, wise and considerate, well balanced men, who will be safe advisers, who have some insight into human nature, who know how to direct and counsel in the fear of God" (E. White, 1893, p. 362). Despite this spiritual counsel, I commonly hear people say, "Everyone tells me I should just pray. If I believed more in God, I would let Him heal these issues that have haunted me all my life." Clients have felt guilty that prayer did not end a wide variety of emotional suffering, that they still live with the coping mechanisms originally used to survive being abused and are unable to have the kind of intimate, healthy relationships to which they aspire.

When they do decide to seek treatment, church members tend to be wary of therapists who are not Seventh Day Adventists or at least members of a Christian denomination. They are concerned that a humanist will encourage them or someone they love to engage in "immoral behavior," such as masturbation. They worry that feminist therapists will destroy the family by telling women who have been in hurtful relationships to leave their husbands or by not expressing shock if someone chooses a gay or lesbian relationship. They see Christian and especially Seventh Day Adventist therapists as being people who would uphold their moral standards, or at least not be judgmental of a religious stance.

This suspicion of outsider therapists creates some difficulties. There are few Seventh Day Adventist therapists, and even fewer who have considerable experience knowingly working with issues connected to sexual abuse. I have had Seventh Day Adventists drive 3 hours one way to see me. I have had church members call and ask if they could drive 8 hours one way for a consultation with me. This is not because I am an extraordinary therapist. Unfortunately, it is because for them, I am the only one in New England.

When Adventists have found me, they have been afraid that I would judge them for their behaviors that do not coincide with church values. This illustrates a painful double bind. They want a therapist to support values they aspire to; yet they fear being honest with me because I might judge them disparagingly according to those values.

I have been working with my local church organization to develop a context for the possibility of seeking therapeutic interventions. When I gave the first campmeeting workshop on self-esteem, I talked about the ways in which emotional traumas affect our physical health and ability to function. I discussed ways in which relational injuries affect our ability to relate to God. I shared with workshop participants some concrete ways that they could begin to recover, including professional supports. I received a letter from the conference about an unprecedented volume of positive responses to the workshop and asking if I would return.

The next year I gave a workshop on sexual child abuse. The average workshop attendance for campmeeting is 20 to 30 people. Each afternoon, 50 to 80 people packed the meeting tent. I talked about the long-term effects of sexual child abuse, the ways in which people tend to cope with this kind of relational trauma, and the ways in which people can heal from it. This year, people began to talk about the shame they had felt because their feelings and behaviors conflicted with their relationship to the church. They began to ask questions about the use of therapy.

I speak with Adventists about the ways prayer and clinical modalities can complement each other. I draw analogies to our use of other experts. "If we are physically ill, first we pray, then we find the best physician available. If our cars are emitting black smoke, we pray and find a good mechanic." I discuss prayer as part of a package deal. Isaiah prayed to God and then applied a fig poultice to King Hezekiah. I emphasize that our psyches are no less important than our bodies.

Over the years, I have given campmeeting workshops on some of the issues faced by support people of survivors: anger, communication, and relationships; characteristics of dysfunctional families and how similar they are to traits of people described in the Biblical account of the Edenic fall; family life cycle patterns; and caring for caretakers.

A shift is occurring. Feelings and troubled human relationships are beginning to be discussed in our regional Seventh Day Adventist community. At the same time, we have begun to hear from West Coast church organizations about work they are doing to address sexual abuse.

In churches and educational institutions, Seventh Day Adventist family life educators are beginning to talk about dysfunctional families, substance abuse, and groups. "Recovery" programming has begun to be introduced into campmeetings and church workshops. The recovery programming has given validity to the place of feelings in the lives of individuals and organizations. It has also encouraged people to seek support for the challenges they face.

The needs of individuals, the parameters of the religious community, and the usual variations in how all human beings seek or avoid healing have led to creative uses of clinical supports by some Adventists. Some attend workshops, seminars, recovery intensives, and campmeetings regularly. I'm beginning to think of this as the intermittent psychoeducational group therapy model. Many of these people do not have regular individual or group therapy in any traditional sense of the word. Recently, some departments of the regional organized church have begun to offer weekend intensive groups for female and male survivors of sexual child abuse. Participants have said that other participants in weekends for Seventh Day Adventist survivors of sexual abuse in other parts of the country seemed to expect an end to their pain and confusion by the end of the workshop. We have told them that the workshops are part of a longer process that could be augmented by individual therapy, ongoing groups, and/or psychoeducational classes.

Some people see me for one or two sessions to talk about how they can work with their religious beliefs and their non-Adventist therapist. Some refer their therapist or pastor to me for consultation about religious or abuse issues. And of course, with some Adventist clients, I hold fairly traditional individual weekly therapy sessions.

Therapy

As therapeutic work begins, it can be useful to frame spirituality and religious structures as part of a healing network. It is important to understand the community as a family. Loyalty binds about exposing issues specific to Adventists can hinder therapy.

Seventh Day Adventism is a culture, not just a religion. Our culture touches every aspect of life, not just a day of the week or a season of the year. If you are not an Adventist, it might be helpful at some point in the therapy for your client to refer you to a "consultant" to help understand some of the more subtle issues, such as the uses and abuses of the writings of the church prophet, Ellen White. If no such consultant is available, your client may be able to serve this function.

During individual therapy, items that are usually "grist for the mill" take on special meaning because of the community context. Confidentiality is often a deep concern. The worldwide organization is known for having the gossip capabilities of a small town. I emphasize my commitment to confidentiality in workshops and in therapy. In an individual relationship, I also say that I know they cannot trust this aspect of my commitment without first experiencing it. Trust building may take time.

The issue of boundaries, always complicated, is quite tangled in this small community. I happen to be a therapist who lectures, preaches, gives workshops, attends concerts, teaches classes, and is well known by the regional organization. This makes me accessible to local Adventists in a way not typically experienced by other therapists. This community thinks I belong to them. Through church directories, they have access to my personal phone numbers.

Clients have contact with me in a variety of roles. This variety has benefits and challenges. I am constantly trying to balance my personal limits with my understanding of my function as a member of the community. When Seventh Day Adventists meet me in my teaching role, they have a chance to assess my values, my grasp of the subject, my personality, my place in the community, and my commitment to confidentiality from a safe distance. Teachers are an integral part of the Adventist culture, but they have little privacy. Their services are available most hours of most days and weeks. In addition to the usual boundary issues, clients feel culturally betrayed and demeaned when I explain to them that it is not helpful for them to include me in their friendship or dinner circle.

Adventists gauge their interest in a cause by the amount of time spent working on it. Clinically, this accentuates the feelings of rejection if I stick to the 50-minute hour. As is usually true with other clients, however, sticking to the boundaries we have established also adds to the sense of safety.

When I consult with pastors or organizational leaders, Adventists come to trust me as a therapist because they see me supporting the church structure and they see the church structure acknowledging my worth. However, if a client has been abused in a religious context, having a therapist supported by that context can add to the transferential confusion and fear that I will hurt or abandon him or her.

As a consultant, I give people information about referral and treatment resources. When church members want to ask me about ways to support people who are my clients, I find myself on a delicate walk in the realm of confidentiality. Being a therapist in the Seventh Day Adventist community is, in many ways, like being a family practitioner in a small town—everyone wants to know how George is feeling since his stroke.

While traveling, Adventists often visit churches other than the one they usually attend. Mine is in the middle of a tourist area. Clients have been known to see me at potluck lunches, praying, laughing, preaching, playing with my friends. I almost always handle their knowledge of me directly. "So, what was it like for you to see me fixing lunch for 50 people?"

One of the benefits of this shared context is the belief that we are family and have an obligation to support each other. Many clients have their seminar fees or therapy costs paid by other members of the church. These "sponsors" have told me that they believe they are members of a team. As team members, they occasionally want information about therapy that I will not give them. This boundary can be difficult for them to understand. The supports and difficulties of these "sponsorships" are an ongoing issue in the work. Recently, when one of my clients became suicidal and assaultive to his wife, several members of his church called and asked what they could do. I gently informed them that I couldn't tell them anything but that they could probably call my client or his wife if they wanted to know.

CASE HISTORIES

Leigh Ann

This case study concerns a client traumatized by ritual abuse. To date, I have had few cases of reported ritual abuse among my Seventh Day Adventist clients. I have included this case because it highlights issues that are relevant to all Adventist survivors. It may also be of interest to therapists working with non-Adventist survivors of ritual abuse.

Leigh Ann made an appointment to see me because of depression. She found herself crying uncontrollably for several hours each day. Her local church Bible worker told her I would be a good person to speak with because I was a Seventh Day Adventist and also understood a variety of family issues. Early in treatment, I stressed my commitment to confidentiality. Leigh Ann also needed reassurance that her experiences and stories would be valued, even if there were things about her that did not make her a perfect Adventist.

Leigh Ann's mother's family have been members of the Seventh Day Adventist Church for three generations. Her father was raised Catholic and does not attend any church. She is the middle of three daughters. She attended a home school run by her mother's brother's wife for kindergarten through second grade, and then she attended an Adventist elementary day school and an Adventist boarding secondary academy. She was 3 months pregnant when she graduated. She is proud that she was the first Seventh Day Adventist to graduate pregnant from that school—other girls were expelled. Leigh Ann married the baby's father. They divorced after 4 years when Leigh Ann discovered her husband sexually abusing their daughter. He has no visitation rights. She moved back to her mother's home and lived there about 3 more years. She moved out because she repeatedly caught her mother touching her daughter's vulva in sexual ways.

She married Harry, a convert to the Seventh Day Adventist church, 1 year later, and he adopted the children. He told Leigh Ann that part of the reason he married her was because he wanted to be part of a "solid Christian family." He works for a denominational institution and is a deacon in the local church. Leigh Ann wanted to bar her children from seeing her parents, but they obtained a court order for regular twice-weekly visits with their grandchildren.

Leigh Ann told me her son was very upset after spending nights at his grandmother's house. He reported her insistence that he sleep in the same bed with her, while she wore short nightgowns with no underwear. Leigh Ann tearfully reported her concern and anger over the situation and felt helpless to prevent it because of the court order. After checking with our local protective services, I told her that if she did not do something about the visits, I would be legally obliged to report her, and I referred her to a reputable family lawyer. She thanked me profusely for having obligated her to seek help outside the family. This took the onus of breaching a family code of loyalty off her shoulders. Within a few weeks the visitation was stopped. Leigh Ann contracted for another 6 weeks of therapy.

She then began to talk about her own past and why she had felt so helpless about taking her mother to court. She said it seemed like she had more memories than she could recall at the time, but did remember being told she was stupid, being given pills that made her groggy until she was old enough to hide them and spit them down the toilet, and having her mother wiggle her fingers in her vagina while her father held her down. Her mother had told her she was checking to make sure she was clean.

When I helped Leigh Ann define this treatment as sexual abuse, she began to cry. She said she thought that what she had experienced was sexual abuse, but she didn't trust her instincts because her family had always told her she was stupid.

Over a period of months, Leigh Ann shared more memories. She described being locked in a pantry and peeking out the window while adults in her family wandered in and out of her next-door neighbor aunt's house in various degrees of undress. She remembered resisting the forced administration of drugs and being relieved to go away to the academy because she didn't have to fight the pills any more. Leigh Ann mentioned a "strange black and purple quilt with odd markings or letters on it" that had been passed down through her mother's family. She asked me if it was normal for home schools to wrap children in burlap bags and stick them in the ground. Her abuse had happened at such an early age and her isolation had been so complete, she lacked a clear sense of normalcy. I told her that what had happened to her was not normal and was never acceptable behavior.

Leigh Ann attended some of my classes on sexual abuse at a local church. She said she was tired of feeling isolated and wanted to talk to other women who had experienced sexual abuse. I told her about some of the professionally facilitated groups offered in the area. She insisted on attending the peer-facilitated Incest Survivors Anonymous group being held at a nearby Seventh Day Adventist college because it was connected with the church.

About 4 weeks into the group, Leigh Ann came to the session pale and quiet. The night before, a peer facilitator had distributed a graphic article on ritual abuse to the group. Leigh Ann had highlighted several sections of the document and waved it in my face, saying, "This is my family! That happened to me!" More concrete memories emerged: red circles drawn on trees and cars, people dressed in white sheets, dead animals, and campfires with weird laughter. Leigh Ann was deeply disturbed that members of the local Seventh Day Adventist church were also present. "My family was crazy, but why would a church member be there?" She needed to be reminded that church members were human beings and quite fallible.

Leigh Ann began to experience more intense flashbacks, flooding, insomnia, and paranoia. She was afraid that her husband was poisoning her, that he somehow was part of her family and "the conspiracy." Harry called me and described Leigh Ann's increasingly erratic behavior. The children were disturbed when they came home from school and found her sitting in a rocking chair, speaking words they could not recognize. I told Harry that Leigh Ann might need to be hospitalized. Leigh Ann and Harry wanted to use the local Seventh Day Adventist hospital. I talked with them about the difference between services offered at the facility they were considering and treatment at hospitals with expertise in treating severe psychological trauma. They eventually agreed to try one of the trauma units I had recommended. By the time Leigh Ann saw me on her way to the hospital, she was expressing concern that I might be part of the conspiracy. I did what I could to allay her fears.

During her inpatient treatment, Harry asked me if I thought she was demon possessed. I said her symptoms were consistent with the mind's reactions to severe trauma. I suggested family therapy to relieve the children's stress. Although Harry would have preferred to bring them to an Adventist counselor, he accepted my referral to a trusted colleague who was familiar with Seventh Day Adventists. After their first session, he reported that my colleague seemed nice, although she wore makeup and jewelry. Harry refused to seek professional counseling for himself, preferring to turn to his friends in the church.

Leigh Ann left the hospital with a prescription for antipsychotic medication. She was upset both because Adventists rarely use psychiatric medications and because of the role of drugs in her own abuse history. I asked her if she would be willing to try an experiment: noting the differences between her use of medication as an adult and the way drugs were forced on her as a child. I emphasized her choice in the matter. I asked her if these medications were helpful to her, if she felt less scared and was more able to sleep. Leigh Ann agreed to try this medication for a while. The psychotic symptoms ceased. Leigh Ann is presently on low doses, and severely decompensates when she tries to wean herself entirely from the medications.

To help Adventists overcome a total rejection of psychoactive medications, I gradually educate them about biochemistry, the effects of trauma, and the potential for medications to relieve distress. I draw a parallel between use of psychological medications and medications for diseases such as diabetes and hypertension. However, I always respect their choices.

Leigh Ann's adolescent children complain regularly about the changes in their mother. They long for the mother they used to have before she entered therapy, the mother who cooked elaborate meals for them and accompanied them unquestioningly to church.

Leigh Ann says she is not angry with God but is fed up with church and "churchy people." One of the few times she did go to church, her pastor gave a sermon exhorting members to "quit wallowing in their past and get on with their lives in Christ." Leigh Ann was furious. "Just how am I supposed to do that! These people just don't understand!" I encouraged her to talk this over with her pastor. She felt guilty about her anger, and she was relieved when I told her she had a right to be angry. This sermon was obviously ignorant of the level of injury she had experienced.

Leigh Ann says sometimes she wants to take her name off the church books as an official member. I tell her it's her choice, but that she might want to wait a year before she makes that major decision. She says that despite the church injunction against suits between members, she has decided to sue her mother for psychological damages.

Leigh Ann remembers using the symbol of the cross to feel safe during her childhood, painting crosses on all her fingers and toenails. Over the past few months, she has wanted to wear a cross despite the proscriptions of the church about jewelry and the concerns of her husband. The level of intensity with which she craved this symbol of safety overrode their objections. In recent sessions, Leigh Ann has arrived with a cross around her neck.

During some sessions, Leigh Ann would tense into a ball of psychotic terror. She asked for and was soothed and consoled when we sang a hymn about the protection of the cross. In several sessions, she requested that we sing the hymn repeatedly. The sounds of that hymn seemed to ease her terror and give her a dose of protection that helped carry her until our next meeting. Now she sings this hymn to herself when her anxiety levels increase or new memories surface.

Leigh Ann and I have been working together for about 2 years. She sleeps better and is able to work part time. She says Harry still "freaks out" when she tries to tell him about the abuse she has suffered. Leigh Ann is an artist and regularly talks about sculpting some of the events she has experienced. She longs for a "regular," relaxed summer. I cannot predict how Leigh Ann will grow and change, or what her relationship with the church or God will become. I have consistently admired her courage and her honesty in dealing with her own issues and with the ways these have interfaced with her church and religious community.

Lacey

Lacey lives 2 hours from my office and has been an intermittent long-distance client for 18 months. She is married to an administrator of one of our denominational institutions. She met me 20 years ago when she was attending a boarding academy run by one of the most conservative branches of the Seventh Day Adventist church. Members of this branch eat a vegan diet, use only natural remedies for illness and injury, are highly patriarchal, are concerned about women having too much of a leadership role in church structure, believe women should wear only dresses, have their own medical and educational institutions, and are wary of the "worldliness" of the mainstream Seventh Day Adventist church. Both her parents are multigenerational members of the church and are well known in its national structure. She said she turned to me for help because she had known of me for many years, and she knew of my reputation as a "plain-spoken" clinician and educator.

Lacey said she was dealing with the effects of being repeatedly raped by her older brother during her latency years. Her sister had reported sexual assaults by the same brother and their father. Both women were ostracized by their family, who said these men were incapable of such behavior.

Lacey expressed outrage at her family, fury at a church that would shield an offender, and confusion with a God who would not protect her. It was important to her that I validated her anger, helped her articulate its sources, and underscored the truth that this anger did not mark her as a horrible person.

Lacey worried about jeopardizing her husband's career by disclosing her brother's abuse to the church organizational structure. Additionally, she no longer wanted to feel compelled to attend church, an unspoken requirement of dutiful denominational wives. I encouraged her to discuss these concerns with her husband, who said he loved her and emphasized that her safety and welfare were his priority. He said they would handle the consequences together.

Lacey called the international organization of the church when they were about to send her brother to a boarding academy post in South America and told them of his abusive history. They rescinded "the call" (job offer). For several months, Lacey was blamed by her family for his career difficulties.

Recently, during a visit, Lacey spent many hours talking with an older sister. This sister began to believe what she said and called together other members of the family. At Lacey's request, they called me long distance to consult. I encouraged them to develop new ways to respect their family members who had been abused. I talked with them about the variety of behaviors that can violate boundaries or fail to protect family members. Some of the older siblings decided to have a family gathering to discuss the abuse issues with their parents. Lacey and her sister chose not to attend. Their father denied all wrongdoing and said he was concerned about his son. Their mother was quiet. The siblings said they wanted to open up communication lines with the abused sisters and they were going to do it with or without their parents' approval.

Currently, Lacey is considering the ways she wants to be involved with her extended family. In this case, my role has been mainly that of a consultant to help Lacey handle larger family and systemic issues. She has begun ongoing individual therapy with a nearby non-Adventist clinician.

Mark

Mark is a convert to the church who met me during one of my seminars. He and his wife were separated because he had hit her and verbally terrified his children. He said he could not keep living this way; he wanted his home back and he needed to face the personal history that fueled his anger and inappropriate responses to his family.

Members of Mark's local church donated payment for 7 months of therapy and a place to live during the separation of his family. When he felt suicidal at one point in the therapy, his hosts said they were not equipped to deal with these kinds of issues, and they sent him home to his family. Other church members have provided short-term "time-outs" for Mark or his wife and children.

Mark was raised in a nonreligious home. He was physically abused by his father and sexually abused by his mother and foster father. He still lives in the area where he grew up. He does not see his parents, and he sees his brothers infrequently. He said the church has become his family. After 2 years of therapy that was mostly concerned with maintaining his stability in the here and now, he recently began addressing issues with his family of origin.

Russell (1986) has noted high rates of religious defection among women who were abused sexually in childhood. Research into the rates of sexual abuse among converts in evangelical churches like ours would be most helpful. I believe that Mark's entrance into the church, like that of many converts, was partially a search for family.

My work with Mark has included addressing his rage at his past and working on constructive ways to vent his feelings. He refused antidepressant medication for a year because he "didn't want to take drugs." He thought he should be able handle his difficulties with therapy, prayer, and other supports. He has been hospitalized twice and separated from his family twice. He is now taking medication and structuring his time to manage past and present stresses. At this writing, Mark and his family are reunited.

Some members of his church have worried that I might be "too New Age" to be working with him, and wondered if anyone who believes in psychology can be biblical. He says it is hard for him to feel pulled between them and me, but decided for himself that I was safe to work with.

Mark adheres strictly to conservative church dietary beliefs. He grows angry with himself when he is less than perfect in this regard. A few weeks ago, he told me he had been bingeing. I asked him what that meant. He had salad at night, and Ellen White said we should not eat dinner. I reminded him that she said we should not fall "into one ditch or the other." Maybe the salad was better than the dozen cookies he had eaten in the past when stressed. Using a discussion of food as a vehicle for introspection, we worked on loosening up some rigid internal demands.

Mark has wanted to press charges against his foster father. However, he worried that this would conflict with his belief in the necessity of forgiving "our trespassers." I talked with him about the ways that both the Old and New Testaments address violations of power and relationship. I noted that this choice could serve to protect other children. After several discussions, Mark told me he believed he would not misdirect rage toward his family if he could concretely address his anger toward one of his perpetrators. Since his most recent hospitalization, he began the process to indict this man, and in fact this does seem to be contributing to a drastic reduction in rageful episodes in the family.

In sessions, I have directly addressed Mark's violence toward his family. I balance the need to do this with awareness of his intense shame around breaking what he considers to be a sacred marriage oath to protect and care for his family. It has been a delicate struggle to confront both the violent behavior and the person in Mark who was victimized. Mark feels both personal and religious shame. I quote the text, "We have all sinned and come short of the glory of God." I say it is the human condition. At the same time, we have a responsibility to change hurtful behavior.

Strengthening the Community

Breaking the silence is the beginning of prevention. Every Seventh Day Adventist schoolteacher, Sabbath school teacher, Pathfinder leader, medical provider, pastor, church elder, administrator, and home school curriculum designer needs to learn the warning signs of sexual abuse and ways to facilitate and respond to disclosures.

We need prevention workshops for all volunteer and professional personnel who work with children. Liability insurance carriers are beginning to demand that sexual abuse reporting policies be included in church policies and procedures. I believe that these policies should be given to every pastor, medical and educational administrator, and church leader.

We need more campmeeting workshops; training for teachers, parents, and students throughout the educational system; and discussions in church literature. We need to refer to the topic as sexual abuse—an abuse of power—and not as interference in private sexual matters.

The prohibition against the use of alcohol and other intoxicating substances is one of our community strengths. However, it also means that the sexual abuse that does occur may have a different flavor than that which happens "under the influence." This topic cries out for research.

We need to study closely and change the contexts and circumstances that encourage boundary violations and the misuse of power in our organization and community. Seventh Day Adventists have a cultural expectation that requests for service should always be honored. Survivors with whom I have worked have often stated that they feel like they need to honor any request asked of them, even those that are self-damaging. They have had no education in the value of saying "no" for their own good. I believe it is important for this message of self-care and boundaries to be inculcated into our religious culture.

A pamphlet on sexual abuse called "When The Unthinkable Happens" (Women's Ministries, 1994) was recently mailed to every registered Seventh Day Adventist home in North America. It suggests that families teach children that their bodies are special and should be protected, that offenders are usually people whom children know, that children have the right to say "no," and that they should be believed and not blamed when they disclose. This is the most direct and best piece of literature distributed by the church on this topic that I have seen. I know of no other church that has taken a similar step to contact its membership in such a way about sexual abuse.

Children in every activity of the Adventist church should have the opportunity to learn about "good touch/bad touch," body boundaries, and ways to disclose. They need to know that they will not be blamed.

This is an enormous task. The church has just begun to open the door of the closet. Changes will take time and persistence, but I believe they are possible.

Gay Males and Sexual Child Abuse

DOUG AREY

There is a child's game where the player is given a marble that is placed on a maze. The goal is to commandeer the marble through the puzzle, exploring various traps and dead ends, by gently rotating two handles that tilt the board, allowing gravity to work its miracle on the rolling ball. When it seems the end is reached, the marble drops through a hole beginning another journey along a whole new puzzle previously unseen by the player. Several layers must be negotiated before the marble reaches its destination and comes through the exit hole at the bottom of the wooden enclosure. Practice, patience, close attention, and coordination help the player get the marble to its destination with greatest satisfaction and minimal aggravation.

The marble game is like doing therapy work with gay male survivors of sexual child abuse in many ways. Experience in dealing with adult survivors of incest and child abuse is essential for getting past the initial levels. It is common to discover unique and hidden layers; stumbling blocks, twists, and turns along a developmental path that differ from the heterosexual norm. Seemingly odd "familial" and social connections and structures may present themselves. In the course of the "game," the therapist/player may discover much about himself or herself (values, judgments, countertransference feelings, or limitations in training and skill) that challenges, disturbs, and ultimately interferes with enjoyment of the work. First-time "players" may discover the need for extra consultation and homework lest their clients be placed in the role of guide for the therapist through the maze of gay male subculture.

This chapter will explore social, cultural, and institutional traps, dead ends, and barriers that hinder service delivery to gay men who were abused sexually as children. Readers may gain better appreciation for a unique developmental process facing all gay people who live in North America, and for the role clinicians can play in guiding gay abuse survivors back along a developmental path interrupted by both cultural homophobia and their abuse.

History

To understand some of the unique issues facing gay male survivors of childhood sexual abuse, therapists first need to know something about what it means to be a gay man in the United States today—the social and cultural context in which our clients work, do their shopping, pay their bills, meet and socialize with friends, and live their lives. To understand gay culture today, one first must know something about how gay people have been regarded by others (and how gays regarded themselves) throughout history, and how this has influenced current attitudes and beliefs about gay and lesbian people.

Throughout the generations, social scientists, astrologers, clergy, and psychologists have speculated on the "causes" of homosexuality. Theories have developed based on such beliefs as the positions of the planets at birth, past lives, diet, and that homosexuality is a way for the species to keep its numbers in check, to name just a few (Fletcher & Saks, 1990).

Today, in most circles, it is recognized that homosexuality has existed in human beings since the beginning of recorded time (Greif, 1982). However, it was not until the late 1800s that homosexuals were labeled and were perceived as a category of people identifiable by their sexual orientation (Katz, 1983). Homosexuality has been viewed differently by various cultures throughout history and has experienced varied levels of cultural acceptance. The Greek "tradition" of male-male sexuality is one example of a time many centuries ago when sex and love between men was commonplace (Blumenfeld & Raymond, 1988).

In many Native American cultures (as well as some African cultures), gay men held honored status in a tribe, often recognized for having special talents and skills necessary for the survival of tribal members. They were called "bardache"; they were "sorcerers" or, in some tribes, the "medicine man"; and they were often excluded from the usual hunting and gathering duties expected of other tribesmen (Grahn, 1984; Katz, 1976).

In European cultures, where Christian leaders encouraged persecution of "pagans" and other nonconformists, lesbians were labeled "witches" and were burned at the stake in public forums as a message to all considering alternative lifestyles (Grahn, 1984). Gay men were also targeted. The derogatory term "faggot," associated with gay men today, has been traced to the practice of burning gay men with the witches, as their bodies, along with faggots (literally meaning "bundle of sticks"), were thrown on the fires as "kindling" (Rutledge, 1987).

Prior to the late 1880s, love between men and between women enjoyed a certain openness and protection, falling into the romanticized early Victorian concepts of love described in popular and religious literature of the time. Presumed "chaste" (and therefore sexless), the "true man" or "true woman" could love either man or woman openly and passionately

> with no fear of impropriety—because these true loves were thought to include no nasty lust. . . . According to [the] Victorian sexual world-view, lust was cordoned off from love, segregated in the separate spheres of procreation or prostitution, or even more rarefied realms of sapphism or sodomy. (Katz, 1983, p. 140)

Throughout U.S. history, when sex between men or between women was discovered and reported to authorities, homosexuals faced severe judgment and consequence. Records dating back to the first settlements in the United States include accounts of the courts imposing sentences of public whippings, mutilation, and/or death by hanging for violators of early "sodomy" laws (a catchall term for any form of sexuality considered "unnatural") (Katz, 1983).

Documentation has been discovered on homosexuality in colonial America. Letters, poems, journal entries, ship's logs, and folklore from as early as the late 1600s tell thinly veiled stories of passionate, committed, loving "friendships" between men on farms, on the prairie, at sea, in the military, and among clergy, statesmen, and politicians. Perhaps because it was not acknowledged or discussed openly in "polite society," men who came to terms with their homosexuality may have enjoyed less open hostility or discrimination than some gays and lesbians today. With their sexuality essentially unacknowledged, they were whimsically referred to as "confirmed bachelors," and lesbians were considered "spinsters" or "old maids." It is likely that many gay men from that earlier era had male lovers as well as a wife and family. Alexander Hamilton, Walt Whitman, Ralph Waldo Emerson, and Abraham Lincoln are just a few famous early Americans known to have had gay relationships (Greif, 1982).

Around the turn of the century, the idea of the "homosexual" and "heterosexual" was constructed in response to women's changing role in industry and society, according to Katz (1983):

> The historical construction and use of the terms "homo-" and "heterosexual" from the 1890s on, indicates an increasing stress on two eroticisms distinguished essentially by the genders of their parties. . . . The distinguishing of a "same-sex" from an "opposite-sex" eroticism reflected an increasing social emphasis in the late-nineteenth century on the differentiation of females and males. . . . The invention of "homosexuality" and "heterosexuality" registers an increasing stress by doctors of the 1890s and early twentieth century on the supposedly innate differences between females and males. In terms of social function, that stress on sexual differentiation was clearly an effort to contain the contemporary movement of women out of the traditional women's sphere and into the world of wage work, social reform, and electoral politics. . . . The homosexual/heterosexual distinction is now so deeply ingrained that it is difficult for us to think in other terms. (pp. 147-149)

Freud believed that homosexuality in adults was evidence of "immaturity," and a "neurotic" condition arising from children growing up in family configurations of dominant or overly protective mothers and passive or absent fathers (Blumenfeld & Raymond, 1988). Although he believed this, he wrote that homosexuality "cannot be classified as an illness; we consider it to be a variation of the sexual function produced by a certain arrest of sexual development" (Katz, 1983, p. 506). He believed psychoanalysis could be effective in providing "a means of living contentedly, uninhibitedly, and efficiently as homosexual," but could not provide a "cure" (Katz, 1983, pp. 506-507).

Because the lives and experiences of gays and lesbians have been talked about more openly in recent times, and accelerated greatly since the beginning of the AIDS epidemic in the early 1980s, to some it has seemed that homosexuality is on the rise. More likely, awareness about the existence of gay and lesbian people has risen. In his groundbreaking study on male sexuality,

Kinsey (1948) reported that approximately 10% of the adult male population was exclusively homosexual. Several recent replications of that study have reconfirmed the 10% statistic, showing no increases in men reporting to be homosexual in the past 45 years.

Not widely discussed in historical literature about the Holocaust is the treatment of gay men during World War II in Nazi Germany. Following one of the most liberal periods known in European history in terms of tolerance of homosexuality, over 50,000 gay men were interned, tortured (in many cases, castrated), and murdered in concentration camps alongside Jews and political dissidents as part of Hitler's program of ethnic and cultural cleansing (Blumenfeld & Raymond, 1988). The pink triangle (a current symbol of gay pride reclaimed by the gay rights movement) was the emblem assigned to homosexuals identifying their status in the camps; the counterpart to the six-pointed yellow Star of David that identified Jewish prisoners. Jewish gay men wore stars made from a pink triangle over a yellow triangle. Concentration camp survivors have reported that when Allied forces overtook the Nazis, Jews were liberated from the camps but homosexual prisoners were left behind. Reportedly, the "liberators" thought there was just cause for homosexuals to continue being locked away (Blumenfeld & Raymond, 1988).

Minority ethnic and class groups in this country often can pinpoint a moment in history when they became organized against oppression by the majority; when they realized they'd suffered enough abuse and decided they weren't going to take it anymore. The movement for civil rights of homosexuals was well under way by the end of World War II, and several public demonstrations had occurred in cities throughout the United States in the early 1960s (Katz, 1983). The understanding of most Americans, however, including gay and lesbian Americans, is that the official gay rights movement began in New York City in June of 1969. The particular event followed years of "cleanup" operations including raids, arrests, harassment, and beatings carried out by New York City police and ordered by an administration wishing to rid the streets of gays, transvestites, and other "undesirables" to make New York more attractive to the throngs of visitors to the city's World's Fair. On the night one of the great icons of a segment of gay subculture, Judy Garland, died, a dozen or so grieving gay men and transvestites found their angry inner voice and fought back as police carried out a raid of the Stonewall Inn, a gay bar in Greenwich Village. Years and generations of pent-up frustration, pain, and persecution were released. Cars were overturned, fires were set, and rioting continued for 10 days in the Village as more and more gays and transvestites realized they were fed up with hiding, being subjected to humiliating and demoralizing treatment by police, the courts, family members, employers, the mental health profession, and society as a whole (Blumenfeld & Raymond, 1988).

Since that day, a vast political and cultural movement throughout the United States has mushroomed. Most major cities, scores of college campuses, and some smaller cities and towns now have openly gay organizations: annual gay pride parades, church groups, social groups, sports teams, political groups, professional organizations, business guilds, teen groups, AIDS care organizations, and gay and lesbian community centers. These institutions contribute to a greater sense of individual and group empowerment and a reduction in self-abuse and self-loathing. More and more individuals have chosen to come out of the closet to family, at work, and in their communities.

Gays and the Mental Health Profession

The mental health profession as a whole owes many apologies to the gay community. Generations of misunderstanding and misdiagnosis have resulted in generations of mistreatment, emotional abuse, and psychological torture of gays and lesbians. The field of psychology convinced gay people and their loved ones that homosexuality was a "disease." Consequently, for many decades, the mental health professions have been among the primary causes and the most violent perpetrators of societal homophobia.

Once originated, the disease concept of homosexuality opened the door to, among many things, a myriad of "cures," consisting of everything from years of psychoanalysis to sedation, castration, hysterectomies, lobotomies, electroconvulsive therapy, and numerous degrading behavior modification programs, including aversive conditioning with electrical shocks. Of the studies conducted to evaluate the effectiveness of any therapy where conversion to heterosexuality was the treatment goal, none has ever been reported to be effective even 3 years following the end of the treatment (Hall, 1985). It is likely they caused gay people in treatment (and gay people who learned about these treatments) to feel deepening levels of isolation, despair, self-loathing, fear, and shame. The view of homosexuality as a disease tore families apart and contributed to elevated levels of substance abuse and suicide among gay people, as well as increases in incidents of violence against gay people.

In 1979, the American Psychiatric Association finally removed homosexuality from the list of psychological disorders in the DSM-III. However, this has not stopped some in the mental health profession from offering treatments claiming to "cure" homosexuality or from perpetuating the myth of homosexuality as a disease or abnormality in need of a cure. This practice continues today throughout the United States, although others now believe that certain mental health professionals are afflicted with a disease (called homophobia) that has been "countertransferred" onto gay and lesbian psychotherapy patients (Hall, 1985).

Today, across the United States, discriminatory practices toward gay clients continue, more commonly in less overt forms. For instance, when a gay person seeks counseling, the mental health professional often may assume the root of the problem is the client's homosexuality, regardless of the presenting problem.

In one example, Donald broke up with his lover of 7 years after discovering his partner's infidelity with a mutual friend. Six months later, Donald continued having angry dreams at night, and listlessness and depression during the day. Friends convinced him he needed help, so he went to the only clinician on his insurance plan's provider list who had openings. Donald describes the therapy:

> The therapist was warm and friendly. He told me he had gay clients before me, and assured me my being gay wasn't a problem for him. At first, things seemed fine. He asked about my relationship with David, and details about how we separated. It felt good to talk about it. About the third session, he asked a lot of questions about how I knew I was gay and if I had ever been in a relationship with a woman. He wanted to know all about my coming out to my family, people at work. That was fine. He wanted to know what I thought about AIDS, and did any of my friends have it, and did I think I might have it? I explained these were things I had thought about already. After a while, I felt like I was reassuring him I had these things under control. I wanted to talk about breaking up with Dave, and he wanted to talk about HIV testing. The straw that broke the camel's back was after the sixth session, when he handed me an article he'd found about gay men who chose to live a celibate lifestyle. I asked him why he was giving this to me. He said he thought I'd like to know there was support out there for people "in my position." He assumed I was so afraid of

getting AIDS I wouldn't want to have sex again or look for another relationship. I had never said anything like that to him.

I have listened to numerous stories about gay clients' previous therapy experiences with well-intentioned therapists who believed strongly that their gay clients could not be happy living a gay lifestyle. Some reports were of subtle homophobia, including one man who reported that he thought his therapist said "all the right things" but seemed to wince whenever they discussed gay sex directly. Another client reported having gone to see a psychiatrist in order to stop having sexual fantasies about men. He remembers the psychiatrist shaming him directly, telling him he was "only half a man" if he couldn't become aroused sexually by the sight of a woman, and that he "might as well commit suicide" rather than live an openly gay lifestyle, reportedly because he would "be dead of AIDS within five years" if he didn't "convert." Upon hearing this from the therapist (with whom he'd worked in weekly psychotherapy for over 3 years), this client made a serious suicide attempt that resulted in hospitalization, where he learned for the first time that his homosexuality was not a disease after all.

When gay people enter therapy, many do so wary that they will be judged, misunderstood, and not accepted by their therapists. Many have heard the horror stories, and, consequently, they hold off seeking help until they feel quite desperate. Many gay people have stayed closeted throughout their therapy to protect themselves, changing the names and pronouns of their significant others. Others have come out to their therapists only after first putting him or her through several tests for tolerance and sophistication about the issue. For instance, when therapists made incorrect assumptions when referring to the gender of their clients' significant others, this revealed a heterosexist bias that gay clients consciously or unconsciously interpreted as unsafe, and therefore felt unable to be their true selves in therapy.

In an ideal world, the sexual orientation of a therapist would be less important to the outcome of the therapy than the quality of the therapeutic relationship. Male survivors of sexual abuse have unique safety needs in their therapy. Gay male psychotherapy patients, whether or not they are abuse survivors, also have unique safety needs. A therapist's sexual orientation is often an important consideration that may need direct discussion before any gay client or any male survivor can form a trusting bond with his therapist. When gay survivors (and gay therapy clients in general) express a wish to be matched either with a gay therapist or with a heterosexual therapist, or a male or female therapist, I believe that these requests need to be given merit and respect, and that referrals should be made to accommodate such requests whenever possible. When a gay man is in treatment with a nongay therapist, the possibility of transferring to a gay therapist may need to be reviewed periodically as he progresses in his recovery and through his coming-out process.

What It Means to Be a Gay Man

The images held out to little boys about what it means to "be a man" rarely include falling in love with and settling down with another man. Masculinity in our culture is often linked with attributes of strength, power, and independence, especially in relationships with other men. A boy learns that strength and power are important for when he needs to defend himself against, or compete with, other males. Socialization as a male in this culture is often in conflict with the inner nature of a gay man, who, instead of wishing to dominate and compete against other members of his gender, yearns instead to be close, cooperative, and intimate.

Homosexuality is often equated by many heterosexuals (and by some gay people) with being nonmasculine, although masculinity and femininity are not directly related to sexual orientation. Men who choose nontraditional professions or who pursue nontraditional or feminine interests and hobbies often face direct or indirect "discomfort" or hostility from others because of their choices. This discomfort is based on the underlying questions about the man's masculinity, often expressed as, "Are you gay?"

All who grow up in North America suffer from some degree of homophobia. Homophobia glues us into traditional roles as men and women. Homophobia is the irrational fear and hatred of homosexuals (or people thought to be homosexual), and things associated with homosexual people or a homosexual lifestyle (Weinberg, 1972). All of us consciously or unconsciously make daily decisions in part so that we are not seen by others as homosexual.

In that the force behind the oppression of gay people is a "phobia," and not an "ism," it differs significantly from oppression of other minorities. Average European Americans don't harbor private fears that they may really be Black, Asian, or Latino. If Kinsey's research is correct, close to 80% of the population is bisexual to some degree and may have reason to "fear" same-gender attractions and affections. For the many people who handle their same-gender attractions by denying and repressing, out-of-the-closet gays and lesbians represent an unacceptable resolution to their internal conflicts about sexuality.

A common myth about gay people that nurtures this phobia is the idea that gay men and lesbians "recruit" little boys and girls into a gay lifestyle. Many people mistakenly associate homosexuality with pedophilia. The myth that gays and lesbians are predators and defilers of America's youth persists despite the fact that heterosexual men constitute the overwhelming majority of perpetrators of sexual abuse of children (93%)! Many Americans associate all homosexuality with NAMBLA (the North American Man/Boy Love Association), an organization of pedophiles who prey on boys that officials in the Christian Right have strategically targeted to justify their campaigns to "Save the Children" and deny gays and lesbians their equal civil rights.

Growing up gay can be quite frightening. Mark is a 17-year-old client from an adolescent coming-out group:

> Growing up gay is like being the only Black kid in an all White school, only different. First, no one else may suspect you're gay, and you live in dread someone will figure it out, knowing if they do you're dead meat. Second, you don't get a break when you get home. Your family is different from you, too, and you don't know if they're going to treat you any better if they find out.

Most gay people intuitively know it is not a safe world for "out" gays and lesbians. Most learn at early ages what parts of their behavior could incite homophobic violence, scorn, or ridicule, and quickly become experts at hiding who they are, even from themselves. At the core of what it means to be a gay man in America is a focus on building safe networks of friends and colleagues who are tolerant or accepting; and choosing careers, relationships, and neighborhoods based on a balance between "What I really want" and "What can I get without getting beaten up, disowned, fired, losing custody of my children, or evicted?"

Although young people today have a great deal more information about what it means to be gay than just a generation ago, seldom do they have thorough or accurate information. Most gay men identify the lack of visible, healthy role models as the greatest obstacle to coming to healthy terms with themselves and their gay identity (Bawer, 1993):

Gay people are for the most part not born into gay families. They suffer oppression individually and alone, without benefit of advice or frequently even emotional support from relatives or friends. This makes their case more comparable in some way to that of the blind or left-handed, who are also dispersed in the general population. (Boswell, 1980, p. 269)

At times, clinicians working with gay survivors may find it difficult to assess whether a client is presenting symptoms of disempowerment as a gay man or disempowerment stemming from his childhood abuse. It is important to note that our gay clients also suffer from homophobia or, in their cases, more accurately, "internalized oppression." Unless they have done a great deal of sorting through and resolving the myriad of issues associated with membership in an oppressed subculture, many gay clients will have consciously or unconsciously accepted second-class citizenship, which may be revealed in a number of ways.

Josh: My landlord is such a prick. He wants me to move out. He doesn't know what to make of me. I must make him nervous.
Therapist: What makes you believe your landlord wants you to move?
J: Oh, he's always on my case about leaving my bicycle in the hall, and he never bothers the other tenants about the stuff they leave out there. (J. looks down and sighs.) And that's not all. It's a bunch of little things. He has a real condescending tone.
T: How do you feel when he uses that condescending tone?
J: Like I want to just disappear. I hate feeling like that. I'd do anything to not feel like that.
T: What do you do when one of these conversations happen?
J: I usually agree to whatever he wants and just try to keep it short.
T: And then what happens?
J: I usually go off and obsess about it. I hate it. I'm such a little wimp sometimes. I think about what I'd really like to say.
T: And what's that?
J: (Laughs) I'd really like to break into his apartment with a bunch of my friends and redecorate it. That would show him. His worst nightmare. . . . The gay Mafia pays him a visit. We'd show him a thing or two about good taste!
T: That's really funny! I wonder, though, if by making a joke of it you might not be taking your own feelings seriously. It really must feel bad to be treated that way.

J: Yeah, but what can I do? I can't move again so soon. This isn't a good time to get people to help, and there aren't any good apartments left in my neighborhood. I looked 3 months for this one.

Josh sees himself as a "wimp," or too weak to stand up for himself. He believes that if he is assertive, his landlord will evict him. He sees no viable option other than to endure what he perceives as hostile and unfair treatment from his landlord, whom he believes has singled him out because he suspects that Josh is gay. His fantasy is to "just disappear."

Many gay men feel powerless when it comes to standing up to gay bashers. From childhood memories of being targeted for abuse for being "different" on the playground without allies for protection, to the current reality for most gay men in the United States of having no legal protection or recourse, a mind-set is created and reinforced that, "If you're gay, you can keep your job, your home, your family, and safety as long as you don't rock the boat and you agree to hide your sexual orientation." Although this is slowly changing, therapists must keep in mind that their gay clients may not have the same options available as their nongay clients for standing up for themselves.

Was Josh's story really about his encounters with his landlord's homophobia, or could his perception have been distorted by sexual abuse? In some way, was he telling the therapist about how he felt as an 11-year-old being raped by his stepfather while his mother lay passed out on the couch in the next room?

T: It feels to you like there isn't much you can do about your landlord.
J: Yes. (Pause) Why, do you know something I can do?
T: You've told me about many times when you felt just like this.
J: Heh . . . story of my life.
T: Yes. This goes back a long way.
J: I know what you're getting at. (Long pause) Maybe it was my "child" talking with the prick landlord?
T: Does that seem right?
J: Yes, I guess it does. I was having flashbacks all that day. I just didn't need his crap. (Another long pause) I think I may have set myself up for that one. I knew better than to leave the bike out. I guess he had a right to have an attitude.
T: Did it feel like attitude he'd give anyone, or did it feel like he was being homophobic?
J: Oh, he's homophobic. No question.

T: What do you think your "adult" would like to say to a homophobic landlord? (Pause) Also, what might you need in order to feel safe enough to say what you really wanted to say?

J: I guess I'd like to call him on his stuff. Ask him if he has a problem with me living there. See if he admits he's prejudiced. I don't know what could help me feel safe.

T: I wonder if the "child" knows the answer to that? What did he want when he felt like that as a kid?

J: He wanted his mother to get up off the damn couch and check out what was happening in the den.

T: It would feel much safer if you felt you had an ally, wouldn't it?

J: Right. Hey, maybe Rick would go with me!

The simultaneous reality for Josh is that he suffers from posttraumatic stress disorder (PTSD), and he is a member of an oppressed minority group. Sometimes these issues overlap in his life. He gets confused and has difficulty accessing personal power when his symptoms surface, especially in situations that replicate the dynamics of his childhood abuse.

It was important for Josh to have both realities validated by the therapist in this session. The gentle suggestion was that Josh didn't have to accept disrespectful treatment from the authority figure, and he need not bash himself for not feeling "man enough" to handle a confrontation on his own. This message spoke directly to his feelings of shame as a male survivor and his internalized homophobia.

Coming Out and Coming to Terms with Incest

I always knew I was different when I was a kid. I was too scared to figure out what the difference was. I just knew I had to learn how to act like the other guys even if I hated what they did. I didn't question it. It all fell apart my second year in college when I met some gay people and realized I was just like them. I wanted to kill myself 'cause I didn't want to be like them. I tried so hard for so long not to be like them. At first I thought it meant I would automatically get AIDS. Eventually I got over it, and now it's no big deal. But I went through some tough times. (John, 25 years old)

I always thought gay guys wanted to be women and wanted to dress like women and wear makeup. I never wanted to do that, and I liked being a male. It was pretty confusing. There weren't any books and nothing on TV like there is today; only what you overheard people saying. It took me a long time to know what I was feeling was gay. (Toby, 55 years old)

"Coming out" is the term used by most gays and lesbians to refer to the process by which a gay person discovers and accepts his or her homosexuality. As the coming-out phenomenon is explored further, readers may notice how it parallels the steps of coming to terms with an identity as an incest survivor.

Although one may hear a gay person say, "I came out when I was twenty," most will agree that coming out is not a one-time event. Instead, it is a lifelong process. Every time a gay man tells someone else about his sexual orientation, he has once again "come out."

Several models have been developed that describe and identify stages of the coming-out process (e.g., Cass, 1979). Clinicians will need to know about the stages of coming out in order to assess accurately where their gay clients are in their psychosexual development and to understand the impact of the client's childhood abuse on this process.

A model that I believe matches gay men's coming-out process best was proposed by Coleman (1981), who identified five distinct stages: pre-coming out, coming out, exploration, first relationships, and integration.

Most of us are familiar with age-stage theories of psychological development. Regardless of which stage theory you may personally favor, it is important to understand that most gay people do not progress through the usual stages in the same order or chronological time frame as heterosexuals. Just as sexual abuse in childhood can interrupt a heterosexual's psychosexual development, discovering a same-sex orientation in a heterosexist society can also deter or postpone progression through normal stages of growth for gay people. Gay survivors of abuse, most of whom were molested in the early part (usually the first three stages) of their coming-out process, have several extra hurdles that must be jumped before they can reach the end goal of health and "integration."

Surveys have shown that most gay men first identified their same-sex attraction around 14 years of age, and most lesbians at 18 years of age (Jay & Young, 1979). I have witnessed in my gay clients that childhood sexual trauma sometimes either retarded or accelerated identification of a gay sexual orientation. I have come to believe that for those for whom their abuse has slowed their coming out, it was for one of two reasons. First, many survivors cope with their molestation by denying or repressing, avoiding "allowing" themselves to explore any sexual feelings, thus avoiding stimulating memories that they are not ready to handle. Second, if they remember the abuse and the perpetrator was a man, they may have believed that the same-sex attraction was a symptom of having been abused, rather than a "real" homosexual orientation, thus preserving hope that one day they would "become" heterosexual.

Some whose coming-out process was accelerated by their abuse experienced a recognition of homoerotic pleasure during the experience. Under normal circumstances, they would not have discovered these feelings for many years because they lacked a framework to understand or label their sexuality. Although gay male survivors often will reframe their abuse experiences in a positive light in order to deal with a potentially overwhelming experience (Gelinas, 1983), this does not imply that the survivor benefited from the abuse. Problems almost always arise for people who are introduced to sexuality before they are developmentally ready. It is often the therapist's task in these instances to help the gay survivor explore his abuse and begin to understand how the experience was hurtful to him or how it may have been the root cause for the symptoms he came to treatment to resolve.

When a young gay man begins to understand his sexual feelings, he will often experience some level of personal crisis because of the hostility he perceives about gay people from his environment. He is faced with a critical developmental "choice": to nurture or repress his sexuality.

Nurturing his developing gay identity can be dangerous on many levels: He risks losing support from his peers, family, and community; he may be at risk for physical danger; and he consequently may realize that he is isolated and be at risk for depression and suicide. With the increase of information about what "gay" really means from movies, books, and television shows that deal with gay themes, it is becoming somewhat more common for gay youth to come out at earlier ages. An obvious drawback to identifying homosexuality as a teen is the lack of an accepting environment, putting some youth at risk.

Repressing or denying his identity to himself and keeping it from others will result in a gay adolescent's deviation from a normal developmental path. It is rare that an adolescent gay person has an accepting environment ready to provide safe, healthy, and age-appropriate avenues for exploring his identity. Many gay youths who deny or repress their homosexuality, whether or not they are abuse survivors, cope by overcompensation: They become extremely active in pursuing heterosexual relationships or sexual experiences, and they may act out violently against gay people. Some become focused on developing other parts of themselves by becoming extremely studious, involved in hobbies and friends, or in volunteer work. Others cope by turning to suicide, alcohol and drugs, promiscuous or compulsive sex, or other forms of antisocial behavior to manage pain and express their inner turmoil. Gay and lesbian youth are believed to be at three times greater risk for suicide than straight teens and to have a three times greater chance of becoming addicted to drugs or alcohol (Kus, 1988, p. 25).

Many gay people postpone dealing with their sexual identity until they are at a time and place in their lives when they are better prepared emotionally to cope with the crisis that coming out often triggers in their lives and families, and until they have discovered support resources for gays. It is common for gay men to come out after leaving home for college or becoming financially independent from their families. Having years of practice at hiding their sexual attraction, it is not uncommon for gay men to come out in midlife after leading an outwardly heterosexual life and raising a family. Likewise, it is common for gay male survivors to put off coming out until they can get help for abuse issues that may emerge concurrently with dealing with their sexuality.

Developmental Stages of the Coming-Out Process

Stage 1: Pre-Coming Out

According to Coleman, prior to having words or concepts to explain feelings of same-sex attraction, many gay men know they are "different" from other boys without knowing just what the difference is. Coleman has called this the "pre-coming-out stage."

Tim reports knowing as early as kindergarten that he didn't fit in easily. He felt drawn to quieter activities than other boys, preferring arts and crafts to tag or kickball:

> The closest I came to figuring out I was gay until I came out at nineteen was when I was in junior high. I was thirteen. A friend asked me over to his house after school and was excited to show me something, but wouldn't tell me what. When we got there he showed me a *Playboy* magazine he'd found somewhere. I remember feeling there was something very wrong that I wasn't interested in looking at the pictures of nude women.

In this stage, which can occur at any chronological age, it is common to see symptoms of depression in gay clients and to hear reports of social isolation. Therapists can assist by making the therapy environment "gay friendly," a safe place to begin exploring what those "different" feelings are all about.

Several of my heterosexual male clients who were molested by men prior to coming to terms with a heterosexual identity report worrying a great deal that their abuse experiences would "make them be gay." Likewise, it is common for gay male survivors who were molested during their pre-coming-out stage to believe they are gay because they were molested. I have noticed this in gay survivors regardless of the gender of the abuser(s).

Perhaps because homosexuality is often stereotyped as "sick," bad, or perverted, it is easy to understand why homosexuality is so often associated with just about any kind of "undesirable" sexuality. As part of their healing, all survivors attempt to understand, integrate, and master their abuse experiences. In doing so, some may conclude that the bad feelings they have from being molested are "gay." In his screening interview for a group for male survivors, Rick said, "I was molested when I was eight by a female baby-sitter. That experience was so disgusting I could never imagine having sex with a woman again. So I became gay."

To fully heal from sexual abuse, it is important to help gay abuse survivors become clear that sexual orientation is not caused by sexual abuse. The clients I have observed who have the greatest difficulty letting go of these long-held beliefs also have the greatest difficulty accepting that a homosexual orientation is healthy and "normal." These clients also have more difficulty with self-esteem and self-abusive behavior. Their gay identity seems to be associated, consciously or unconsciously, with having been molested.

I have found it important to explore with clients the ways in which abuse experiences may influence how and under what circumstances they express themselves sexually. In Rick's case, for instance, over time he was able to understand that although being molested by a woman did not make him homosexual, it may have lessened his interest in nurturing any bisexual inclinations he may have had toward women. He also began exploring whether his need to be "in charge" in adult sexual situations was related to having felt fear when sex was forced on him by the baby-sitter. After looking at these issues, Rick reported feeling less homophobic and more appreciative of his gay friends. With further therapy, he was able to become less rigid and in charge when being sexual with his lover.

Stage 2: Coming Out

Coming out is the second stage, entered when a homosexual person labels his same-sex attraction. According to Coleman, the developmental task for this stage is to share the self-labeling with another person.

A therapist is often the first person to whom a gay client will come out. Therapists can be helpful in this stage by having a positive initial response and by exploring with the client whom else in his social network he could safely tell about his sexual orientation. Coleman believes that having the first experiences of disclosure of a gay identity be positive is crucial in the ongoing development of a positive gay identity.

I have observed that when a gay child or adolescent is molested when he is in his coming-out stage, it is likely that he will negatively associate his sexual orientation with the abuse. However, he is less likely to make this association if the perpetrator was female. Therapists should look for themes or worries that his being gay "caused" him to be molested.

In the coming-out stage, most gay men and lesbians are emotionally vulnerable. They are experiencing a major adjustment in their worldview and self-identification, and they likely need to grieve the loss of things associated with believing they would be heterosexual. Don remembers thinking:

> There goes the family and kids and station wagon ideal. I couldn't imagine how my life would turn out. I only had images of being alone, or hanging around a dark, smoky bar. I didn't think gay people had real relationships. I couldn't imagine it 'cause I'd never really seen it anywhere.

Jamie was molested by a taxi driver when he was 12 years old:

> I knew I was gay since I was 8 or 9, but I never told anyone. I lived in the city and we usually took busses or taxis to get around. Once I was alone coming home from a music lesson and the taxi driver was very friendly to me. He asked all about my music lessons, where I lived, and what school I went to. He seemed nice, and I liked the attention. I looked for him the next week, and he was there to give me a ride. He let me sit in front with him. I felt I'd made a friend. I guess he'd figured me out, and it wasn't long before he asked me if I knew what "gay" meant. You can fill in the rest of what happened from there. I felt so

dirty and stupid. My wanting a gay friend was what got me in trouble. He wouldn't have asked me to his house if I didn't tell him I was gay. He probably never would have picked me up at all if I was a jock coming home from football practice instead of a little pansy taking clarinet lessons.

Sam was raped by two older boys when he was 14 years old and away at summer camp. He was targeted as a "sissy" and remembers hating camp:

Kids used to pick on me. Two muscle guys, counselors-in-training from one of the other cabins, made it a point to follow me around and were always hassling me and making sexual comments. They threatened to cut my balls off if I didn't give them both blowjobs one day. I believed them, of course. I couldn't tell anyone. They made me believe they could make things worse if I told.

Whereas heterosexual boys may believe they were molested because they were weak or naive and feel shame about not being "man enough" to have kept it from happening, gay boys sometimes feel they deserved their abuse because "after all, I'm just a fag. What did I expect?" Several clients have reported having such feelings confirmed by police, parents, or friends, although often indirectly. Sam, for instance, eventually told his school counselor what happened at the summer camp. His parents were brought in for a conference. Sam remembers one of his father's comments: "You should learn to walk more like a guy. They probably thought you were a girl."

Clinicians seeing gay male survivors who were molested when they were working through their coming-out stage will need to help their clients understand sexual abuse as an abuse of power, not a "crime of passion." Assuming that a part of themselves so basic as their sexual orientation stems from the violence they experienced as children leaves many survivors feeling self-loathing and places them at high risk for depression and self-abusive behavior. Many see their homosexuality as a lifelong reminder of their victimization; a version of the "damaged goods" syndrome common to many survivors.

Stage 3: Exploration

The "exploration" stage of the coming-out process, according to Coleman, is best understood as a gay person's "adolescence." No matter what age he is when he comes to terms with his gay identity, when he first starts to validate his feelings by putting them into practice, he necessarily faces similar developmental tasks as those faced by most teenagers, including learning to socialize; exploring whom he finds attractive and who finds him attractive; and learning how to ask someone out on a date and how to behave on a date.

As in the previous stage, gay men who were abused sexually during this stage of coming out may also negatively associate their abuse with their homosexuality. If, for instance, a young gay man connects with an older gay man for friendship or to explore his sexuality and agrees to try sexual behavior he later regrets or is coerced into, he may feel he brought this upon himself for having wanted a friend or a sexual experience. Many gay teens talk about feeling extremely isolated and desperate for contact with other gay people. Not knowing how to find others their age, some seek out the only gay people readily identifiable to them.

Therapists can help their gay clients during this stage in several important ways: In general, gay people who are coming out need approval of their sexuality. They may be lucky enough to be accepted by friends and family for their gay identity, but few report having support from their straight friends in becoming sexual with other men. When it comes to encouraging a gay friend, son, or brother to become sexual, the limits of acceptance often become clear. "Okay in theory, but do you really have to do that?" In a surrogate parent role to a gay client who is coming out, therapists are often in the best position to offer this badly needed approval and encouragement. This is also a place where many therapists become more acutely aware of their own homophobia, and they should seek out appropriate supervision. The therapist may also be called upon during this stage to act as a resource for a gay client needing information about where to find other gay people, services for gay people, reading material for gay youth, and information about "safe sex."

The developmental task at this stage is to have a homosexual experience. Especially with gay clients who are abuse survivors, the therapist will need to be prepared to help the client learn how to choose partners for having safe, self-affirming sexual experiences. Given that many gay men who are survivors may have a somewhat skewed sense of sexual expression because of their abuse, attention may need to focus on helping the client clarify what he feels is healthy, affectionate sexuality.

Many survivors will need help in therapy in determining the degree of their responsibility, if any, for the abuse. A gay adolescent seeking a sexual experience from an adult, for instance, may have difficulty understanding that he was not responsible for the adult's decision to become sexual with a minor, and that the adult is responsible for the minor's feelings of having been victimized. Usually, once able to understand his own behavior in the context of a "healthy teen needing to explore, without access to age-appropriate resources," he will be better able to hold his perpetrator(s) accountable.

It is common in our culture for men to turn to pornography for images, information, and models to inform their sexuality. I suggest that clinicians counsel their gay clients away from seeking answers about healthy gay sexuality from the many pornographic materials currently available for the following reasons. First, gay men are extremely impressionable at this stage of their coming out, and the images presented may leave indelible impressions that influence their sexual response patterns for many years, potentially creating future problems when they work through later stages (Money, 1988). Few of the films and magazines available portray gay sex in the context of a caring and intimate relationship. Instead, they promote and reinforce a sexual response pattern that is based on depersonalized, anonymous sexual encounters that later can become a barrier to enjoyment of sexual intimacy with a partner. (For some gay men, the "actors" portrayed in pornographic videos are the first gay role models they have!) Second, much of the gay pornographic material available contains violent imagery and themes of dominance and submission, suggesting an association of sexual arousal with violence and the use and abuse of power. For gay survivors, this can often be traumatizing, and it may confirm their worst fears and negative images about gay sexuality: "I am destined to a lifetime of nothing but hurtful, uncaring sexuality!" Finally, in comparing themselves to the models used in these films and magazines, most clients will end up feeling inadequate about their bodies, which will hinder the completion of the developmental tasks of this important stage.

Stage 4: First Relationships

Coleman's fourth stage is "first relationships." The developmental task at this stage is to find and learn the skills to function in a relationship with another gay man. Although it is beyond the scope of this article to cover the unique relationship issues facing gay couples, it will be useful for clinicians in their work with clients at this stage to become acquainted with the challenges of gay partnerships. Several good resource books are available for gay couples and for clinicians doing couples work.

Only infrequently will clinicians need to assess a gay male survivor who was sexually abused during the "first relationships" stage of his coming-out process. It is rare that gay people have an opportunity to be in a (nonabusive) gay relationship while young enough to become a sexual abuse victim. On such occasions, the treatment will again need to focus on issues stemming from a negative association of the abuse trauma and the gay sexual orientation, as well as on other, more typical issues facing male abuse survivors regarding violation of trust and confused boundaries.

Regardless of the stage of coming out, a client may have experienced sexual trauma. If he is in a relationship when he seeks treatment, therapists should readily consider involving the client's partner in the therapy, just as he or she would with heterosexual survivors who are in relationships. A major barrier to successful relationships identified by gay couples is not being given consideration as a "legitimate couple" by their nongay family members, friends, social institutions, and service providers. Gay couples commonly report that invitations, greeting cards, and credit applications will be sent to only one member of a couple. They report, for instance, being expected to separate on family holidays to each visit his own family, whereas their heterosexual siblings will be assumed to accompany their spouses to these same gatherings. Therapists can be aware of this and convey their respect for the legitimacy of their gay clients' relationships by equal and consistent treatment planning for their gay and nongay clients who are in couples.

Stage 5: Integration

The final stage of coming out is called "integration" and is achieved when a gay person has melded his private and public "selves" into a unified personality. At this stage of his development, he will consider himself a gay person wherever he goes and in whatever he chooses to do. Although he will not likely wear signs announcing his sexuality, neither will he go to great lengths to hide who he is.

Many gay people never achieve this stage. For practical reasons, they may never feel it is safe or wise to come out in their workplaces, to homophobic family members, to ex-spouses (for fear of losing custody or visitation of children), or in their communities. Therapists may need to help their gay clients at this stage explore whether the fears they express about taking this last step are reality based or vestiges of internalized homophobia.

It is unlikely that a gay male survivor will present for therapy who was abused as a child while in this final stage of coming out. The youngest gay person I have met who seemed well integrated in terms of his sexuality was in his mid-20s.

Other Issues in Treatment With Gay Survivors

Separate from the coming-out issues outlined above, gays, like many other oppressed minority groups (and like incest survivors in general), suffer from substance abuse at much higher rates than the average population. For this reason, gay clients should always be assessed thoroughly for substance abuse and other addictions. I have discovered that many of my gay clients who are survivors will suffer from addictive sexual acting out (often coupled with alcohol or drug abuse), or the opposite, total sexual abstinence (or "sexual anorexia"). In fact, several gay male survivors with whom I have worked entered therapy not knowing they had been molested until after several months of sobriety from their addictions.

I have often found it helpful to reframe for my clients their "relationship" with substances, sexual acting out, and other addictions as a valuable "friend" they discovered to help them manage the pain they experienced from their abuse or their coming to terms with their sexuality when nothing and/or no one else was available to them. I have suggested that they consider letting go of these relationships, much as they would a friend whom they had outgrown or who had misused them, because this old "friend" was now getting in the way of their healing and moving forward in their lives.

Twelve-step programs have been a valuable resource for my clients. Many larger communities have Alcoholics Anonymous (AA), Sex and Love Addicts Anonymous (SLAA), Adult Children of Alcoholics (ACOA), and Survivors of Incest Anonymous (SIA) for gays and lesbians only. Some gay men and lesbians report feeling more comfortable in 12-step groups that are for gays and lesbians only, finding these a nurturing context for all aspects of themselves. Others appreciate a mixed group. Twelve-step programs can provide a ready-made community for gays and lesbians who may not yet have found a network of other gays and lesbians. These groups can meet many of the needs of gay people in early stages of recovery and coming out. Several reputable treatment centers currently exist that gear their programs exclusively to the gay and lesbian population. Whenever possible, I recommend referring gay clients to one of these facilities or to hospitals that recognize unique recovery needs of gays and lesbians and who advertise having a special track or special programming for gay and lesbian patients.

For many gay men, sexuality is split off from the rest of how they define themselves. In my practice, I have talked with many men who reported that they had been sexually active with other men for several years before they realized they were gay. Many communities have public places rumored or known to offer opportunities for men to meet and have sex anonymously. Many of these public sex areas draw men who are married and who, even though they are sexual with other men several times a week, define themselves as heterosexual. Gay men who frequent such places sometimes experience a sense of belonging and community they have never known before. Although they may not know the names or other personal information about the men they meet there, they have intimate knowledge about each other sexually, and over time develop a sense of camaraderie, familiarity, and a thrill from having shared the experience and risk of this illegal and potentially dangerous activity. Some report feeling for the first time that they "fit" in a group of men and don't have to worry about feeling odd or different.

In some regions, the only opportunities for gay men to meet is at public sex areas or through other anonymous means. Many gay men who frequent these meeting places prefer the anonymity agreements among the participants because they claim it heightens their eroticism. They may be "turned on" by the idea that they are doing something clandestine and "naughty," for which they might get arrested, or might end up meeting a stranger who may be rough with them. For others, perhaps those who have much to lose if their sexuality was known by others in their community, frequenting cruising areas is frightening and a deep source of shame and humiliation. They may travel many miles away from their hometowns to avoid meeting up with someone who could report back to their families and coworkers. Although I would not recommend that therapists help their gay clients find these places, I would encourage them to understand the function that these places or networks serve to closeted gay people, and to realize and explore with the client the realistic costs involved in taking further steps toward coming out in a fuller way versus being found out.

Not all gay men who "cruise" public sex areas are abuse survivors. Likewise, not all are sex addicts. Therapists of gay clients who cruise must approach this issue with their clients only after they have been able to build a trusting relationship, and then only with a truly open, nonjudgmental stance.

Many men will not experience their membership in the cruising community as harmful, and will not wish to give it up. They may view their participation as a healthy expression of freedom from oppressive messages about "normal" (meaning heterosexual) sexuality. For gay clients who understand their cruising behavior as harmful and who wish to change, therapists should be aware that some grieving may accompany the change. Clients may first need to have a clear understanding of alternatives for getting these specific needs met elsewhere and then work through the various issues perceived as barriers to the alternatives. Whereas cruising offers quick and easy (although limited) intimacy, joining gay social groups calls for courage, strength, and positive self-esteem, which a client may believe he lacks. Professionally facilitated gay men's therapy or support groups (and programs such as SLAA) often provide the only safe, transitional access to other aspects of the gay community for these men.

Once trust is established, therapists should question their gay clients about other forms of sexual addiction, including telephone sex (1-900 numbers), the use of personals advertisements to meet other men for compulsive sex, or computer sex networks (for meeting men or to exchange writing about sex in "real time," often for hours at a stretch).

Gay Culture

Some of the traps and dead ends in the matrix of this healing "game" with gay male survivors are yet to be discovered. No easily identifiable "gay subculture" exists. Instead, there are many subgroups, sometimes having little in common with each other. Every city and region, and every cultural and ethnic group of gay people within these regions, are likely to have formed their own social, political, and cultural networks, each with individual values, codes of behavior, and cultural norms. Even if it were possible to learn about all the different aspects of the norms of the subgroups in any region, they all would likely change in a short time.

It is commonly understood that the gay movement in the United States is still in its adolescence. Although present throughout history as an identified subculture in the United States, it has only "come out of the closet" in the past 25 years. As we know, adolescence is a time for finding one's identity and for great and rapid change and development. Since 1969, the gay community in the United States has gone through many transformative stages. For responsible assessment, it is important for clinicians to know how their gay clients may have participated or been affected at various stages of their personal growth by the development of the gay community. For instance, knowing when and in what context the client came out, and what cultural factors may have influenced his values and his lifestyle, can help the clinician understand how the client views himself and his sexuality.

Most large cities have a gay community that often consists of some of the following: gathering places, such as gay bars, restaurants, coffeehouses, or community centers; church groups, which are either subgroups of mainstream churches, or are gay and lesbian only, and include Christian, Jewish, Pagan, and other spiritual sects; social groups, such as community potluck dinner clubs, gourmet clubs, "Gays for Patsy" (Patsy Cline fan club), video and book clubs; activity organizations, including gay and lesbian outdoor clubs, gay sports teams, antique car owner clubs, motorcycle clubs, ballroom or western dance clubs, and gay and lesbian community choirs; service organizations, such as helpers for people with AIDS, community-sponsored Big Brothers/Big Sisters for gay and lesbian teens, and gay and lesbian business guilds; and political groups, such as Act-Up, Queer Nation, Black Men/White Men Together, and other groups that promote racism consciousness raising or offer support for ethnic and racial minorities within the gay community, or local groups that form to work on promoting a gay rights agenda or to organize local gay rights marches.

It is essential for clinicians working with gay clients to be informed about the organizations existing in their area and nearby areas to help clients reduce their isolation. This information often can be found in gay publications, distributed in bookstores, libraries, and gay bars. Many communities have a "gay hotline" service advertised in the yellow pages that disseminates information about community events and services. Colleges and universities often have gay student organizations that collect information on a variety of services in the larger community.

If we allow our impressions of gay culture to be based solely on portrayals in the mainstream media, we would believe limiting and harmful stereotypes. Aspects of gay culture most often highlighted by the mainstream media paint mixed, confusing images of gay people: on one hand, laughable and meek, on the other, dreaded militants posing a dangerous threat to the moral fabric of society; either a mincing, effeminate hairdresser, or an angry, radical AIDS terrorist; cross-dressing drag queens, or sadomasochistic leather men. Whereas it would seem strange for many of us to read in a newspaper headline: "Heterosexual Man Robs National Bank," we often fail to question the relevance when a headline reads: "Gay Man Arrested for Disturbing the Peace."

In truth, gay people are as varied in dress, manner, appearance, career choices, interests, and proclivities as their heterosexual counterparts. The vast majority of gay people would not stand out in a crowd as different in any noticeable way. Many gay people pay high emotional costs to hide themselves, and most are quite behind the scenes and invisible in our culture.

Those who have found the courage to "go public"—some out of need (gay men who are HIV positive and fighting for funding of AIDS research, for example, or others who are unable to "act straight"), or some out of self-love and affirmation (having achieved Coleman's "integration")—are typically the ones who have television or news photographers' cameras turned on them. In their willingness to offer themselves as public role models, they have helped form a visible, although somewhat skewed, picture of the gay male subculture.

CASE HISTORIES

Jeff

Jeff was an intelligent, attractive, 18-year-old, first-year student at the local university when he was referred to me for counseling by the university health services for support with coming-out issues. Jeff knew he was gay when he was in high school, and he attended a support group for gay teens. He had been having difficulty fitting in socially with the university gay scene and was presenting at health services several times a week with a range of somatic complaints.

During our first session, it was clear that Jeff was worried about making a positive first impression. He had difficulty making eye contact, talked rapidly, and asked many personal questions. I learned that he had asked to be referred to a gay therapist but was not told directly that I was gay. His questions hinted at wanting to know my sexual orientation. When I asked if my being gay would make a big difference to him, he admitted he likely would be frightened if he knew this about me. We explored this further, and Jeff eventually shared that he believed I would want to be sexual with him if I was gay, yet he also said he believed I couldn't help him if I wasn't gay. After assuring Jeff that I would not be sexual with him, or in any other way inappropriate, we agreed together that initially I would not tell him my orientation, and that he could ask again if he remained curious once he had a sense about whether I could be trusted, understanding, and helpful. He seemed relieved, and we were able to proceed with the interview.

Jeff asked about my orientation again after our third session. After reiterating my commitment to never make sexual advances or be inappropriate in any other way, and sharing that I am gay, our working relationship began to grow and develop rapidly. Jeff took many risks in being honest about his feelings toward me and perceptions about me in our work together. Jeff felt shame about virtually all of his feelings. A session in which Jeff took a particularly large risk often would be followed by one in which he would feel mistrusting. Jeff responded well to my assurances that he need not trust me too much or too soon, and that he would likely feel safest if he knew he was staying vigilant about keeping himself safe. Jeff admitted that he continued to feel suspicious of me throughout most of the first year in therapy.

Jeff initially presented a puzzling image. Although he appeared on the surface as an appropriate 18-year-old college student in terms of interests, intellect, awareness of social issues, and physical appearance, beneath the surface he was anxious and tended to regress to a very young stage of development in his worldview and problem-solving abilities. He would often become distressed when people were not kind or fair toward him or with each other and didn't follow the rules or act as he believed they should. He tried establishing a "teacher's pet" relationship with his professors and reported often feeling rejected by his peers. He had only a few friends he considered to be close.

Jeff was the oldest of three boys from a working-class family. His parents divorced when Jeff was 6 years old. His mother remarried soon after and divorced again when Jeff was 10 years old. Initially, Jeff described his relationship with his mother as positive and supportive. He had difficulty being away at school and away from her. Other than times when he had visited with his father, his being at the university was the first time he had ever been away from his mother.

As Jeff grew more trusting, he revealed a history of physical and emotional abuse from his father, which he had been told had precipitated his parents' divorce. Both his father and stepfather were alcoholic, as were his grandfathers on both sides. Early in treatment, Jeff disclosed that he, too, drank to excess regularly, and agreed he had a drinking problem. Jeff started attending Alcoholics Anonymous soon after and remained sober throughout the next 4 years of our psychotherapy work together.

Alcohol had served as a means for Jeff to relax his fears and socialize with other gay students. His excessive drinking and immature (and

sometimes promiscuous) behavior when he was drunk eventually resulted in social alienation from Jeff's peer group. Once sober, many
fears regarding closeness with other men came to the surface. Jeff
reported several incidents when he was drinking where he felt overpow-
ered sexually. Once sober, Jeff had great difficulty being around men to
whom he felt attracted. He felt afraid that he would again be overpow-
ered and unable to set limits with men he wanted to date. He realized
that he had unreasonably high expectations that the men he met would
take care of him emotionally and physically. He reported that he felt
most attracted to men close to his father's age.

After several months of sobriety, Jeff disclosed that he had compulsive desires to dye or cut his hair, to wear T-shirts with pro-gay slogans
on them, and to dress in ways that provoked homophobic men on
campus and in town to sneer or threaten violence. He developed a
fascination with hitchhiking and used poor judgment in entering cars
late at night. Inevitably, when Jeff was harassed or threatened, he
reported in therapy that he did not understand what role he played in
these things happening to him. At first, he blamed his victimization on
societal homophobia and saw no connection between his behavior and
the reactions. Eventually, with my gentle confrontations, he started
accepting some responsibility for keeping himself safe. I used "inner-
child" concepts and language with Jeff throughout my work with him.
It was useful to remind him occasionally of the commitment he had
made during an early session to keep his "inner child" safe from further
trauma. Jeff agreed to approach his compulsive behaviors using a
12-step model, similar to how he gained mastery over his other identified addictions, and experienced great success in a short amount of time.

Jeff also realized that he was a compulsive eater and masturbator.
As the compulsive behaviors were revealed throughout his treatment,
Jeff was able to understand that he had a deep-seated need to feel abused
and frightened, as he had been as a child, and then to soothe the feelings
with behaviors that masked or distracted from the distress and pain.
Through exploring Jeff's transference feelings in therapy (approximately 9 months into his sobriety), Jeff was able to share fantasies he
had about the therapy relationship that included sex. Eventually, Jeff
revealed that it was confusing and painful for him to allow himself to
feel cared for by me without having a sexual connection. Around this
time, Jeff started having his first clear memories of his father sexually
abusing him. He came to understand that he had associated being cared
for with sex because of the incest with his father.

Over several months, we explored Jeff's childhood memories in our sessions, keeping the therapy environment a "safe place" through clear boundaries and positive regard. Jeff came to remember that from age 4 until his parents' separation at age 6, his mother worked an evening shift and Jeff was left alone with his father. He remembered his father's suspicion, jealousy, and anger at his mother for working. Jeff's father drank heavily and became emotionally and physically abusive with Jeff. Eventually, Jeff was made to perform oral sex on his father. Months later, in treatment, Jeff reported he had painful sensations in his rectum that lasted hours at a time, and this went on for weeks. He saw a doctor, who could not diagnose a medical explanation for the symptom. In therapy, hypnosis helped uncover a memory of anal rape by Jeff's father when Jeff was 5 years old. Once this was revealed, the physical symptom cleared and Jeff made the courageous decision to confront his father about the abuse.

Jeff attempted to gain support from his mother for confronting his father and discovered in the process that he had strong feelings about his mother's passive involvement in the abuse. She expressed doubt about the validity of his memories. She denied remembering Jeff begging her not to leave him alone with his father. She finally admitted that her decision to end the marriage came only after an incident where she was raped by his father, not as a result of his abusive behavior toward Jeff, as he had been told. Jeff's mother was not supportive of his work in therapy, and at one point she cautioned him about therapists who planted "false memories" in their patients. Later, she directly asked Jeff to stop exploring the past because she could not handle what he was uncovering. After making several attempts to establish appropriate boundaries with her that she repeatedly violated, he severed all contact with her. Jeff concluded that his mother had behaved in an "emotionally incestuous" way with him for many years.

Jeff's father denied the accusations of sexual abuse. He had in recent years become a born-again Christian and had stopped drinking. The accusations were extremely threatening to him, and he immediately obtained a lawyer to protect himself. Jeff eventually decided not to file formal charges, primarily because of the expense of legal representation, the time it would take away from his studies, and the lack of support he felt to go through with the process. He considered it a personal triumph, however, that he had told his father what he remembered and how he felt about what had been done to him. It represented a step away from a lifelong pattern of victimization and became a model that he would often use for asserting himself when faced with fear.

For most of Jeff's early life, he had wished for a caring relationship with an older man who would provide unconditional love, safety, and support, and who would help him define and maintain appropriate distance from his mother—the very things he did not get from his father. When he came out to himself at age 15, Jeff's emotional needs blended with his sexual feelings and needs, and his ideal father image became his model for an ideal lover.

Understandably, Jeff had strong transference feelings in therapy. Many sessions focused on helping him work through his disappointment and anger at my unavailability to either adopt or become lovers with him. Although these feelings felt painful and shameful, working through this grief was an important part of his recovery.

Jeff also struggled with confusion that came from a deeply rooted association of sex with violence. He was often uncomfortable when he dated men who were not in some way abusive toward him or whom he could not provoke to become violent or emotionally abusive.

Because Jeff had been sexually abused in his "pre-coming-out" stage of sexual development, when he later came out as gay and discovered incest memories, he initially believed the abuse was the cause for his homosexuality. Later, when he accepted that the abuse likely had no bearing on his orientation, his worries instead focused on beliefs that he was abused because his father sensed he was gay. (A variation on the common theme of survivors assigning responsibility for the abuse to themselves.) Jeff remembered being shamed by his father for being effeminate and being compared with his brother, who was more athletic and gender traditional in his interests. As far as Jeff knows, his brother was not molested. Jeff remembered that, as a child, he had often wished he were a girl, believing that as a girl he would have been spared his father's abuse and shaming.

Jeff's progress in working through his abuse issues paralleled his growth and progress through his psychosexual development, as well as other developmental processes. When Jeff gave up drinking and started working the steps in Alcoholics Anonymous, he began to feel more self-reliant and more secure living away from home. His need to ally himself with his professors lessened, and his fear of peer friendships decreased. When Jeff accepted that his behavior had a direct impact on his safety, he began holding his parents accountable for their behavior toward him. Jeff realized he wasn't ready for sexually intimate relationships, and that feelings associated with having sex were too much to cope with while he was in therapy. He chose to become celibate, thus putting on hold his working through the experimentation stage of his coming-out process. This freed him to focus on completing tasks from earlier stages of the coming-out process and other unresolved developmental issues. Jeff improved at discerning potentially dangerous people from safe people, and felt less a victim in his world and more successful in his studies and his personal friendships. When Jeff finally grieved and then accepted the loss of ideal, caring parents, he proved more willing and better able to take care of himself.

When Jeff ended treatment, he was "sober" from alcohol, overeating, compulsive masturbation, and negative attention seeking. He reported feeling good about his friendships, his sense of himself as a male and as gay, and his ability to maintain boundaries with family and friends. Jeff was confident about finding a good job when school ended, and he had made sound choices about his future that took personal safety and other emotional needs into consideration. Although still not ready for relationships, Jeff had a positive outlook about eventually meeting and developing a meaningful relationship with a man.

Jeff experienced a setback in maintaining safe boundaries with his mother when he graduated from college. His desire to have family attend his graduation activated a new level of grief. Ultimately, Jeff felt it best to withdraw an invitation made to his mother to attend the ceremony, although only after experiencing a great deal of turmoil and some "slipping" in his addictions. As of our final session (2 months after college graduation), Jeff planned to have no contact with his family and was considering moving far away from his parents.

Jack

Jack, 38 years old, had worked through some of the layers of treatment with gay survivors in previous therapy with another clinician. The oldest of five siblings, Jack grew up in a Catholic family, characterized by an alcoholic and abusive father and a passive, codependent mother referred to by friends and family as "saintly" in her devotion to her family and to the church. Jack married his high school sweetheart when he graduated from college, and within the first year of marriage, his wife was pregnant with their first child. Jack experienced a great deal of stress and some depression after the birth of a second child, and sought counseling from a therapist referred by their parish priest. The therapist targeted his having grown up in an alcoholic household as a major factor in Jack's depression and referred Jack to Adult Children of Alcoholics, which he attended regularly for 3 years.

When Jack was 34 years old, he was arrested for having sex with a man in a public rest area. At this point, Jack had been having sex with

men on a regular basis for 8 years. His wife had believed he was at
ACOA meetings all that time he was away from home. Jack and his wife
started couples counseling with the same therapist Jack had seen before.
The issue of Jack's arrest had been regarded by the therapist only as a
symptom of communication problems in the marriage because of Jack's
history as an adult child of an alcoholic.

After a year and a half of working with the therapist individually
and with his wife, and shortly following the death of his father, Jack was
able to recognize that he was gay. Previously, he had believed that as
long as he did not kiss another man, he was still heterosexual. Jack now
believes that the therapist's investment in keeping the marriage viable
was a major barrier to his coming out.

Jack came to see me for therapy when he responded to a flyer I had
distributed about a therapy group for gay men. During the screening
interview, he had many questions regarding homosexuality and much
anxiety about joining a group for gay men. Jack had known many gay
men, but he had talked with only a few. He was determined to make his
marriage work and was concerned that joining the group would sabotage
his chances, although he knew he needed to explore what he referred to
as his "gay side."

After 10 group sessions, Jack indeed felt threatened by feedback
from several group members who, like Jack, had once been married but
who left their wives after realizing they were gay. Jack chose to pursue
individual therapy with me instead of further work in the group. We
explored the issue of his sexual acting out. I learned that even though
he had curtailed his visits to public rest areas for many months after his
arrest, he felt as if he were "going crazy" and "had to get back there to
make the feelings go away." At the point of our starting individual
therapy, Jack reported he was going to the cruising area on a daily basis.
He reported feeling much more shame and fear about this activity since
his arrest. Before the arrest, Jack had had sex with men to manage stress,
but after being arrested, it became a source of stress.

The cruising area was the only place Jack reported feeling accepted
for who he was and where he felt his world was not falling apart.
Pleasing men sexually in an anonymous atmosphere had become a way
for Jack to feel he belonged to a community of men, and as long as he
could keep it secret, his "cruising" was an outlet for his homosexual
orientation without concern that his self-identity as a good (i.e., heterosexual) Catholic family man would collapse.

It was several more months before Jack could admit to his wife that
he was continuing to have sex with men. His greatest fear was that she

would leave him (which to Jack would mean that he had failed as a heterosexual and a good Catholic), and that he would end up an alcoholic like his father. Both Jack and his wife wanted the marriage to work, and began working together with me in couples therapy. Jack's wife was referred to a support group for women who were married to gay men. Although still hesitant about giving up sex with men in rest areas, Jack agreed to attend Sex and Love Addicts Anonymous to explore the compulsive aspects of his sexuality.

Eventually, Jack accepted that he was a sex addict and began working with a sponsor in SLAA who helped him establish a "bottom line" for his sex addiction. After 7 months of "sobriety," Jack expressed interest in joining the support group for gay men again and began exploring alternative, self-affirming avenues for meeting other gay men. He joined a Catholic gay men's organization and, with the support of other group members, started experiencing improved self-esteem. Jack made a gay friend for the first time. He was able to communicate with his wife that he no longer felt able to be sexual with her, whereas previously he had held onto hope for a sexual component of their marriage. Meanwhile, with group support, Jack's wife was getting stronger in stating what she needed from the relationship.

Several months later, Jack developed an attraction for a man he met at the Catholic gay men's group and asked this man out on a date. As the relationship grew stronger and became sexual, Jack experienced a flashback for the first time that dated back to his ninth birthday. He remembered going on a camping trip with a much-loved uncle who was a Catholic priest, and being coerced into having oral sex with the uncle. After the initial memory, he remembered several incidents of his father coming into his room drunk and passing out on his bed, and at least on one occasion waking up and feeling his father fondling his genitals. Jack has since focused his treatment on sexual abuse issues, and he recently joined a mixed (gay and straight) therapy group for male survivors.

Jack recalls feeling attracted to his uncle prior to his being molested. He had been grateful for the invitation by the uncle to go camping and was excited when their conversation became sexually focused. He realizes now that he felt betrayed, overwhelmed, and "numb" after the uncle had sex with him, and recalls the uncle blaming him and making him pray for forgiveness for the "sin" he committed.

Because Jack was in his "pre-coming-out" stage of development when he accepted the invitation from his uncle to go camping, the sexual abuse by the uncle caused him to bury some of the gay feelings that had started to surface but had not yet been named. For many years, Jack fought against the memories of his abuse by repressing the memory (as other children his age often do) and by denying his gay sexuality (by "acting straight" and "bargaining" that as long as he hadn't kissed another man, he was really heterosexual). Jack's Catholic, antigay upbringing, and the fact that he was abused by a priest who labeled the incest as Jack's "sin," helped reinforce the shame of Jack's victimization and homosexuality. Jack unconsciously attempted to heal from the repressed memories of abuse by "mastering," or repetitively and compulsively being sexual with men and acting out dynamics of his abuse. Jack began to work through and deal with his sexual orientation in therapy only after his father died, and when he was able to reduce the addictive activities that had numbed his feelings. Memories of the incest by his uncle and his father began to surface. When he had come to healthier terms with his sexual orientation, Jack began to heal from the abuse and from the many other issues associated with his alcoholic father.

The sexual abuse experiences, combined with being raised in a repressive family background, caused Jack to remain in his pre-coming-out stage of sexual development for many years into adulthood. Sexual abuse and dysfunctional family dynamics also contributed to stunting his emotional growth, leaving him feeling like a young adolescent much of the time in terms of general problem-solving abilities and social skills. Both aspects of Jack's developmental needs required attention in treatment before he could begin integrating his experiences and feel like he was moving ahead with his life.

Currently, Jack is still married, has come out to his children as a gay man, and is involved in an organization for married gay men as well as my gay men's therapy group. With support from his Catholic gay men's group, he has reconciled that he can be good, gay, and Catholic, and he continues to negotiate a viable (although nonsexual) relationship with his wife while recognizing and validating his orientation toward men. He occasionally struggles with compulsive sexual activity at cruising areas, but he is working toward the goal of finding and establishing a sexually monogamous relationship with another man, perhaps one who is also married to a woman. He is currently free from serious depression and most PTSD symptoms, and generally reports less conflict in his self-esteem and self-worth.

Conclusion

Effective treatment of gay male sexual abuse survivors requires that clinicians become familiar with the unique psychosexual developmental issues facing gay and lesbian people. Sexual abuse will likely affect a gay youth differently depending on the interplay of two important factors: his age (or stage in chronological development) and the stage in his coming-out process, in addition to the usual influences affecting all survivors of childhood abuse and incest. Assessing the impact of abuse from this dual developmental perspective is essential in planning a treatment approach for the gay client's healing process.

As adult survivors seeking treatment for childhood abuse, gay male clients present a unique challenge to nongay clinicians, who may be unfamiliar or uncomfortable with the gay male subculture or who may not have examined or resolved the homosexual feelings or experiences that they have had. Cultural homophobia, heterosexism, and internalized oppression often surface in treatment. Historical oppression of gays by the mental health profession is an obstacle for gay male survivors seeking help and a challenge for clinicians in the field to rectify and overcome. The gay and nongay communities must commit to creating safe and affirming environments, especially for gay youth, and alternatives to settings that reinforce use and dependence on drugs, alcohol, and compulsive sex.

Clinicians and protective caseworkers who wish to be useful to gay clients are advised to examine their own prejudices and homophobia; know about community resources for gay clients; consult with and refer to gay clinicians; help make their agencies "gay friendly"; and read literature about the gay community and about clinical issues with gay clients.

9

Lesbians and Sexual Child Abuse

MARYELLEN BUTKE

The inclusion of this chapter on lesbians and sexual abuse in a book on multicultural issues in sexual abuse is both relevant and timely. Specific concerns for and about lesbians are often overlooked in the literature. Social service providers may not know what to do because of this gap. For decades, lesbian women have "passed" as heterosexual and therefore have not been studied extensively as a group in their own right.

Although there is some reference to lesbians and sexual abuse in the published literature (Bass & Davis, 1988; Courtois, 1988; Davis, 1991; Dinsmore, 1991; Loulan, 1987; Maltz & Holman, 1987), adequate review of the salient issues faced by lesbians who were abused sexually is lacking. Lesbian survivors face particular concerns that may differ from those of their heterosexual peers. In an extensive study of 930 women conducted in the San Francisco area, Russell (1986) found that 38% of the women she surveyed had been sexually abused before the age of 18. Loulan (1987) conducted a survey of 1,566 lesbian women and also found that 38% of the women in her survey had been abused sexually. Thus, because there is a one-in-three chance

Author's Note:

The author would like to acknowledge the assistance of and careful critiques from her colleagues at Women's Psychotherapy Associates, particularly Lynn McCarthy and Lee Weille, as well as Jean Twomey and Cathy Curtis. She would also like to thank the women who agreed to be interviewed for this chapter and who shared their experiences as lesbians who have been abused sexually. Finally, she would like to thank the lesbian abuse survivors she treats, for their continued courage and strength.

236

of a woman being abused sexually as a child, and because all lesbians are women, there is a high likelihood that a vast number of lesbians are affected in some way by the issue of sexual abuse—either as survivors, as partners of survivors, or as friends of someone who has been abused sexually.

This chapter is based on my clinical work with lesbians who are survivors of childhood sexual abuse. Currently, approximately one third of my work is with lesbians who were abused sexually. I work in a women's psychotherapy practice in Providence, Rhode Island, and am identified as a lesbian. The quotes throughout this chapter come from a variety of sources, including interviews with clients, friends, and colleagues. All clinical material in this chapter has been disguised to protect confidentiality.

History and Cultural Context

Lesbians and gay men have been referred to as the "last invisible minority" (Hartman, 1993). The year 1994 marked the 25th anniversary of the Stonewall revolt in New York City, which served as a pivotal marker in the history of lesbians and gay men. Stonewall was a turning point in which gay men and lesbians demanded recognition and fought back against years of discrimination and oppression. More recently, with the tragedy of the AIDS epidemic, lesbians and gay men have organized to form a collective voice. Initially, the fight focused on the need to find a cure for AIDS. With increasing power in numbers and community strength, the work has become more political and all encompassing. The election of President Clinton and the heightened attention to gays and lesbians in the military have brought gay and lesbian issues to center stage. Certainly, it is a time of "revolution and backlash" (Hartman, 1993). Lesbians and gay men are demanding the same rights as their heterosexual peers—the right to work, live, form partnerships, raise children, and love, free from discrimination.

In most of the United States, the rights of lesbians and gay men are not protected by law. Lesbians and gay men have been fired from their jobs, lost children in custody battles, been physically and verbally assaulted, lost housing, and been kept from marrying because of their sexual orientation. Many lesbians and gay men have been disowned by family members as well because of whom they love. Until 1973, homosexuality was labeled a psychiatric disorder by the American Psychiatric Association, and lesbians and gay men were counseled, often aggressively, in an attempt to alter their sexual orientation (Bayer, 1981).

Today, researchers are studying the "causes" of homosexuality. Krajeski (1986) states that "customarily, the research literature has spoken of the etiology of homosexuality which in itself disclosed an inherent bias since the word etiology is ordinarily used in medicine to refer to disease states" (p. 13). However, behind the question of the causal factors in homosexuality is often the overt or covert question, "Who would *choose* this lifestyle?" This argument fails to view homosexuality as a positive, healthy lifestyle. Although there is current debate about research investigating genetic "causes" of homosexuality, it should be noted that "neither genetic nor other biological origins for sexual orientation have been ruled out" (Krajeski, 1986, p. 14). It is likely that some interaction of environment and biology are at work, perhaps to differing degrees for different people, making the development of sexual orientation complex and multidetermined.

This question of choice is often discussed in the lesbian community. For some women, their lesbianism has been something they have known and felt since they were young children. For others, lesbianism is a choice, an alternative lifestyle that they discovered and chose for themselves instead of heterosexuality. Many women describe their lesbianism as choosing to be with women as opposed to turning away from men.

Shively and DeCecco (1977) describe sexual identity as being composed of a number of different aspects, with sexual orientation being one component. Kinsey (1948) developed a 7-point rating scale that includes both sexual feelings and behaviors and views sexual orientation on a continuum. Exclusive heterosexuality is on one end of the scale and exclusive homosexuality is on the other. Thus sexual orientation is not seen as fixed and dichotomous but rather as a continuum. A person's sexual orientation may change over the life cycle. Because of the climate in our culture and the adverse treatment of lesbians and gay men, sexual orientation as lesbian or gay may not emerge until later in life.

Lukes and Land (1990) have used the term *biculturality* to refer to lesbians and gay men who bridge two different cultures—the heterosexual, dominant culture, and the lesbian or gay culture. In addition, lesbians may belong to another minority group because of their race or ethnicity. Indeed, lesbians have a "culture" of their own, often referred to as "the women's community," which includes its own set of norms, values, belief systems, and taboos. Although cultural norms may vary according to particular subgroupings, it is also possible to see common themes and similarities.

Certainly, one thread of connection among lesbians is the bond formed by being a member of an oppressed minority group. Women in the lesbian community, particularly those identified as feminists, often share an understanding about the roots of oppression, stemming from patriarchy. Perhaps because of this oppression, lesbians have joined together to create their own culture and community. This includes women's organizations and social groups, music, art, sporting events, political events, coffeehouses, bookstores, literature, restaurants, and bars. Out of the bonds of oppression has come a community rich with history and diversity.

Special Issues for Lesbian Survivors

Community Responses to Sexual Abuse

How does the lesbian community view sexual abuse? What supports can members of the lesbian community offer to the survivors and partners among them?

Sexual abuse is discussed openly within much of the lesbian community. Lesbians who also identify as feminists likely share a common understanding about issues of oppression with a keen awareness about the prevalence and impact of violence perpetrated against women and children. Shared beliefs about the troubling aftermath of trauma and the need for intervention and treatment are also likely. Thus disclosing one's history as a survivor in the lesbian community will likely be met with some degree of understanding and support. A woman describes her experience of disclosing her history to her close friends:

> My lesbian friends freaked out at first to learn that I was a survivor, because they couldn't believe that someone would hurt me. Then, they were incredibly supportive and extra attentive to me. They wanted to learn what they could about sexual abuse, and they came with me to talks and workshops. They've never let me down. (Sarah, 34, speech therapist, abused by her father)

Another woman describes her experience as she began to remember past abuse:

> I was worried that no one would believe me, but that wasn't true at all. My friends were incredibly supportive. They often felt the feelings that

I couldn't yet acknowledge about what had happened—like the anger and grief. (Annie, age 32, psychotherapist, abused by her father)

This willingness to acknowledge sexual abuse and support its members through the difficult process of recovery can be seen as a strength of the lesbian community.

At the same time, there are certain taboos in the lesbian community, particularly when it comes to the issue of abuse committed by women. Because abuse is most often perpetrated by men, there can be a tendency to minimize or deny the occurrence of abuse committed by females. Even when this abuse is acknowledged, it may be seen as less harmful than abuse perpetrated by a man. Lesbians have reported feeling silenced when women do not want to hear their stories of abuse by another woman. A woman who was abused sexually as a teenager by an older woman, a teacher and mentor, says:

Everyone knew that there was a relationship between us, but no one seemed to think there was anything wrong with it. After I came out in college, I was reluctant to talk about that relationship, because I didn't think anyone would really see it as a violation. It's seen as cool to have a relationship with an older woman who can introduce you to lesbian culture. But it wasn't cool to me. It was really abusive. (Pam, 29, counselor, abused by her teacher)

In her study of women who were abused sexually by an older, trusted female, Myers (1992) quotes a participant who addressed the need to face abuse by women:

I want people to know what's happening . . . to know it happens. To know that it's just as devastating. I want lesbians to know that women abuse, too. I want feminists to know that women abuse, too. I'm a really strong feminist and I love women, but I'm really tired of the brand of feminism that says men are awful, men are abusive, men are violent, and that women are angels. That's bullshit. Obviously, there's a huge power dynamic that goes on between men and women that isn't there for women and women, but women are abusive. Women are violent. Women are capable of it, too. I want people to know that.

Similarly, a survivor in the lesbian community may have a more difficult time receiving support in addressing the complicated feelings she may have toward her mother, often for her lack of protection. Women, particularly feminists, may tend to emphasize the mother's victimization and her power-lessness, which contributed to her failure to protect her daughter. Although this position may be accurate, it can silence the survivor in her expression of feelings regarding her abuse and lack of protection, and thus may hinder the healing process.

Lesbians and the Mental Health System

In the lesbian community, entering therapy is fairly acceptable in most circles (Brown, 1989). However, upon entering the social service or mental health system, some lesbians are understandably cautious. Although I am known in the community as a lesbian and a feminist, I will often be asked about my experience with and attitude toward lesbians in a telephone screening. At times, clients conceal their sexual orientation from professionals until they feel safe or comfortable enough to disclose this information. This issue may be even more complicated if the woman seeking treatment is a mother. Many lesbians with children fear that their children will be removed if their sexual orientation is revealed. Because most lesbians have suffered from oppression because of stereotyping and denigration of their lifestyle, women want to be assured that in asking for help, they will not be victimized further.

Also, many agencies are not "user friendly" to lesbians, who often find themselves excluded when seeking treatment. This can include initial phone calls from intake staff asking about "marital status" to required forms that are not inclusive of alternative lifestyles.

> Annie reported her reluctance to engage in individual therapy because of a past experience with the mental health unit of an HMO. She told of attending an initial screening but finding that the questionnaire she was required to fill out left no place for her to openly say who she was. The client, an "out" lesbian, had to scratch out questions and write answers between the lines so she could accurately represent her lesbian lifestyle and relationship with her woman partner.

As therapists, we must ensure that our language, forms, and waiting room create an atmosphere that is friendly to lesbian clients and that invite clients to tell us about their lives. Without this awareness, we may inadvertently display an assumption of heterosexuality, which serves to reenforce a lesbian's invisibility—particularly harmful for lesbians who feel they have been rendered invisible and voiceless by sexual abuse.

In considering issues of lesbians seeking treatment, it is important to look at other cultural issues as well concerning a woman's comfort level upon entering the mental health system. Even though therapy may be acceptable in the lesbian community, it may be taboo based on the cultural norms of the lesbian's ethnic group or social class. It is essential to understand from our client's perspective what it is like for her to be entering treatment. What are her values and beliefs regarding asking for help? What are the values of her family of origin? This understanding will further our ability to work with our clients and alert us to obstacles that may emerge in the treatment process.

Family Ties

Family issues may be central in the lives of lesbian clients who are also survivors. It is essential to assess a client's relationship with both family of origin and family of creation. Issues such as the identity of the person who abused, the extent of family knowledge of abuse, and the family's reaction to the woman's disclosure are paramount. In addition, issues regarding the client's lesbianism must be explored. Has she come out to her family of origin? If so, how was this information handled? Is she welcome to come home for family events? Can she bring her partner with her? Are there cutoffs from family of origin? If so, who initiated these disconnections and toward what end?

Regardless of whether the family of origin can be counted on for support, lesbians often create family for themselves. These families of creation can act as surrogate family and can offer support and comfort. This created family serves the function of family and should be called upon when assessing a client's supports. Families of creation should have equal status to the client's family of origin and should be active participants in the treatment process if the client so desires. This family can include partners, friends, ex-partners, and children.

Disclosures of Abuse and Sexual Orientation

Issues of disclosure as a lesbian and as a survivor of childhood sexual abuse may become entangled. The process of coming out—telling another person about one's sexual orientation—is repeated throughout the life cycle of a lesbian. As lesbians meet new people and form new relationships, they are consistently challenged with deciding whether to disclose their sexual orientation. A similar challenge may occur as well in dealing with issues of sexual abuse. Survivors of abuse often feel a need and desire to come out as well, sharing their history with those close to them. Disclosing one's sexual abuse history may be an important part of the healing process. Black (1982) coined the phrase "double duty" to refer to people who carry not just one label, such as "survivor," but have another one with which to contend as well. For lesbian survivors who are members of racial or ethnic minorities, this may extend to "triple duty."

If family members know about both the sexual abuse and sexual orientation, it is important to understand their response. One survivor said, "My mother thought I was accusing my stepfather of sexual abuse because, as a lesbian, I hated all men and was just trying to get back at them." Some women have reported that their families have chosen to face one issue and have minimized or denied the other. After disclosing her abuse history and her sexual orientation to her mother, a college student in treatment for abuse issues stated,

My mother seemed much more upset about my lesbianism than she did about my sexual abuse history, even though it was her father who abused me. I think that she couldn't deal with the abuse, so she focused on the lesbianism instead.

In my clinical experience, many lesbian survivors have been concerned that if they come out about both their sexual abuse and lesbianism, the two will become linked in the minds of those who hear them. One woman stated that when others found out about her sexual abuse history, a comment would often follow that suggested that she was a lesbian because of her sexual abuse experience. She understood this as a causal link that suggested that if she had not been "damaged" by the abuse, she would have been heterosexual and therefore "normal." Another woman stated that in forming new friendships, she often found herself coming out about both the sexual abuse history and her lesbianism in the same conversation. "It's like taking the friendship to a new level and sharing secrets about your life. If I'm going to tell one, then I'm going to tell the other, too." Thus, for a lesbian who has also been abused sexually, the issues of self-disclosure may be complex.

The Effects of Sexual Abuse on Sexuality

Sexual abuse often leads to questioning about all aspects of one's sexuality. How a woman views her sexual self and her feminine identity can all be affected by a history of abuse.

A woman coping with sexual abuse may have a distorted image of her body and her ability to function sexually. In a study on the long-term impact of childhood sexual abuse on sexual functioning in lesbian women, Johnson (1993) found that of 27 respondents, the majority indicated being affected in the areas of trust and intimacy in interpersonal relationships, level of enjoyment in sexual relationships, sexual inhibition, difficulty achieving orgasm, arousal problems, and inhibited sexual desire. However, in Loulan's (1987) survey of 1,566 lesbians, she found no significant differences in sexual functioning between women who reported a history of sexual abuse and those who did not. For those survivors who do experience difficulties, these can emerge as difficulty partnering because of trust and intimacy problems, continual reexperiencing of past traumatic events when being sexual, difficulty feeling comfortable experiencing bodily pleasure, or shutting down when being intimate. Maltz (1991) addresses ways in which survivors can alleviate the common sequelae of sexual trauma.

Feminine identity and self-concept can be affected by abusive experiences as well.

> I didn't want to be a woman because that meant being weak and getting hurt. I worked out a lot so that I could be strong and more masculine. I was never going to let myself get hurt again. (Paula, 21, student, abused by her father)

A woman's history of sexual abuse may make her ability to know, acknowledge, and accept her sexual orientation more difficult than it might be otherwise. I extend a caution, however, against viewing this in a linear and causal fashion, as in "this woman is a lesbian because she has been sexually abused by a man and therefore is not comfortable interacting with men sexually." This explanation is both overly simplistic and does not take into account the multidetermined factors connected with sexual orientation previously discussed. Also, because one in three women has been abused sexually and because the vast majority of abuse is perpetrated by men, we would expect a much higher percentage of lesbians in the population if a lesbian identity resulted from sexual abuse.

Johnson (1993) quotes a participant who is involved in an 8-year relationship with a woman but continually questions whether or not she is a lesbian. This woman asks, "How am I supposed to know what I would have been before the abuse? That choice was taken away from me. I'm not sure that I'll ever really be able to know the truth." Thus, even though this woman was involved in a long-term relationship with another woman, she continued to question her orientation, wondering if it was due to her abuse history. It is important to note that the majority of the lesbians with whom I work, and those with whom I met for this chapter, felt that their sexual orientation had not been determined by their sexual abuse history. Davis (1991) quotes a survivor as saying, "If I'm a lesbian because I was sexually abused, at least something good came out of it" (p. 205).

Ultimately, the goal of treatment for women who may struggle with this issue is to resolve their questions and confusion regarding whether or how their sexual orientation has been affected by their abuse. It is important that therapists refrain from encouraging a survivor toward any sexual orientation, and that they view lesbianism, heterosexuality, and bisexuality as well as a respite from sexuality as healthy alternatives. A therapist's erroneous conclusion that a woman's lesbianism is caused by her abuse history can leave the client feeling misunderstood and mistrustful of mental health professionals:

When Annie was in her 20s, she went for an initial screening at an HMO with a male psychologist. In the 30-minute interview that followed, the therapist asked her detailed questions about her relationship with her father and about her abuse history. Near the end of the interview, he concluded that her lesbianism was caused by her abuse history and by her lack of adequate male connection. The client left feeling angry, ashamed, and misunderstood. She never followed up with treatment and waited several years before seeking treatment again.

Many lesbians who are survivors of abuse will seek out lesbian therapists, wanting to begin the work with a clear understanding that their sexual orientation is not the focus of the treatment. A number of lesbians have contacted me for therapy to deal with abuse, stating that they do not want to have to explain or account for their lesbianism. Regardless of the sexual orientation or gender of the therapist, an exploration of the impact of abuse on the various aspects of a survivor's sexuality is essential.

Therapeutic Issues

Although safety and trust issues are key in our work with all abuse survivors, there are some special considerations in work with lesbian survivors of abuse. I will elaborate on two of these: boundary issues and issues of transference and countertransference.

Boundaries

Boundary issues are paramount in work with all survivors of abuse. Therapists often will be asked by survivors to self-disclose more than we may wish or be used to in our work. Authenticity is essential in work with abuse survivors. Because of past betrayal of trust, clients need to know that we are who we say we are, and they are likely to test us continually to find out if we are authentic. However, there is a difference between self-disclosure and authenticity. It is essential that we remain aware of our own boundaries and make thoughtful decisions about self-disclosure.

My tendency is to be more authentic in the real, here-and-now relationship. This means naming and taking responsibility for times that I make errors in the therapy. It also means giving a client honest feedback and feeling responses about the material they are discussing and, at times, being more self-disclosing in particular ways. For example, I generally tell clients where I will be going when I leave town. For many, my leaving evokes great fear about my safety and about whether I will come back to see them again. I find it useful to allay fears by providing limited, but concrete, information. I will also disclose very general, concrete information about myself such as my age, where I grew up, my university training, and whether or not I have children. I might also provide clients with some form of transitional object when this is therapeutically indicated. Most clients use this to internalize the soothing function I provide until they are able to soothe themselves.

Whether a therapist is heterosexual, bisexual, gay, or lesbian, his or her sexual orientation may be important to a client, and she may ask about this either in a telephone screening or during the initial session. We must be clear about our own boundaries regarding what we choose to tell our clients about ourselves and our lives (Gantrell, 1992). Because I am known in the community as a lesbian, and because clients have easy access to this information, I will readily disclose my sexual orientation. I also want to know what it means to the client to work with a lesbian therapist, and I do not make assumptions that I know what the meaning is for them. I do not, however, volunteer the information when it is not asked for, as demonstrated in the following example:

> Pam, a lesbian survivor of abuse, was referred to me when she moved to the area. During our first meeting, she spoke of her previous treatment, and how unsafe she felt discussing issues about her lesbian life with a heterosexual therapist whom she felt was homophobic. She asked me if I was homophobic. I told her that I done a great deal of work with lesbian clients and had worked on issues of both external and internalized homophobia. I asked her how she would know for herself whether or not she would be safe to explore these issues in the therapy. We went on to explore her own intuition and sense of trust in herself and her judgments, much of which were clouded because of the abuse. I asked her if she wanted to know about my sexual orientation, and she said that she didn't want that information yet.

All therapists should consider how they will respond to the question of sexual orientation. My colleague, who is heterosexual, recently co-led a therapy group for lesbians who were abused sexually. During the initial screening, several clients referred to their immediate comfort with her because she was a lesbian. She struggled with her need to come out to them as heterosexual, something she was not usually asked and not used to doing in individual therapy.

Another important question we will often be asked is whether or not we have experienced sexual abuse in our own histories. Again, it is important that we determine how and whether we wish to disclose that information. Will we disclose this in the initial interview if a client asks? Will we disclose later in the treatment process? I believe that there is no "right answer" to this question, although an argument can be made about the benefits and hazards. One benefit of a therapist's disclosure about his or her own sexual abuse history was noted by Annie:

> Annie had been exploring her history of sexual abuse for a number of years with a therapist. She struggled with a great deal of shame and self-loathing about her history. As a psychotherapist herself, she often felt isolated and worried that she would be seen as damaged if others knew her history. Eventually, her therapist disclosed that she, too, was

a survivor of sexual abuse. The therapist's comfort with herself in relation to her own abuse history provided a model for this client and served as a positive turning point in her treatment.

This issue of boundaries can present a unique challenge when both client and therapist are lesbians (Gantrell, 1992). In many cities, the lesbian community is small enough that there is a great likelihood that the therapist and client will come into contact with one another outside of the therapist's office. Dual relationships, which can seriously complicate the treatment process, frequently present themselves as challenges. The therapist and client may have friends in common, and it is likely that the client may have access to information about the life and relationship of the therapist.

Gantrell (1992) stresses the need for supervision and consultation regarding boundary issues. She refers to the therapist as the "guardian of the boundaries" in the therapy. Sexual abuse survivors have had boundaries violated and confused. Thus it is essential that therapists are clear about boundaries and limits. I have heard the lesbian community referred to as "incestuous" because of the many intricate connections of its members. Given that this is often the case, it is essential that we maintain appropriate boundaries with our clients. This includes never engaging in a sexual relationship with a client or former client, maintaining clarity about our role in the client's life, and always holding the needs and interests of the client as the priority in the treatment process. At the same time, we must take care not to be rigid and unmoving in our treatment. Hayward (1993) suggests that therapists' overly rigid boundaries and strict adherence to therapeutic rules can interfere with the process of mutuality in the therapist-client relationship.

It is important to address the issue of sexual misconduct within the therapeutic relationship. Statistics indicate that of all forms of abuse of clients by therapists, the second most common form of abuse is female therapists with female clients (after male therapists with female clients), currently comprising 13% of reported cases (Schoener, Milgram, Gonsiorek, Luepker, and Conroe, 1989). This statistic is alarming. Brown (1989) points out that lesbian therapists are often placed in high esteem in the lesbian community and therefore have an ethical responsibility to maintain high ethical standards. Brown also suggests that one possible explanation for the boundary violations may be due to lesbians' position as "members of at least two culturally disempowered groups, women and sexual minorities," which "may lead many of us to experience ourselves as lacking power" (p. 22). She suggests that if lesbian therapists feel disempowered about their role, they may have a decreased awareness about the ways in which they do hold power in the therapeutic relationships with their clients. This issue is further complicated in working with lesbians who are abuse survivors because boundaries have been violated in the past. Brown (1989) suggests that we view boundary violations on a continuum, so that all therapists can become aware of the ways in which they may violate clients' boundaries. Although I have focused on boundary issues with lesbian therapists treating lesbian clients, awareness about boundaries and their violation is essential work for all therapists, regardless of sexual orientation or gender. Boundary violations in the therapeutic relationship are extremely traumatic for people who have turned to a therapist for help. Ongoing supervision is essential. Therapists must also be prepared to treat survivors of abuse who have been further victimized in a therapeutic relationship.

Transference and Countertransference

Therapists often rely on the developing relationship between themselves and their clients to provide information about the clients' past and current relationships. The therapeutic relationship can be a vehicle for tremendous healing and transformation. Being aware of the development of a client's transference and the therapist's own countertransference feelings can assist the therapeutic process.

Although a thorough discussion about transference is beyond the scope of this chapter, I will raise a few salient issues regarding the treatment of lesbian survivors. As with all clients, many variations of transference may occur, and who we, as therapists, represent to our clients is multidetermined. Herman (1992) discusses the development of traumatic transference, "which [has] an intense, life-or-death quality unparalleled in ordinary therapeutic experience" (p. 136). Because of a client's lack of control and helplessness in the original traumatic relationship, she may have a need to idealize the therapist, seeing her or him as an "omnipotent rescuer." When we are unable to live up to that idealized view, the client may get enraged. "Because the patient feels as though her life depends upon her rescuer, she cannot afford to be tolerant; there is no room for human error" (p. 137). Thus an idealized transference may develop in the therapy, followed by a client's feeling of rage and disappointment when the therapist cannot live up to that image.

This idealized transference may take the form of a parental transference. With many clients, the therapist may become idealized as the all-good parent who was absent in childhood and who is capable of meeting the client's unmet needs. The development of this form of transference can be healing to some clients and may enable them to develop a trusting, nurturing relationship in which they can begin to internalize the functions of the "good enough" parent. However, clients will likely become disappointed and disillusioned when therapists are unable to provide or compensate for what was lost in childhood. The limitations of psychotherapy are inherently frustrating, and the therapist must be present for a client as she explores all aspects of her feelings about the therapist and the therapy relationship.

The therapist may also be ascribed various roles from the abusive dynamic in childhood. One such role is that of the nonprotective parent or caretaker. A therapist in this role may be unable to protect the client or keep her safe from harm in the present. The client may experience the therapist as being passive, as not really listening, or as never being helpful. Another role in the abuse dynamic is that of the abuser. In this form of transference, the client may experience the therapist's interventions, interpretations, and attempts to help as invasive, violating, and even harmful. She may believe that the therapist intends to harm or attack her, physically, sexually, or emotionally. The very nature of the therapeutic relationship lends itself to this type of transference. This is a relationship in which two people are alone together in a room, the client is intimately sharing the details of her life, and the therapist is in a position of power and authority because of his or her role in the relationship (MacKinnon & Miller, 1987).

Another form of transference that can serve as a reenactment of the relationship with the abuser is sexualized transference. It is essential to understand these feelings in context, looking for the ways in which the transference may replicate the client's past history of abuse. For abuse survivors, sexual feelings and loving feelings may become intertwined and can result in confusion about feelings toward the therapist. Other times, clients believe they are valued only for their sexual selves. Sexualized transference and its varied meanings are illustrated in the following example:

> A young woman in treatment was beginning to explore issues of her sexuality as well as her experiences of sexual abuse. As she began to accept her feelings toward other women, she developed a powerful sexualized transference toward me, which was worrisome for her. As we explored these issues in treatment, we began to understand its relationship to both the past sexual abuse as well as to her newly

forming identity as a lesbian. Eventually, she was able to talk about her powerful longings to be held and nurtured by me, but she had never known an intimate relationship that was not sexual. This client's isolation with regard to her lesbianism made me the first lesbian she knew, thus intensifying the transference. The therapy relationship was the first safe place where she could openly express her desires for another woman. As she became more comfortable with her sexual orientation and made contacts in the community, the sexualized transference rapidly diminished. Simultaneously, she was able to verbalize her maternal longings and began to separate this from her desires of a sexual nature. (Paula, age 26, counselor, abused by female caretaker)

It is likely that various forms of transference may occur throughout the therapeutic relationship. The form that the transference takes may or may not be affected by the gender and sexual orientation of the therapist. The identity of the offender may influence the client's reaction to the therapist. A number of the women I treat were abused by other women. As a therapist, I come to represent a woman in power who may use my power to harm them. Therapists must be aware of these issues and attend to them. Discussion of the transference dynamics in the therapy relationship can greatly enhance the work.

Therapists' countertransference feelings can serve as important tools to sort out what is happening in the treatment. In the above example with my client, Paula, I was unaware of having any sexual feelings toward her, although she was intensely sharing details about sexual feelings toward me. Instead, my countertransference feelings were consistently maternal, and I felt extremely protective of this client. I continually felt that what she really wanted was to get those maternal needs met in the treatment. Thus my own feelings toward my client enabled me to better understand her process and wishes.

Regardless of our sexual orientation or gender, therapists must be aware of their own feelings and attitudes about lesbianism and internalized or externalized homophobia. The following example is from my own experience:

A number of years ago, when I was working in a private psychiatric hospital, I used my office there to see private clients. I began to treat a young lesbian who was an abuse survivor. This woman was open about her lesbianism, and she often dressed in black leather, adorned with numerous buttons and stickers that revealed her sexual orientation. I shared a waiting room with the rest of the outpatient department, and I remember the anxiety that began prior to the arrival of my client. Would she come early? How long would she be sitting in the waiting room? Were there other people in the waiting room? What would the receptionist and my colleagues think about me because I was treating her? Although I was open at work about my sexual orientation, I watched my own internalized homophobia surface in relation to this young woman, wondering if *I* would be judged in some way because of my relationship to her.

Our countertransference reactions, including homophobia, will certainly differ depending on what we bring to the work. This includes our own sexual orientation, age, gender, race, ethnicity, social class, and cultural context. We must continually check in with ourselves to ensure that the clinical choices we make are in our clients' best interests and not in service of having our own needs met. Are we afraid of our client's anger toward us? Are we afraid that setting clear limits will place us in the role of the depriving parent? Are we pulled to rescue? Do our own dependency needs interfere with allowing our clients' dependency issues to emerge? If a client does place us in the role of the abuser, the victim, or the nonprotector, how do we respond? Awareness of our own internal reactions will enable us to avoid getting trapped in these roles. We are also less likely to act on our feelings of helplessness, sadism, dependency, or our need to rescue if we can understand and predict these possible dynamics.

Therapies

Individual Treatment

Most lesbian survivors who seek treatment usually end up in some form of individual psychotherapy. I believe that the therapeutic relationship in individual treatment provides the frame and healing environment in which powerful change can occur. Our clients come to us to address their issues of abuse, often at the hands of those whom they loved and trusted. By entering into a therapeutic alliance, these clients risk trusting again to explore the past and make changes for the future. Our task in treatment is to create a place of safety where clients can unfold. We need to convey our utmost respect for their undertaking. Establishing safety, especially for the severely traumatized client, can take a very long time. Together, we come to understand how she can develop this necessary sense of safety and trust. She can then apply this learning to other relationships.

The role of the therapist on the client's journey is one of support, witness, and guide. Herman (1992) writes about our role as "bearing witness" to the horrors our clients have suffered. The therapeutic relationship is the ship in the harbor for this journey of healing. Kurtz (1990) described the therapy relationship as follows:

> A healing relationship is special. When you are in one, you feel it. There is an incredible delicacy that you do not dare to disturb. There is a connection with yourself that allows you to relax, be curious and wait. There are intuitions that pop up easily and make powerful contributions to the work. There is a basic warmth and friendliness. There's a basic wakefulness that informs both therapist and client. There is no question of healer and healed. Both are parts of something greater taking place. Both feel this. Each is healed. (p. 64)

Couples Therapy

As previously stated, because so many women have been abused sexually, lesbian couples will have a greater likelihood of dealing with the aftereffects of abuse than heterosexual couples. Sexual abuse can significantly affect relational issues of trust, intimacy, and sexuality. Couples in which one or both partners are abuse survivors may face numerous challenges in their relationship (Maltz, 1991).

When one member of the couple is a survivor and the other is not, there may be extended periods of time when the survivor needs to prioritize her own healing over the needs of the relationship. This can create a dynamic where the survivor is seen as the "sick" or "needy" member of the couple and the partner is the healthy caretaker who is there to meet the survivor's needs. The partner may see her own needs as less important or pressing than the needs of the survivor. As one lesbian partner of a survivor asked:

> How can I make my needs a priority in this relationship? She's the one that was hurt so badly. She had a horrible childhood. My childhood was okay, and my problems seem pretty small compared to hers. I feel selfish when I make my needs known. (Elizabeth, age 40, college professor)

Important issues to consider when treating a couple where one partner is a survivor and the other is not include taking care to focus on both the needs of the survivor and the needs of the other partner. Identifying and addressing these imbalances can assist the couple in developing a relationship where the needs of both partners are valued equally.

It may be necessary to assist the couple in finding adequate supports for the partner who is not a survivor. This can be a challenge for the lesbian partner, who may not feel comfortable or understood in a partners' group that is exclusively or predominantly male and heterosexual. Find out what is available in your community or nearby. If there is a partners' group, find out if there are lesbians in that group. If the partner wants to join a group but none is available, assist her in networking with other lesbian partners of survivors to form her own support group.

Couples treatment may be advisable at different stages in a survivor's healing. In the early stages of treatment, education helps the partner understand the process of healing and recovery. The early stage of treatment, coined the "emergency stage" by Bass and Davis (1988), may be a time when the survivor's needs feel urgent. The couple will likely need to discuss how they will manage their relationship during this time. Most often, survivors in the early stages of their healing are not ready to handle issues of sex and intimacy. These issues will likely need to be put on hold while the survivor works through her abuse recovery. Many survivors go through a period when they need to stop being sexual or wish to refrain from particular sexual activities that seem to trigger memories of past abuse. Again, the partner's needs must be recognized and acknowledged during this period while also honoring the decisions made by the survivor in her healing. Ultimately, the partner who is not a survivor needs to decide whether she can tolerate waiting until her partner is ready to be intimate again.

Later in the treatment process, once the survivor has worked through her abuse memories, she will probably want to deal with issues of sexuality and intimacy with her partner. The survivor may find herself reexperiencing aspects of the abuse in her current sexual relationship. She may shut down sexually and emotionally, with an inability to be present. She may also mistake her partner for her abuser, confusing acts of intimacy with acts of abuse. Partners often describe feeling hurt and confused by the survivor's response, and by the presence of a third person, the abuser, in the relationship. There also may be a misperception regarding sexual issues in that if a woman was abused sexually by a man, she will not experience sexual difficulties when being sexual with another woman. Thus couples may be surprised to learn that the same triggers are present, even with a loving woman partner. Also, for couples who have unsuccessfully attempted to be sexual, both partners may fear trying again. Concrete work on the issues of sex and intimacy is warranted during this time. Helping the couple begin to create new experiences of sexuality and intimacy, free from abuse, can empower them and strengthen their relationship.

In a couples relationship where both partners are survivors, the relationship may present some additional challenges. At the same time, the partners may show an increased ability to understand and support one another because of the common bond of abuse. If partners are in different stages of healing, they may find that although they understand what the other is going through, they have different needs. If partners are in the same stage of healing, there will likely be times when they need to focus on themselves, perhaps being less available for the needs of the other. Partners may also want to be mindful of the place that issues of abuse hold in their relationship so that the relationship will not become exclusively focused on the abuse, excluding other relational issues.

Lesbian partnerships may be stronger and more able to provide the support and connection necessary during the process of recovery than heterosexual couples. Self-in-relation theory (Surrey, 1991) purports that relationships are essential to women throughout the life cycle. When two women are in a relationship with one another, it is likely marked by a high degree of closeness and intimacy. This strong connection has been pathologized in the past, being named "merger" or "fusion" and viewed as a sign of unhealthy dependency. More recently, the intimacy in lesbian relationships is being reexamined from a health-oriented perspective. Mencher and Slater (1991) propose that merger in lesbian relationships is one way in which the couple attempts to define its own boundaries and defend against a hostile environment. They also suggest that the closeness may show a greater capacity for empathy and connectedness. These qualities may give lesbian couples extra strength to grapple with the issues of being in a couple where one or both partners are survivors of abuse.

Group Therapy

Group treatment for abuse survivors is clearly a treatment of choice at certain stages in the healing process. Breaking silence and ending the isolation so often caused by abuse can be addressed in group treatment. It is necessary to assess the client's stage of recovery to determine the type of group that will be most useful to her. In the early stages of the work, groups that are supportive and educationally focused are most appropriate. In the middle stages of the work, when the client is remembering and integrating her abuse experiences, a group focused on storytelling and feelings is most useful. In the final stages of treatment, when the survivor is focused on moving on and dealing with sexuality, a group of others in this stage, or a generic group focused on relational issues and not on abuse, is most useful (Herman, 1992).

Most groups that focus on the middle stage of the work—storytelling and connecting with feelings—are mixed with both heterosexual and lesbian women. A thorough screening of clients must be conducted prior to their entering the group to assess their ability to tolerate difference among members. This should include discussing the need for acceptance of different lifestyles, sexual orientation, class, culture, religion, and race. Ideally, a group would consist of at least two members of the same minority group so that one member does not feel isolated in the group. There are times when this is not possible, and then the decision rests with the potential group member.

> Gloria was the only lesbian in a long-term survivors' group. Gloria knew upon entering that she was the only lesbian, and she decided that she did not want to wait until a group formed with other lesbians. Although she used the group to talk openly about her issues, including her sexual orientation and her partner, she ultimately found it difficult that the other women in the group did not come from a feminist perspective in understanding their histories of abuse. She believed that lesbian group members would have been more likely to share her feminist outlook. (Gloria, age 38, self-employed, abused by her father)

Mixed groups with heterosexual, bisexual, and lesbian women can benefit from this diversity. There are times when a lesbian's ability to disclose and discuss her sexual orientation in a survivors' group frees other members to talk about the sexual feelings or experiences they may have had with other women. The mixing of people of various orientations in a group may foster more open discussion of sexuality.

One alternative to a mixed group is a group specifically for lesbian abuse survivors. Our women's psychotherapy practice recently held such a group, and members found it extremely useful to be in a group with other lesbians.

Most importantly, they wanted to be assured that they would be safe to discuss their sexual abuse in the context of a shared understanding about their sexual orientation. Although sexual orientation was not a major topic of conversation in the group, members felt that they could openly share their questions and concerns about relationships, dating, and sexuality in a safe and accepting environment.

Protective Issues

There are important issues for those working in child protective services to consider when working with lesbians with children as well as with lesbian teenagers. Many lesbian mothers fear that custody of their children may be threatened if they are open about their lesbianism. Because of this, protective service workers may experience lesbian mothers as secretive and withholding. For example, lesbian mothers may be reluctant to give consent for various agencies and schools to exchange information in an effort to protect themselves and their children.

In addition, there is a common myth that children are at risk for sexual abuse in lesbian households. Although this has not been investigated empirically, children of lesbian parents may actually be unusually safe because most sexual abuse is perpetrated by men, and especially by fathers or father figures (Russell, 1986). Lesbian parents or coparents may worry that protective service workers will hold these prejudicial and unfounded beliefs and try to wrest custody of their children from them.

Another important protective issue involves lesbian teenagers in the system who have been abused sexually. These teens may be particularly vulnerable to revictimization because of both their history of abuse and their lesbianism. Lesbian teens may be targeted for rape, assault, or harrassment if their lesbian identity is known. Lesbian teens may also be at higher risk for suicide given their status as lesbians and lack of support services.

Conclusion

Lesbians who have been abused sexually have special issues that must be taken into account. Oppression and stigma may keep lesbian survivors of abuse from getting the treatment they need and from fully disclosing their identity to professionals. Examination of bias; careful attunement to our own attitudes and feelings; and knowledge about lesbian history, culture, and resources can enhance our ability to provide appropriate and life-affirming service to lesbian clients.

Culturally Informed Interventions for Sexual Child Abuse

LISA ARONSON FONTES

We have considered ideas for prevention and intervention for sexual child abuse in nine cultural groups in the United States. Collectively, they suggest clear paths for agencies, therapists, and policymakers in attending to the needs of diverse communities.

An intervention (be it medical, legal, psychological, protective, or other) for sexual abuse that is culturally sensitive would be—first and foremost—user friendly. The client would feel welcome, respected, and understood:

> It's understanding, it's trust, so we won't feel the fear of speaking with another person. Above all, because of the culture and the betrayal, it's a big deal for many of us to reach out for the first time and say, "I need help." (Puerto Rican woman, abused sexually by her father)

Services, paperwork, and outreach must be readily available in the client's language. Services must fit the schedules, finances, and geographic location of the population. Meaningful links must be established between child protection professionals and community leaders. Personnel must understand the culture and oppression issues of their clients, and also examine the cultural roots of their own values, attitudes, and behaviors.

In an encounter with a culturally competent protective worker, a family (whatever its origins, race, or makeup) would feel validated, supported, and understood. When the worker left the room, the nonoffending family members would turn to each other and say, "This person really cares about us. He or she is going to help us help our child, who has been hurt."

In an encounter with a culturally competent therapist, a child client would feel, "This therapist likes my family and wants to help us." An adult would feel, "It's okay to be me in this office." The validation offered by culturally competent professionals can begin to ease the crushing of the soul caused by sexual abuse and oppression.

Cultural Matching

One hotly debated multicultural topic concerns matching between professionals and clients. I will present the argument in its two extreme forms and then advocate a moderate position, which actually may be the most radical of all because it defies fixed rules and requires attention to individual circumstances.

Proponents of matching believe that it is crucial that therapists and clients be matched for ethnicity (or gender, sexual orientation, etc.), particularly for clients who are members of minority groups (Burstow, 1992). They believe that group similarity facilitates understanding and trust and reduces the burden faced by members of minority groups to explain themselves incessantly to others. Proponents of this viewpoint believe that "psychotherapy with the ethnoculturally different patient frequently provides more opportunities for empathic and dynamic stumbling blocks, in what might be termed 'ethnocultural disorientation' " (Comas-Díaz & Jacobsen, 1991, p. 392). They further argue that nonverbal communication is often misinterpreted by both therapist and client when therapy is a cross-cultural encounter.

The second group believes that ethnocultural differences do not matter. They believe that a skilled therapist can understand and empathize with people's problems regardless of their own group identity. They might believe that the reference group differences between professional and client provide material for the therapy, or they might see these differences as irrelevant. Depending on their training, they may believe that intrapsychic processes, environmental reinforcers, or self-defeating cognitions are important—not culture of origin.

In this area, as in others, I advocate for flexibility and treatment tailored to the specifics of the situation rather than rigid policies of either matching or refusing to match for culture or other factors. For some clients at some times, it may be important to meet with clinicians from the same cultural background. At other points, this may not be important, may not be most important, may not be ideal, or may not be possible. I believe the ethnocultural divide is like the gender divide, or the generation gap, or the myriad other ways in which therapists and clients can differ from each other. It would be ludicrous to try to match therapist and client in terms of all their diverse communities of reference, including gender, age, culture, religion, sexual orientation, politics, marital status, socioeconomic class, and so on. Indeed, if the client and therapist were matched in every way, overidentification might develop.

In my ideal world, clients would have an opportunity to seek out therapists who are like them culturally or in other ways, when they so desire. This may be especially important for members of oppressed groups who do not see favorable reflections of themselves in the media or in the professionals in their lives. A given client may prefer to choose a therapist based on training or professional orientation, rather than group membership characteristics. Another client (or this same client at a different point in life) may decide that having a therapist with similar group membership characteristics is crucial. I would grant this choice whenever possible.

I have been on the giving and receiving end of a variety of therapies, with people who differed or were the same as me in almost every imaginable way including gender, culture, class, sexual orientation, religion, race, physical ability, and age. I believe that the success of the therapy depends less on the identity into which therapists are born than on their skills, knowledge, cultural competency, and genuine comfort with people of diverse cultures.

Awareness of cultural issues is key. I lasted but a short time as a client in the office of a therapist who told me that she didn't think a person's ethnicity mattered, saying, "We are all basically the same." Only a member of the dominant group who has not spoken deeply with members of other groups could make this kind of statement. As Boyd-Franklin (1989) writes, "Even if the therapist does not perceive race or racism as an issue, it is certainly an ever-present reality to many black families" (p. 257). Therapists from dominant groups (Whites, males, mainstream Christians, heterosexuals) have a particular obligation to examine their cultural assumptions and get to know the cultures of their clients so that the therapeutic encounter is not isomorphic to the disempowerment of clients in other spheres.

My clinical and personal experience and research have led me to marvel at the variety of perspectives on culture and at the power of multicultural connections to enrich our lives. In a study of adult Puerto Rican women who had been in therapy to address their molestation as children (Fontes, 1992), I encountered a range of attitudes toward ethnic matching. Some women swore that the fact that their therapists were Puerto Rican ensured the success of the therapy, and others avoided Puerto Rican therapists because they feared the therapists would remind them too much of their families or worried they would gossip in the community. I encountered women who were pleased that their therapists had been Latino(a) but not Puerto Rican because they felt they were able to understand the culture but were not too embedded in it, and others who worried that an Argentine or Chilean therapist would necessarily disdain Puerto Ricans. I encountered women who had excellent working relationships with non-Latino (Anglo, Black, or Jewish) therapists and others who resented their therapists' overly strict boundaries, which they saw as due to culture. I interviewed English-speaking Puerto Rican clients who resented the assumption that they would automatically prefer working with a Puerto Rican therapist, and Puerto Rican therapists who resented being assigned only the Puerto Rican cases. One Puerto Rican client had been in therapy with five different providers over a 20-year period. Only her most recent therapist, who happened to be a White male, finally inquired about sexual abuse. She disclosed her abuse for the first time to him, and they developed a highly successful working relationship.

The richness of multicultural encounters can occur not just in the therapist/client relationship but also in groups. I have spoken with women who were in the minority as lesbians in a group of survivors of sexual abuse and women who were in the minority as heterosexuals in similar groups. Sometimes mixed-gender groups of survivors are indicated, and at other times women-only or men-only groups work best. The professional, class, age, and cultural differences that emerge in survivor groups can enrich all the members. However, there is one proviso, and it is a big one. Sometimes, being in individual or group therapy that is a cross-cultural encounter can feel too threatening, too time consuming, and be a distraction from the issues that most concern the client. In these cases, every effort should be made to accommodate the clients' wishes for cultural matching around the dimensions that they are feel are important.

Diverse and High-Quality Treatment Teams

I advocate strongly for diverse treatment teams that include members of all the major cultures in the area, regardless of whether ethnic matching is employed. A diverse treatment team communicates an openness toward culture that may be key in working in minority communities. Diversifying staff to reflect catchment area has been found to lead to an increased flow of minority clients (Barrera, 1982). When I first began to work in rural western Massachusetts, I was told that my ability to speak Spanish was of no interest to the agency because they had no Spanish-speaking clients. However, when word of my presence spread in the Latino community and at other agencies, I was deluged by clients who spoke only Spanish. If we are unequipped to serve the needs of oppressed groups, we will never be able to assess those needs accurately.

A diverse team (in terms of training, age, gender, class, religion, ethnicity, and sexual orientation) increases an agency's ability to generate creative approaches to diverse client experiences. For a team to reap the greatest benefits from this diversity, team members need contexts in which they can interact and express a range of viewpoints comfortably (Fontes, 1994).

In their efforts to address the needs of cultural minority groups, agencies sometimes unwittingly provide separate and unequal services to minority clients. In Massachusetts, where I worked for several years, agencies would frequently recruit people with undergraduate degrees in psychology or social work from Puerto Rico to work with Latino clients, whereas English-speaking clients would be treated by clinicians with graduate degrees and extensive advanced training. The general attitude was, "These people speak the same language, so they can work with their own." Of course, we would not allow someone to work as a clinician on issues of sexual abuse simply because he or she spoke English! Clinicians must have clinical knowledge, sophistication, and familiarity with issues of sexual abuse. Clients from minority groups are entitled to receive the same quality services as clients from the dominant group (Facundo, 1990). The recruitment, training, and support of diverse people in the helping professions is urgently needed.

Potential Pitfalls of Attending to Culture

Specific treatment recommendations based on the client's culture should not be seen as rigid prescriptions to be used with clients in all cases but rather as suggestions that are worth considering and then accepting or rejecting with each new situation. Some practitioners fear that discussions of culture may lead to sloppy overgeneralizations and simplifications. Culture-specific recommendations are intended to initiate discussions among professionals who then decide their usefulness in any given instance. Every time we approach a family, we are approaching an unfamiliar culture. They may look like people we have known before, but we do not know them just by knowing their race or any other demographic characteristic. The family itself—and some home-work—can guide us.

Child Protection, Culture, and Oppression

Members of minority groups, immigrant groups, and economically op-pressed groups often actively fear the agencies that are designed to help them care for their children (for provocative discussions of child protection agen-cies, see Armstrong, 1993, and Gordon, 1988). These agencies are often perceived as "child-snatchers" who are eager to find fault with and destroy minority families. These fears are not wholly unwarranted:

> Institutions concerned with child abuse prevention have spent a dispro-portionate share of their time dealing with these [minority] groups in ways that have aroused acute suspicion and resentment. They have sometimes been accused of promoting not justice and human well-being, but racism and human oppression. (Derezotes & Snowden, 1990, pp. 161-162)

The biases against members of specific cultural groups can manifest in many ways, both subtle and overt, and have a tremendous cumulative impact. Bias can enter at all points, from the first suspicion of abuse to investigation to legal action; it can be present in all spheres, including protective, criminal, legal, medical, and psychological; and can result in a range of negative outcomes, from failure to substantiate legitimate claims of abuse, thereby leaving children in danger, to falsely "substantiating" abuse and removing children from homes unnecessarily. Bias can emerge because of genuine dislike by providers toward members of certain groups, or less malicious but equally destructive misunderstandings. Such bias can be illegal, legal, or even legally prescribed, as in cases where children are removed from homes because of the sexual orientation of a parent.

Cultural misunderstandings can impede child protective work in ways we do not often consider—from the Anglo American mother who declines to discuss sexuality to the Mexican father who believes the rape of his son by a man indicates that his son is gay to the Orthodox Jewish family who may miss a court date because they are observing a holiday.

Lack of understanding of oppression issues can also impede protective work, in that families are often termed pathological for issues that stem from discrimination or poverty, which results in double victimization. Dumont (1992) movingly describes the struggle of people who live in impoverished city neighborhoods to raise their children well in the face of discrimination; extreme poverty; and inadequate education, housing, and health care. He describes the parallel struggle of protective workers to do their jobs while faced with excessive caseloads and often inadequate training and supervision. The pressure on workers may lead to situations in which families are "punished" by having their children removed because they are seen as unmotivated or uncooperative, or, conversely, children are not afforded adequate protection because parents conform to expectations. Clearly, the more one knows about the workings of the social service system, the easier it is to follow the (often unwritten) rules, putting immigrant and other families who are not from the dominant group at a disadvantage.

Policy and Future Directions

Public policy and funding priorities must change to acknowledge the needs of diverse cultural groups in coping with sexual abuse. Research into culture-specific prevention, detection, and treatment must be funded. The culturally oriented intervention programs that do exist must be given adequate funding so that they can take root and prosper, not limp along from one bake sale or small grant to the next. These programs range from community and school-based child abuse prevention programs to family intervention programs to opportunities for subsidized family, group, and individual therapy.

I am not advocating for the balkanization of intervention into sexual abuse, but the status quo is also unacceptable:

That the experiences of White victims are assumed to be the norm for all minority victims is evident in the lack of ethnicity-based child sexual abuse research. But the assumption that the data on Whites accurately reflect the experiences of the members of all other groups denies the role of cultural differences in people's lives, denies the fact that racism has an impact, and reflects the White bias of most researchers in this field. (Russell, Schurman, & Trocki, 1988, pp. 119-120)

Alliances across cultures provide great strength in numbers and diversity. Examples of "natural" coalitions include nonoffending mothers of children who have been victimized by incest, clergy united to confront sexual abuse, and neighbors for prevention. This unity across groups must include acknowledgment of different as well as common needs.

I am hopeful. From the silence of the sexually abused and the silence of the oppressed have emerged clear, brave voices calling out for every child's right to grow up free from sexual abuse. Change is in the air.

References

Abad, V., Ramos, J., & Boyce, E. (1974). A model for delivery of mental health services to Spanish-speaking minorities. *American Journal of Orthopsychiatry, 44,* 584-595.

Acosta, F. X., & Yamamoto, J. (1984). The utility of group work practice for Hispanic Americans. *Social Work with Groups, 7,* 63-73.

Acosta, F. X., Yamamoto, J., & Evans, L. A. (1982). *Effective psychotherapy for low income and minority patients.* New York: Plenum.

Agtuca, J. R. (1994). *A community secret: For the Filipina in an abusive relationship.* Seattle, WA: Seal Press.

Algarín, M., & Piñero, M. (Eds.). (1975). *Nuyorican poetry: An anthology of Puerto Ricans' words and feelings.* New York: William Morrow.

Allen, C. M., & Lee, C. M. (1992). Family of origin structure and intra/extra-familial child sexual victimization of male and female offenders. *Journal of Child Sexual Abuse, 1,* 31-45.

Amaro, H., Russo, N. F., & Johnson, J. (1987). Family and work predictors of psychological well-being among Hispanic women professionals. *Psychology of Women Quarterly, 11,* 505-521.

267

America's immigrant challenge [Special issue]. (1993, Fall). *Time.*

Aramoni, A. (1982). Machismo. *Psychology Today, 5,* 69-72.

Arditti, R. (1991). But you don't look Jewish! In R. J. Siegel & E. Cole (Eds.), *Jewish women in therapy: Seen but not heard* (pp. 69-77). Binghamton, NY: Haworth.

Armstrong, L. (1993). *And they call it help: The psychiatric policing of America's children.* New York: Addison-Wesley.

Aron, A. (1992). Testimonio: A bridge between psychotherapy and sociotherapy. In E. Cole, O. Espin, & E. D. Rothblum (Eds.), *Refugee women and their mental health: Shattered societies, shattered lives* (pp. 173-189). Binghamton, NY: Haworth.

Asen, K., George, E., Piper, R., & Stevens, A. (1989). A systems approach. *Child Abuse & Neglect, 13,* 45-57.

Babín, M. T. (1973). *La cultura de Puerto Rico.* San Juan, PR: Instituto de Cultura Puertorriqueña.

Bagley, C. (1991). The long-term psychological effects of child sexual abuse: A review of some British and Canadian studies of victims and their families. *Annals of Sex Research, 4,* 23-48.

Baldwin, J. A. (1991). African (black) psychology: Issues and synthesis. In R. L. Jones (Ed.), *Black psychology* (3rd ed., pp. 125-135). Berkeley, CA: Cobb and Henry.

Baldwin, J. A., Brown, R., & Hopkins, R. (1991). The black self-hatred paradigm revisited: An Africentric analysis. In R. L. Jones (Ed.), *Black psychology* (3rd ed., pp. 141-165). Berkeley, CA: Cobb and Henry.

Barnard, C. P. (1984). Alcoholism and incest in the family: Part I: Similar traits, common dynamics. *Alcoholism: A family matter* [Pamphlet]. Pompano Beach, FL: Health Communications Inc.

Barrera, M. (1982). Raza populations. In L. R. Snowden (Ed.), *Reaching the underserved: Mental health needs of neglected populations.* Beverly Hills, CA: Sage.

Barrett, M. J. (1993). Mothers' role in incest: Neither dysfunctional women nor dysfunctional theories when both are explored in their entirety. *Journal of Child Sexual Abuse, 2,* 141-143.

Barrett, M. J., Trepper, T. S., & Fish, L. S. (1990). Feminist-informed family therapy for the treatment of intrafamily child sexual abuse. *Journal of Family Psychology, 4*(2), 151-166.

Bart, P. (1986, Summer). Why Jewish women get raped (Interview with S. W. Schneider). *Lilith, 15,* 8-12.

Bass, E., & Davis, L. (1988). *The courage to heal: A guide for women survivors of child abuse.* New York: Harper & Row.

Baumrind, D. (1972). An exploratory study of the socialization effects on black children: Some black-white comparisons. *Child Development, 43,* 261-267.

Bawer, B. (1993). *A place at the table.* New York: Poseidon.

Bayer, R. (1981). *Homosexuality and American psychiatry.* New York: Basic Books.

Beck, E. T. (1991). Therapy's double dilemma: Anti-Semitism and misogyny. In R. J. Siegel & E. Cole (Eds.), *Jewish women in therapy: Seen but not heard* (pp. 19-30). Binghamton, NY: Haworth.

Becker, J. V. (1990). Treating adolescent sex offenders. *Professional Psychology: Research and Practice, 21,* 362-365.

Bernardez, T. (1987). Gender based countertransference of female therapists in the psychology of women. *Women & Therapy, 6,* 25-39.

Betancourt, G. (1974). The Puerto Rican recipient of mental health services. In D. J. Curren, J. J. Rivera, & R. B. Sanchez (Eds.), *Proceedings of Puerto Rican conferences in human services* (pp. 47-57). Washington, DC: National Coalition of Spanish-Speaking Mental Health Organizations.

Billingsley, A. (1968). *Black families in white America.* Englewood Cliffs, NJ: Prentice Hall.

Bird, H. R. (1982). The cultural dichotomy of colonial people. *Journal of the American Academy of Psychoanalysis, 10,* 195-209.

Birns, B., & Meyer, S. (1993). Mothers' role in incest: Dysfunctional women or dysfunctional theories? *Journal of Child Sexual Abuse, 2,* 127-135.

Black, C. (1982). *It will never happen to me.* Denver: MAC.

Blumenfeld, W., & Raymond, D. (1988). *Looking at gay and lesbian life.* New York: Philosophical Library.

Bolton, F. G., Morris, L. A., & MacEachron, A. E. (1989). *Males at risk: The other side of sexual abuse.* Newbury Park, CA: Sage.

Booth, J. (1993). A college wide prevention program on child abuse and neglect. *The Advisor, 6*(1), 23-26.

Boswell, J. (1980). *Christianity, social tolerance, and homosexuality: Gay people in Western Europe from the beginning of the Christian era to the 14th century.* Chicago: University of Chicago Press.

Boszormenyi-Nagy, I., & Spark, G. (1973). *Invisible loyalties: Reciprocity in intergenerational family therapy.* New York: Harper & Row.

Bowman, B. T. (1992). Culturally sensitive inquiry. In J. Gabarino, F. M. Stott, & Faculty of the Erikson Institute (Eds.), *What children can tell us* (pp. 92-107). San Francisco: Jossey-Bass.

Boyd-Franklin, N. (1989). *Black families in therapy: A multisystems approach.* New York: Guilford.

Brady, K. (1993). Testimony on pornography and incest. In D. E. H. Russell (Ed.), *Making violence sexy* (pp. 43-45). New York: Teachers College Press.

Breer, W. (1992). *Diagnosis and treatment of the young male victim of sexual abuse.* Springfield, IL: Charles C Thomas.

Brown, L. (1991). How is this feminist different from all other feminists? Or, my journey from pirke avot to feminist therapy ethics. In R. J. Siegel & E. Cole (Eds.), *Jewish women in therapy: Seen but not heard* (pp. 41-55). Binghamton, NY: Haworth.

Brown, L. S. (1989). Beyond thou shalt not: Thinking about ethics in the lesbian therapy community. *Women and Therapy, 8*(1/2), 13-25.

Brown, L. S. (1990). The meaning of a multicultural perspective for theory-building in feminist therapy. In L. S. Brown & M. P. P. Root (Eds.), *Diversity and complexity in feminist therapy* (pp. 1-21). Binghamton, NY: Haworth.

Brown, L. S. (1993). Anti-domination training as a central component of diversity in clinical psychology education. *Clinical Psychologist, 46,* 83-87.

Brown, P. (1974). *Toward a Marxist psychology.* New York: HarperColophon.

Burstow, B. (1992). *Radical feminist therapy: Working in the context of violence.* Newbury Park, CA: Sage.

Burstyn, G. (1990, Fall). Jewish identity, anti-Semitism and the battered women's movement. *NCADV Voice,* pp. 1-2. (Available from the National Council Against Domestic Violence, 1012 14th Street, Suite 807, Washington, DC 20005)

Canino, G. (1982). Transactional family patterns: A preliminary exploration of Puerto Rican female adolescents. In R. E. Zambrana (Ed.), *Work, family, and health: Latina women in transition* (pp. 27-36). New York: Hispanic Research Center, Fordham University.

Canino, G., & Canino, I. A. (1982). Culturally syntonic family therapy for migrant Puerto Ricans. *Hospital and Community Psychiatry, 33,* 299-303.

Cantor, A. (Speaker). (1992). *Assimilation as the root of low self-esteem in non-traditional Jewish women* (Cassette Recording No. 92JFP-51). Seattle, WA: Jewish Women's Caucus, Association for Women in Psychology.

Carlson, E. B., & Rosser-Hogan, R. (1993). Mental health status of Cambodian refugees ten years after leaving their homes. *American Journal of Orthopsychiatry, 63*(2), 223-231.

Carney, T. (Ed.). (1977). *Communist party power in Kampuchea (Cambodia): Documents and discussion.* Ithaca, NY: Cornell University Press.

Cass, V. (1979). Homosexual identity formation: A theoretical model. *Journal of Homosexuality, 4*(3), 219-236.

Castro, F. G., Furth, P., & Karlow, H. (1984). The health beliefs of Mexican, Mexican American, and Anglo American women. *Hispanic Journal of Behavioral Sciences, 6,* 365-383.

Chan, C. S. (1987). Asian American women's psychological response to sexual exploitation and cultural stereotypes. *Women and Therapy, 6*(4), 33-38.

Chan, S. (1993). Families with Asian roots. In E. W. Lynch & M. J. Hanson (Eds.), *Developing cross-cultural competence: A guide for working with young children and their families* (pp. 181-258). Baltimore: Brookes.

Civil Rights Digest. (1967). Washington, DC: U.S. Commission on Civil Rights.

Clark, V. R., & Harrell, J. P. (1992). The relationship of type A behavior styles used in coping with racism, and blood pressure. In A. K. H. Burlew, W. C. Banks, H. P. McAdoo, & D. A. Azibo (Eds.), *African American psychology: Theory, research, and practice* (pp. 359-369). Newbury Park, CA: Sage.

Cole, E., Espin, E., & Rothblom, E. (1992). *Refugee women and their mental health.* Binghamton, NY: Harrington Park Press.

Cole, P. M., & Woolger, C. (1989). Incest survivors: The relation of their perceptions of their parents and their own parenting attitudes. *Child Abuse & Neglect, 13,* 409-416.

Coleman, E. (1981). Developmental stages of the coming out process. *Journal of Homosexuality, 7*(2-3), 31-44.

Colon, F. (1980). The family life cycle of the multiproblem poor family. In E. Carter & M. McGoldrick (Eds.), *The family life cycle: A framework for family therapy.* New York: Gardner.

Comas-Díaz, L. (1981). Puerto Rican *espiritismo* and psychotherapy. *American Journal of Orthopsychiatry, 51,* 636-645.

Comas-Díaz, L. (1982). Mental health needs of Puerto Rican women in the United States. In R. Zambrana (Ed.), *Latina women in transition* (pp. 1-10). New York: Hispanic Research Center, Fordham University.

Comas-Díaz, L. (1987). Feminist therapy with Puerto Rican women. *Psychology of Women Quarterly, 11*(4), 461-474.

Comas-Díaz, L. (1989). Culturally relevant issues and treatment implications for Hispanics. In D. R. Koslow & E. Salett (Eds.), *Crossing cultures in mental health*. Washington, DC: Society for International Education Training And Research (SIETAR).

Comas-Díaz, L. (1994). Integrative approach. In L. Comas-Díaz & B. Greene (Eds.), *Women of color: Integrating ethnic and gender identities in psychotherapy* (pp. 287-318). New York: Guilford.

Comas-Díaz, L., & Duncan, J. W. (1985). The cultural context: A factor in assertiveness training with mainland Puerto Rican women. *Psychology of Women Quarterly, 9*(4), 463-475.

Comas-Díaz, L., Geller, J. D., Melgoza, B., & Baker, R. (1982, August). *Attitudes and expectations about mental health services among Hispanics and Afro-Americans*. Paper presented at the annual meeting of the American Psychological Association, Washington, DC.

Comas-Díaz, L., & Jacobsen, F. M. (1991). Ethnocultural transference and countertransference in the therapeutic dyad. *American Journal of Orthopsychiatry, 61*, 392-402.

Comas-Díaz, L., & Padilla, A. (1990). Countertransference in working with victims of political repression. *American Journal of Orthopsychiatry, 60*, 125-134.

Courtois, C. A. (1988). *Healing the incest wound: Adult survivors in therapy*. New York: W. W. Norton.

Davis, L. (1991). *Allies in healing: When the person you love was sexually abused as a child*. New York: Harper Perennial.

De Granda, G. (1968). *Transculturación e interferencia lingüística en el Puerto Rico contemporáneo*. Bogotá, Colombia: Ediciones Bogotá.

De La Cancela, V. (1991). Working affirmatively with Puerto Rican men: Professional and personal reflections. *Journal of Feminist Family Therapy, 2*(3/4), 195-211.

Delgado, M., & Humm-Delgado, D. (1984). Hispanics and group work: A review of literature. *Social Work with Groups, 7*, 85-96.

Derezotes, D. S., & Snowden, L. R. (1990). Cultural factors in the intervention of child maltreatment. *Child and Adolescent Social Work, 7*(2), 161-175.

Dinsmore, C. (1991). *From survivng to thriving: Incest, feminism, and recovery*. New York: State of New York Press.

Doi, T. (1973). *Anatomy of dependence*. Tokyo: Kodansha International Ltd.

Dratch, M. (1992). *The physical, sexual, and emotional abuse of children*. Proposal to the Rabbinical Council of America. (Available from the Rabbinical Council of America, 5625 Arlington Avenue, Riverdale, NY 10471)

Dumont, M. (1992). *Treating the poor.* Belmont, MA: Dymphna.

Ebihara, M. (1985). The Khmer. In D. Haines (Ed.), *Refugees in the United States* (pp. 127-147). Westport, CT: Greenwood.

Edwards, J. J., & Alexander, P. C. (1992). The contribution of family background to the long-term adjustment of women sexually abused as children. *Journal of Interpersonal Violence, 7,* 306-320.

Elliott, D. (1994). The impact of Christian faith on the prevalence and sequelae of sexual abuse. *Journal of Interpersonal Violence, 9,* 95-107.

Engelen-Eigles, D. (Speaker). (1992). *Difficult questions: Understanding how Jewish-American women construct their identities* (Cassette Recording No. 92JFP-12). Seattle, WA: Jewish Women's Caucus, Association for Women in Psychology.

Espin, O. M. (1984). The sexuality of women: Theoretical formulations and therapeutic implications. In C. S. Vance (Ed.), *Pleasure and danger: Exploring female sexuality.* Boston: Routledge & Kegan Paul.

Espin, O. M. (1985). Psychotherapy with Hispanic women: Some considerations. In P. Pedersen (Ed.), *Handbook of cross-cultural counseling and therapy* (pp. 165-171). Westport, CT: Greenwood.

Espin, O. M. (1986). Cultural and historical influences on sexuality in Hispanic/Latin women. In J. Cole (Ed.), *All American women: Lines that divide, ties that bind.* New York: Free Press.

Etcheson, C. (1984). *The rise and demise of democratic Kampuchea.* Boulder, CO: Westview.

Facundo, A. (1990). Social class issues in family therapy: A case-study of a Puerto Rican migrant family. *Journal of Strategic and Systemic Therapies, 9*(3), 14-34.

Facundo, A. (1991). Sensitive mental health services for low-income Puerto Rican families. In M. Sotomayor (Ed.), *Empowering Hispanic families: A critical issue for the 90's* (pp. 121-139). Milwaukee, WI: Family Service America.

Falicov, C. J. (1982). Mexican families. In M. McGoldrick, J. K. Pearce, & J. Giordano (Eds.), *Ethnicity and family therapy* (pp. 134-163). New York: Guilford.

Fanon, F. (1967). *Black skin, White masks.* New York: Grove.

Felman, J. L. (1992). *Hot chicken wings.* San Francisco: Aunt Lute Books.

Finkelhor, D. (1979). *Sexually victimized children.* New York: Free Press.

Finkelhor, D. (1984). *Child sexual abuse: New theory and research.* New York: Free Press.

Fischman, Y. (1991). Interacting with trauma: Clinicians' responses to treating psychological aftereffects of political repression. *American Journal of Orthopsychiatry, 61,* 179-185.

Fish, V., & Faynik, C. (1989). Treatment of incest families with the father temporarily removed: A structural approach. *Journal of Strategic and Systemic Therapies, 8*(4), 53-63.

Fitzpatrick, J. P. (1971). *Puerto Rican Americans: The meaning of migration to the mainland.* Englewood Cliffs, NJ: Prentice Hall.

Fletcher, L., & Saks, A. (1990). *Lavender lists.* Boston: Alyson.

Fontes, L. (1992). Considering culture and oppression in child sex abuse: Puerto Ricans in the United States (Doctoral dissertation, University of Massachusetts, 1992). *Dissertation Abstracts International, 53,* 1797A.

Fontes, L. (1993a). Considering culture and oppression: Steps toward an ecology of sexual child abuse. *Journal of Feminist Family Therapy, 5*(1), 25-54.

Fontes, L. (1993b). Disclosures of sexual abuse by Puerto Rican children: Oppression and cultural barriers. *Journal of Child Sexual Abuse, 2*(1), 21-35.

Fontes, L. (1995). Sharevision: Collaborative supervision and self-care strategies for working with trauma. *The Family Journal, 3*(3).

Freire, P. (1967). *Educação como prática da liberdade* (Education as a practice of freedom). Rio de Janeiro, Brazil: Paz e Terra.

Freire, P. (1970). *Pedagogy of the oppressed.* New York: Seabury.

Gallagher, V., & Dodds, W. F. (1985). *Speaking out, fighting back.* Seattle, WA: Madrona.

Gantrell, N. (1992). Boundaries in lesbian therapy relationships. *Women and Therapy, 12*(3), 29-50.

Ganzarain, R., & Buchele, B. (1986). Countertransference when incest is the problem. *International Journal of Group Psychotherapy, 36,* 551-566.

García-Preto, N. (1982). Puerto Rican families. In M. McGoldrick, J. K. Pearce, & J. Giordano (Eds.), *Ethnicity and family therapy* (pp. 164-186). New York: Guilford.

García-Preto, N. (1990). Hispanic mothers. *Journal of Feminist Family Therapy, 2,* 15-21.

Gardner, F. (1990). Psychotherapy with adult survivors of child sexual abuse. *British Journal of Psychotherapy, 6,* 285-294.

Gelinas, D. J. (1983). The persisting negative effects of incest. *Psychiatry, 46,* 312-332.

Gelinas, D. J. (1988). Family therapy: Critical early structuring. In S. M. Sgroi (Ed.), *Evaluation and treatment of sexually abused children and adult survivors: Vulnerable populations* (Vol. 1, pp. 51-76). Lexington, MA: Lexington Books.

Gelles, R. J. (1993). The doctrine of family reunification: Child protection or risk? *APSAC Advisor, 6*(2), 9-11.

Gibbs, J. T. (1991). Black American adolescents. In J. T. Gibbs, L. N. Huang, & Associates (Eds.), *Children of color: Psychological interventions with minority youths* (pp. 179-223). San Francisco: Jossey-Bass.

Giller, B., & Goldsmith, E. (1980). *All in the family: A study of intra-familial violence in the Los Angeles Jewish community.* Unpublished master's thesis, Hebrew Union College/University of Southern California.

Gillum, R., Gomez-Marin, O., & Prineas, R. (1984). Racial differences in personality, behavior, and family environment in Minneapolis school children. *Journal of the National Medical Association, 76,* 1097-1105.

Gin, H. (1978). *Corporal punishment and the Chinese culture.* Paper presented at the First Multicultural Training Conference on Child Abuse and Neglect, Sacramento, CA.

Giraldo, D. (1972). El machismo como fenómeno psicocultural. *Revista Latino-Americana de Psicología, 4*(3), 295-309.

Glaser, D. (1991). Treatment issues in sexual child abuse. *British Journal of Psychiatry, 159,* 769-782.

Gluck, B. (1988). Jewish men and violence in the home—Unlikely companions. In H. Brod (Ed.), *A mensch among men* (pp. 162-173). Freedom, CA: Crossing Press.

Gold, M. (1992). *Does God belong in the bedroom?* Philadelphia: Jewish Publication Society.

Gomez, A. G. (1982). Puerto Rican Americans. In A. Gaw (Ed.), *Cross cultural psychiatry* (pp. 109-136). Boston: John Wright.

Gordon, L. (1988). *Heroes of their own lives: The politics and history of family violence.* New York: Penguin.

Grahn, J. (1984). *Another mother tongue.* Boston: Beacon.

Greif, M. (1982). *The gay book of days.* Secaucus, NJ: Main Street Press.

Greve, H. (1987). *Kampuchean refugees between the tiger and the crocodile: International law and the overall scope of one refugee situation.* Unpublished master's thesis, University of Bergen, Norway.

Hadar, E. (1993). *Incest and molestation in Jewish families.* Unpublished study proposal.

Hale, J. (1982). *Black children: Their roots, culture, and learning styles.* Provo, UT: Brigham Young University Press.

Hall, M. (1985). *The lavender couch: A consumer's guide for lesbians and gay men.* Boston: Alyson.

Hamilton, J. A. (1989). Emotional consequences of victimization and discrimination in "special populations" of women. *Psychiatric Clinics of North America, 12,* 35-51.

Hamilton, J. A., & Jensvold, M. (1992). Personality, psychopathology, and depressions in women. In L. S. Brown & M. Ballou (Eds.), *Personality and psychopathology: Feminist reappraisals* (pp. 116-143). New York: Guilford.

Hamilton, V. (Ed.). (1988). Arrivals in resettlement countries, [19]87, [19]88, and cumulative since 1975. In *Refugee Reports, 9*(12), 7.

Hartman, A. (1993). Out of the closet: Revolution and backlash. *Social Work, 38*(3), 245-246.

Haugaard, J. J., & Reppucci, N. D. (1988). *The sexual abuse of children.* San Francisco: Jossey-Bass.

Hayward, C. (1993). *When boundaries betray us: Beyond illusions of what is ethical in therapy and life.* New York: Harper.

Heras, P. (1985). *Acculturation, generational status, and family environment of Pilipino-Americans: A study in cultural adaptation.* Unpublished doctoral dissertation, California School of Professional Psychology, San Diego.

Heras, P. (1992). Cultural considerations in the assessment and treatment of child sexual abuse. *Journal of Child Sexual Abuse, 1*(3), 119-124.

Herman, J. L. (1981). *Father-daughter incest.* Cambridge, MA: Harvard University Press.

Herman, J. L. (1992). *Trauma and recovery: The aftermath of violence—from domestic abuse to political terror.* New York: Basic Books.

Herz, S. M., & Rosen, E. J. (1982). Jewish families. In M. McGoldrick, J. K. Pearce, & J. Giordano (Eds.), *Ethnicity and family therapy* (pp. 364-392). New York: Guilford.

Heschel, S. (1991). Jewish feminism and women's identity. In R. J. Siegel & E. Cole (Eds.), *Jewish women in therapy: Seen but not heard* (pp. 31-39). Binghamton, NY: Haworth.

Hicks, G. (1993, February 18). Ghosts gathering: Comfort women issue haunts Tokyo as pressure mounts. *Far Eastern Economic Review,* pp. 32-37.

Hidalgo, H., & Hidalgo Christensen, E. (1979). The Puerto Rican cultural response to female homosexuality. In E. Acosta-Belén (Ed.), *The Puerto Rican woman*. New York: Praeger.

Hiegel, J. P. (1984). Collaboration with traditional healers: Experience in refugees' mental care. *International Journal of Mental Health, 12*(3), 30-43.

Hill, R. B. (1972). *The strength of black families*. New York: Emerson Hall.

Ho, M. (1987). *Family therapy with ethnic minorities*. Newbury Park, CA: Sage.

Ho, M. K. (1992a). *Minority children and adolescents in therapy*. Newbury Park, CA: Sage.

Ho, M. K. (1992b). Social work practice with Asian Americans. In A. T. Morales & B. W. Sheafor (Eds.), *Social work: A profession of many faces* (pp. 534-554). Boston: Allyn and Bacon.

Holton, J. K. (1993). Preventing sexual child abuse in the African American community without reinventing the wheel. *APSAC Advisor, 6*(1), 25.

Hosch, H. M., Chanez, G. J., Bothwell, R. K., & Muñoz, H. (1991). A comparison of Anglo-American and Mexican-American jurors' judgments of mothers who fail to protect their children from abuse. *Journal of Applied Social Psychology, 21*(20), 1681-1698.

Hunter, M. (1990). *Abused boys: The neglected victims of sexual abuse*. Lexington, MA: Lexington Books.

Hu, H. C. (1975). The Chinese concepts of face. In D. G. Haring (Ed.), *Personal character and cultural milieu* (pp. 446-467). Syracuse, NY: Syracuse University Press.

Huang, L. N. (1989). Southeast Asian refugee children and adolescents. In J. T. Gibbs, L. N. Huang, & Associates (Eds.), *Children of color* (pp. 278-321). San Francisco: Jossey-Bass.

Huang, L. N., & Ying, Y. (1989). Chinese American children and adolescents. In J. T. Gibbs, L. N. Huang, & Associates (Eds.), *Children of color* (pp. 30-66). San Francisco: Jossey-Bass.

Ima, K., & Hohm, C. (1991). Child maltreatment among Asian and Pacific Islander refugees and immigrants. *Journal of Interpersonal Violence, 6*(3), 267-285.

Ishisaka, H., & Takagi, C. (1982). Social work with Asian and Pacific Americans. In J. Green (Ed.), *Cultural awareness in the human services* (pp. 121-156). Englewood Cliffs, NJ: Prentice Hall.

Jackson, A. M. (1992). A theoretical model for the practice of psychotherapy with black populations. In A. K. H. Burlew, W. C. Banks, H. P. McAdoo,

& D. A. Azibo (Eds.), *African American psychology: Theory, research, and practice* (pp. 321-329). Newbury Park, CA: Sage.

Jay, K., & Young, A. (1979). *The gay report: Lesbians and gay men speak out about sexual experiences and lifestyles.* New York: Simon & Schuster.

Jenkins, A. H. (1990). Dynamics of the relationship in clinical work with African-American clients. *Group, 14*(1), 36-43.

Johnson, J. (1993). *The long term impact of childhood sexual abuse on sexual functioning in lesbian women.* Unpublished master's thesis, Smith College, Northampton, MA.

Jones, E. E. (1985). Psychotherapy and counseling with Black clients. In P. Pedersen (Ed.), *Handbook of cross-cultural counseling and therapy* (pp. 173-179). Westport, CT: Greenwood.

Kalichman, S. C. (1992). Clinicians' attributions of responsibility for sexual and physical child abuse: An investigation of case specific influences. *Journal of Child Sexual Abuse, 1,* 33-47.

Kanuha, V. (1990). *Sexual assault in Southeast Asian communities: Issues in intervention.* Minneapolis, MN: Community-University Health Care Center.

Kaschak, E. (Speaker). (1992). *First there are questions* (Cassette Recording No. 92JFP-1). Seattle, WA: Jewish Women's Caucus, Association for Women in Psychology.

Katz, J. (1976). *Gay American history: Lesbians and gay men in the U.S.A.* New York: Avon.

Katz, J. (1983). *Gay/lesbian almanac: A new documentary.* New York: Harper & Row.

Kaye/Kantrowitz, M. (1991). The issue is power: Some notes on Jewish women and therapy. In R. J. Siegel & E. Cole (Eds.), *Jewish women in therapy: Seen but not heard* (pp. 7-18). Binghamton, NY: Haworth.

Kim, B. C., Okamura, A., Ozawa, N., & Forrest, V. (1981). *Women in shadows.* La Jolla, CA: National Committee Concerned With Asian Wives of U.S. Servicemen.

Kinsey, A. (1948). *Sexual behavior in the human male.* Philadelphia: W. B. Saunders.

Kinzer, N. (1973). Women in Latin America: Priests, machos, and babies, or Latin American women and the Manichean heresy. *Journal of Marriage and the Family, 35,* 299-312.

Klem, Y. (Speaker). (1992). *This is no ordinary bath: The mikvah and recovery from childhood sexual abuse* (Cassette Recording No. 92JFP-34). Seattle, WA: Jewish Women's Caucus, Association for Women in Psychology.

Knopp, F. H. (1982). *Remedial intervention in adolescent sex offense: Nine program descriptions.* Orwell, VT: Safer Society Press.

Knopp, F. H. (1984). *Retraining adult sex offenders: Methods and models.* Orwell, VT: Safer Society Press.

Korbin, J. (Ed.). (1981). *Child abuse and neglect: Cross-cultural perspectives.* Berkeley: University of California Press.

Korbin, J. (1987). Child abuse and neglect: The cross-cultural context. In R. Helfer & R. Kempe (Eds.), *The battered child* (pp. 23-41). Chicago: University of Chicago Press.

Korbin, J. E. (1979). A cross-cultural perspective on the role of the community in child abuse and neglect. *International Journal of Child Abuse and Neglect, 3*(1), 9-18.

Korbin, J. E. (1991). Cross-cultural perspectives and research directions for the 21st century. *Child Abuse & Neglect, 15*(Suppl. 1), 67-77.

Krajeski, J. (1986). Psychotherapy with gay men and lesbians: A history of controversy. In T. Stein & C. J. Cohen, *Contemporary perspectives on psychotherapy.*

Kuoch, T., & Scully, M. F. (1984). *Cambodian voices and perceptions: A collection of materials, experiences and cross-cultural understandings.* Unpublished master's thesis, Goddard College, Vermont.

Kurtz, R. (1990). *Body-centered psychotherapy: The Hakomi method.* Mendocino, CA: LifeRhythm.

Kus, R. J. (1988). Alcoholism and non-acceptance of gay self: The critical link. *Journal of Homosexuality, 15*(1-2).

Lechner, N. (1992). Some people die of fear: Fear as a political problem. In J. E. Corradi, P. W. Fagen, & M. Garretón (Eds.), *Fear at the edge: State terror and resistance in Latin America* (pp. 26-35). Berkeley: University of California Press.

Lee, E. (1988). *Ten principles on raising Chinese American teens.* San Francisco: Chinatown Youth Center.

Lee, S. A. (1995). *The survivor's guide.* Thousand Oaks, CA: Sage.

Lew, M. (1988). *Victims no longer: Men recovering from incest and other sexual child abuse.* New York: Nevraumont.

Lewis, D. K. (1978). The black family: Socialization and sex roles. In R. Staples (Ed.), *The black family: Essays and studies* (pp. 215-225). Belmont, CA: Wadsworth.

Lewis, G. (1974). *Notes on the Puerto Rican revolution: An essay on American dominance and Caribbean resistance.* New York: Monthly Review Press.

Locke, D. C. (1991). *A model of cross cultural counseling understanding.* Unpublished manuscript.

Looney, J., & Lewis, J. (1983). *The long struggle: Well-functioning working-class black families.* New York: Brunner/Mazel.

Loulan, J. (1987). *Lesbian passion.* San Francisco: Spinsters Ink.

Lukes, C., & Land, H. (1990). Biculturality and homosexuality. *Social Work, 35,* 155-161.

Lyon, E. (1994). Hospital staff reactions to accounts by survivors of childhood abuse. *American Journal of Orthopsychiatry, 63,* 410-416.

MacKinnon, L. K., & Miller, D. (1987). The new epistemology and the Milan approach: Feminist and sociopolitical considerations. *Journal of Marital and Family Therapy, 13,* 139-155.

Maletzky, B. M. (1991). *Treating the sexual offender.* Newbury Park, CA: Sage.

Maltz, W. (1991). *The sexual healing journey: A guide for survivors of sexual abuse.* New York: HarperCollins.

Maltz, W., & Holman, B. (1987). *Incest and sexuality: A guide to understanding and healing.* Lexington, MA: Lexington Books.

Mann, D. (1989). Incest: The father and the male therapist. *British Journal of Psychotherapy, 6,* 143-153.

Marín, G. (1989). AIDS prevention among Hispanics: Needs, risk behaviors, and cultural values. *Public Health Report, 104,* 411-415.

Marín, G., & Triandis, H. (1985). Allocentrism as an important characteristic of the behavior of Latin Americans and Hispanics. In R. Diaz-Guerrero (Ed.), *Cross-cultural and national studies in social psychology* (pp. 85-104). Amsterdam: Elsevier North-Holland.

Marqués, R. (1972). *El Puertorriqueño dócil.* Barcelona: Editorial Antillana.

Martin, J., & Martin, E. (1985). *The helping tradition in the Black family and community.* Silver Spring, MD: National Association of Social Workers.

Martin, T. C., & Burpass, L. L. (1989). Recent trends in marital disruption. *Demography, 26,* 37-51.

Martinez, K. J. (1994). Cultural sensitivity in family therapy gone awry. *Hispanic Journal of Behavioral Sciences, 16,* 75-89.

Martinez, R., & Wetli, C. (1982). Santería: A magico-religious system of Afro-Cuban origin. *Journal of Social Psychiatry, 2,* 32-39.

Matousek, M. (1991, March/April). America's darkest secret. *Common Boundary,* pp. 16-25.

Matsakis, A. (1992). *I can't get over it: A handbook for trauma survivors.* Oakland, CA: New Harbinger.

McAdoo, H. P. (1981). Black families and child interactions. In L. E. Gary (Ed.), *Black men* (pp. 115-130). Beverly Hills, CA: Sage.

McAdoo, H. P. (1989, March). *African American family patterns.* Paper presented at the Black Family Summit, University of South Carolina, Columbia.

McGill, D. W. (1992). The cultural story in multicultural family therapy. *Families in Society, 73,* 339-349.

McGoldrick, M., Pearce, J. K., & Giordano, J. (1982). *Ethnicity and family therapy.* New York: Guilford.

McGoldrick, M., & Rohrbaugh, M. (1987). Researching ethnic family stereotypes. *Family Process, 26,* 89-100.

McKenry, P. C., & Fine, M. A. (1993). Parenting following divorce: A comparison of black and white single mothers. *Journal of Comparative Family Studies, 24,* 99-111.

Memmi, A. (1965). *The colonizer and the colonized.* Boston: Beacon.

Mencher, J., & Slater, S. (1991, July 1). *Uncharted waters: Developing a model of the lesbian family life cycle.* Presentation at Smith College School for Social Work, Northampton, MA.

Mendez, P., & Jocano, F. (1974). *The Filipino family in its rural and urban orientation.* Manila, Philippines: CEU Research and Development Center.

Meyers, H. F. (1982). Research on the Afro-American family: A critical review. In B. A. Bass, G. E. Wyatt, & G. J. Powell (Eds.), *The Afro-American family: Assessment, treatment, and research issues* (pp. 35-68). New York: Grune & Stratton.

Mokuau, N., & Tauili'ili, P. (1992). Families with native Hawaiian and Pacific Island roots. In E. W. Lynch & M. J. Hanson (Eds.), *Developing cross-cultural competence: A guide for working with young children and their families* (pp. 301-318). Baltimore: Brookes.

Mollica, R. F., & Lavalle, J. P. (1988). Southeast Asian refugees. In L. Comas-Díaz & E. H. Griffith (Eds.), *Clinical guidelines in cross cultural mental health* (pp. 262-293). New York: John Wiley.

Money, J. (1988). *Gay, straight, and in-between.* New York: Oxford University Press.

Montalvo, B., & Gutierrez, M. (1983). A perspective for the use of the cultural dimension in family therapy. In C. J. Falicov (Ed.), *Cultural perspectives in family therapy.* Rockville, MD: Aspen Systems Corp.

Myers, K. (1992). *The experience of adult women who, as children, were sexually abused by an older, trusted female: An exploratory study.* Unpublished master's thesis, Smith College, Northampton, MA.

Nagata, D. K. (1989). Japanese American children and adolescents. In J. T. Gibbs, L. N. Huang, & Associates (Eds.), *Children of color* (pp. 87-113). San Francisco: Jossey-Bass.

Neighbors, H., & Taylor, R. (1985). The use of social service agencies by Black Americans. *Social Service Review, 59,* 259-268.

Neighbors, H. W. (1990). The prevention of psychopathology in African Americans: An epidemiologic perspective. *Community Mental Health Journal, 26,* 167-179.

Nguyen, N. A., & Williams, H. (1989). Transition from east to west: Vietnamese adolescents and their parents. *American Academy of Child and Adolescent Psychiatry, 28*(4), 505-515.

Nieves-Falcón, L. (1972). *Diagnóstico de Puerto Rico.* Río Piedras, PR: Editorial Edil.

Nobles, W. W. (1978). Toward an empirical and theoretical framework for defining black families. *Journal of Marriage and the Family, 40,* 679-688.

Nolen-Hoksema, S. (1987). Sex differences in unipolar depression: Evidence and theory. *Psychological Bulletin, 101,* 259-282.

Oaklander, V. (1988). *Windows to our children.* Highland, NY: Real People Press.

O'Connell, M. A., Leberg, E., & Donaldson, C. R. (1990). *Working with sex offenders: Guidelines for therapist selection.* Newbury Park, CA: Sage.

Ogbu, J. U. (1981). Origins of human competence: A cultural ecological perspective. *Child Development, 52,* 413-429.

O'Hara, M. (1989). Person-centered approach as conscientizaçao: The works of Carl Rogers and Paulo Freire. *Journal of Humanistic Psychology, 29,* 11-35.

Okamura, A. (1992, January). *Ethnicity and physical discipline.* Paper presented at the San Diego Conference on Responding to Child Maltreatment, San Diego, CA.

Okamura, A. (1993, February). *Asian American adolescents.* Paper presented at the Adolescent Psychiatry Review Course, American Society of Adolescent Psychiatry, San Diego, CA.

Parker, H., & Parker, S. (1986). Father-daughter sexual abuse: An emerging perspective. *American Journal of Orthopsychiatry, 56,* 531-549.

Payne, M. A. (1989). Use and abuse of corporal punishment: A Caribbean view. *Child Abuse & Neglect, 13,* 389-401.

Phipps, L. (1991, September). Confessions of a young WASP. *New York,* pp. 24-31.

Pierce, L. H., & Pierce, R. L. (1984). Race as a factor in the sexual abuse of children. *Social Work Research and Abstracts, 20,* 9-14.

Pinderhughes, E. (1982). Afro-American families and the victim system. In M. McGoldrick, J. K. Pearce, & J. Giordano (Eds.), *Ethnicity and family therapy* (pp. 108-122). New York: Guilford.

Plummer, C. A. (1984). *Preventing sexual abuse: Activities and strategies for those working with children and adolescents.* Holmes Beach, FL: Learning Publications.

Pogrebin, L. C. (1991). *Deborah, Golda, and me: Being female and Jewish in America.* New York: Anchor.

Ponchaud, F. (1977). *Cambodia: Year Zero.* New York: Holt, Rinehart & Winston.

Priest, R. (1992). A preliminary examination of child sexual victimization in college African American populations. *American Journal of Orthopsychiatry, 63,* 367-371.

Ramos-McKay, J., Comas-Díaz, L., & Rivera, L. (1988). Puerto Ricans. In L. Comas-Díaz & E. H. Griffith (Eds.), *Clinical guidelines in cross cultural mental health* (pp. 204-232). New York: John Wiley.

Rao, K., Di Clemente, R. J., & Ponton, L. D. (1992). Child sexual abuse of Asians compared with other populations. *Journal of the American Academy of Child & Adolescent Psychiatry, 31,* 880-886.

Reid, A. (1992, May 22). Neighbor charged in rape, slaying of Revere girl, 5. *Boston Globe,* Sec. 4., p. 1.

Rogow, F. (1991/1995). Prayer [untitled]. In J. R. Spitzer, *When love is not enough: Spousal abuse in rabbinic and contemporary Judaism.* New York: National Federation of Temple Sisterhoods.

Rohter, L. (1994, January 31). A Puerto Rican boom for Florida. *New York Times,* p. A10.

Root, M. P. P. (1992). Reconstructing the impact of trauma on personality. In L. Brown & M. Ballou (Eds.), *Personality and psychopathology: Feminist reappraisals* (pp. 229-265). New York: Guilford.

Ross, C. E., Mirowsky, J., & Cockerham, W. C. (1983). Social class, Mexican culture, and fatalism: Their effects on psychological distress. *American Journal of Community Psychology, 11,* 383-399.

Rothenberg, A. (1964). Puerto Rico and aggression. *American Journal of Psychiatry, 120,* 962-970.

Rotter, J. B. (1966). Generalized expectancies for internal versus external control of reinforcement. *Psychological Monographs, 80*(1, Whole No. 609).

Round table discussion: Jewish women talking about incest. (1991, Spring). *Bridges,* pp. 26-34.

Rush, F. (1980). *The best kept secret: Sexual abuse of children.* New York: McGraw-Hill.

Russell, D. E. H. (1986). *The secret trauma: Incest in the lives of girls and women.* New York: Basic Books.

Russell, D. E. H., Schurman, R. A., & Trocki, K. (1988). The long-term effects of incestuous abuse: A comparison of Afro-American and White American victims. In G. E. Wyatt & G. J. Powell (Eds.), *Lasting effects of child sexual abuse* (pp. 119-134). Newbury Park, CA: Sage.

Rutledge, L. (1987). *The gay book of lists.* Boston: Alyson.

Schmidt, M. G. (1991). Problems of child abuse with adolescents in chemically dependent families. In E. S. Sweet (Ed.), *Special problems in counseling the chemically dependent adolescent* (pp. 9-24). Binghamton, NY: Haworth.

Schoener, G., Milgram, J. H., Gonsiorek, J. C., Luepker, C. T., & Conroe, R. M. (1989). *Psychotherapists' sexual involvement with clients: Intervention and prevention.* Minneapolis, MN: Walk-In Counseling Center.

Schwartz, M. (Speaker). (1992). *Unraveling the truth beneath the symptom: Issues of Jewish women in therapy* (Cassette Recording No. 92JFP-13). Seattle, WA: Jewish Women's Caucus, Association for Women in Psychology.

Serafica, F. (1990). Counseling Asian-American parents: A cultural developmental approach. In F. C. Serafica, A. I. Schwebel, R. K. Russell, P. D. Isaac, & L. J. Meyers (Eds.), *Mental health of ethnic minorities* (pp. 224-244). New York: Praeger.

Sgroi, S. (1988). *Handbook of clinical intervention in child sexual abuse.* Lexington, MA: Lexington Books.

Shively, M. A., & DeCecco, J. P. (1977). Components of sexual identity. *Journal of Homosexuality, 3*(1), 41-48.

Simkins, L. (1993). Characteristics of sexually repressed child molesters. *Journal of Interpersonal Violence, 8,* 3-17.

Sluzki, C. (1982). Migration and family conflict. *Family Process, 18*(4), 379-390.

Sommers-Flanagan, R., & Walters, H. A. (1987). The incest offender, power, and victimization: Scales on the same dragon. *Journal of Family Violence, 2,* 163-175.

Spiegel, M. C. (1988, Summer). The last taboo—Dare we speak about incest? *Lilith, 20,* 10-12.

Staples, R. (1973). *The black woman in America.* Chicago: Nelson-Hall.

Staples, R., & Mirande, A. (1980). Racial and cultural variations among American families: A decennial review of the literature on minority families. *Journal of Marriage and the Family, 42*, 887-903.

Steiner, S. (1974). *The islands: The worlds of the Puerto Ricans.* New York: HarperColophon.

Stevens, E. (1973). Machismo and marianismo. *Transaction-Society, 10*(6), 57-63.

Stevenson, H. W. (1992). Learning from Asian schools. *Scientific American, 267*(6), 70-77.

Stone, E. (1988). *Black sheep and kissing cousins: How our family stories shape us.* New York: Penguin.

Sue, D., & Sue, D. (1990). *Counseling the culturally different: Theory and practice.* New York: John Wiley.

Sue, S., & Morishima, J. K. (1982). *The mental health of Asian Americans.* San Francisco: Jossey-Bass.

Sue, S., & Zane, N. (1987). The role of culture and cultural techniques in psychotherapy: A reformation. *American Psychologist, 42*, 37-45.

Surrey, J. L. (1991). The "self-in-relation": A theory of women's development. In J. V. Jordan, A. G. Kaplan, J. B. Miller, I. P. Stiver, & J. L. Surrey (Eds.), *Women's growth in connection* (pp. 51-66). New York: Guilford.

Sussman, L. K., Robins, L. N., & Earl, F. (1987). Treatment seeking for depression by black and white Americans. *Social Science and Medicine, 24*, 187-196.

Tharinger, D., Krivacska, J. J., Laye-McDonough, M., Jamison, L., Vincent, G. G., & Hedlund, A. D. (1988). Prevention of child sexual abuse: An analysis of issues, educational programs, and research findings. *School Psychology Review, 17*, 614-634.

Thompson, V. S., & Smith, S. W. (1993). Attitude of African American adults toward treatment in cases of child sexual abuse. *Journal of Child Sexual Abuse, 2*(1), 5-19.

Torres-Matrullo, C. (1976). Acculturation and psychopathology among Puerto Rican women in mainland United States. *American Journal of Orthopsychiatry, 46*, 710-719.

Tran, T. V. (1988). The Vietnamese American family. In C. H. Mindel, R. W. Habenstein, & R. Wright, Jr. (Eds.), *Ethnic families in America* (pp. 276-299). New York: Elsevier.

Trask, H. (1990). Politics in the Pacific Islands: Imperialism and native self-determination. *Amerasia Journal, 16*(1), 1-19.

Trepper, T. S., & Barrett, M. J. (1986). Vulnerability to incest: A framework for assessment. In T. S. Trepper & M. J. Barrett (Eds.), *Treating incest: A multiple systems perspective.* Binghamton, NY: Haworth.

Trepper, T. S., & Barrett, M. J. (1989). *Systemic treatment of incest: A therapeutic handbook.* New York: Brunner/Mazel.

Trepper, T. S., & Traicoff, E. M. (1985). Treatment of incest: Conceptual rationale and model for family therapy. *Journal of Sex Education and Therapy, 11,* 18-23.

Tsui, A. (1985). Psychotherapeutic considerations in sexual counseling for Asian immigrants. *Psychotherapy, 22,* 357-361.

Union of Pan Asian Communities. (1982). *Pan Asian child rearing practices: Filipino, Japanese, Korean, Samoan, Vietnamese.* San Diego, CA: Pan Asian Parent Education Project, Union of Pan Asian Communities.

U.S. Bureau of the Census. (1990). *Census of the population and housing.* Washington, DC: U.S. Department of Commerce, Bureau of the Census, Data Users Services Division.

Vasquez, M. (1994). Latinas. In L. Comas-Díaz & B. Greene (Eds.), *Women of color: Integrating ethnic and gender identities in psychotherapy* (pp. 114-138). New York: Guilford.

Vernon, G. (1994). Verbal report. Child Sexual Assault Treatment Program, San Diego County Department of Social Services, Childrens Services Bureau Statistics, San Diego, CA.

Veroff, J., Douvan, E., & Kulka, R. A. (1981). *The inner American.* New York: Basic Books.

Wakefield, D. (1960). *Island in the city: Puerto Ricans in New York.* New York: Corinth.

Wali, S. (1991). *Rape trauma and its effect on refugee women and their communities.* Washington, DC: Refugee Women in Development.

Weinberg, G. (1972). *Society and the healthy homosexual.* New York: St. Martin's.

White, E. (1893). *2nd selected messages.* Washington, DC: Review and Herald Publishing Association.

White, E. C. (1985). *Chain chain change: For black women dealing with physical and emotional abuse.* Seattle, WA: Seal Press.

Williams, L. M. (1986). *Race and rape: The black woman as legitimate victim* (Research Rep. No. MH15161). Durham: University of New Hampshire, Family Violence Research Laboratory.

Williams, R. M., Jr. (1970). *American society: A sociological interpretation.* New York: Alfred A. Knopf.

Wilson, M. (1994). *Crossing the boundary: Black women survive incest.* Seattle, WA: Seal Press.

Wilson, M. N. (1992). Perceived parental activity of mothers, fathers, and grandmothers in three-generational black families. In A. K. H. Burlew, W. C. Banks, H. P. McAdoo, & D. A. Azibo (Eds.), *African American psychology* (pp. 87-104). Newbury Park, CA: Sage.

Wittoker, E. D. (1970). Trance and possession states. *International Journal of Social Psychiatry, 16,* 153-160.

Wolf, M. (1991, February). Sitting shiva for my parents. *Valley Women's Voice,* Amherst, MA, pp. 7-8.

Wolf, N. (1991). *The beauty myth.* New York: Doubleday.

Women's Ministries. (1994, February). When the unthinkable happens. *The Adventist Review* [Pamphlet]. (Distributed by the North American Division Office of Women's Ministries, 12501 Old Columbia Pike, Silver Spring, MD 20904)

Wong, D. (1987). Preventing child sexual abuse among Southeast Asian refugee families. *Children Today, 16*(6), 18-22.

Wong-Kerberg, L. (1993, May). *Children's memories: Current knowledge, implications for effective intervention—Cultural perspectives.* Paper presented at the California Consortium for the Prevention of Child Abuse, Giarretto Institute, Berkeley.

Wyatt, G. E. (1982). Identifying stereotypes of Afro-American sexuality and their impact upon sexual behavior. In B. A. Bass, G. E. Wyatt, & G. J. Powell (Eds.), *The Afro-American family: Assessment, treatment, and research issues* (pp. 333-346). New York: Grune & Stratton.

Wyatt, G. E. (1985). The sexual abuse of Afro-American and White-American women in childhood. *Child Abuse & Neglect, 9,* 507-519.

Wyatt, G. E. (1988a). The relationship between child sexual abuse and adolescent sexual functioning in Afro-American and White-American women. *Annals of the New York Academy of Science, 528,* 111-122.

Wyatt, G. E. (1988b). Re-examining factors affecting Afro-American and White-American women's age of first coitus. *Archives of Sexual Behavior, 18*(4), 269-296.

Wyatt, G. E. (1990). Sexual abuse of ethnic minority children: Identifying dimensions of victimization. *Professional Psychology: Research and Practice, 21*(5), 338-343.

Wyatt, G. E., & Mickey, M. R. (1988). The support by parents and others as it mediates the effects of child sexual abuse: An exploratory study. In G. E.

Wyatt & G. J. Powell (Eds.), *Lasting effects of child sexual abuse* (pp. 211-226). Newbury Park, CA: Sage.

Wyatt, G. E., & Peters, S. D. (1986a). Issues in the definition of child sexual abuse in prevalence research. *Child Abuse & Neglect, 10,* 231-240.

Wyatt, G. E., & Peters, S. D. (1986b). Methodological considerations in research on the prevalence of child sexual abuse. *Child Abuse & Neglect, 10,* 241-251.

Wyatt, G. E., Peters, S. D., & Guthrie, D. (1988a). Kinsey revisited, part I: Comparisons of the sexual socialization and sexual behavior of white women over 33 years. *Archives of Sexual Behavior, 17*(3), 201-239.

Wyatt, G. E., Peters, S. D., & Guthrie, D. (1988b). Kinsey revisited, part II: Comparisons of the sexual socialization and sexual behavior of black women over 33 years. *Archives of Sexual Behavior, 17*(3), 289-332.

Zavala-Martinez, I. (1981). *Mental health and the Puerto Rican in the United States: A critical literature review and comprehensive bibliography.* Unpublished comprehensive examination project, Department of Psychology, University of Massachusetts, Amherst.

Zavala-Martinez, I. (1988). En la lucha: The economic and socioemotional struggles of Puerto Rican women. *Women and Therapy, 6,* 13-24.

Zborowski, M., & Herzog, E. (1952). *Life is with people.* New York: Schocken.

Index

About the Editor

Lisa Aronson Fontes, Ph.D., is Assistant Professor of Family Therapy at Purdue University in West Lafayette, Indiana, where she teaches about family violence, qualitative research, and other topics. She supervises family therapists and has worked as a family, individual, and group therapist in a variety of settings including managed care, emergency services, and protective outreach services. She researches multicultural issues in  family violence, particularly with Latinos, and she is currently conducting related research with migrant farm workers in the U.S. and with shantytown residents in Chile. She also facilitates workshops for professionals on the impact of working family violence on their own personal lives. She is on the editorial boards of *Child Maltreatment, The Journal of Feminist Family Therapy,* and *The Family Journal.* She obtained her doctorate in counseling psychology from the University of Massachusetts in Amherst. She welcomes correspondence about matters related to this book.

About the Contributors

Veronica D. Abney is a clinical social worker on the staff and clinical faculty at the University of California, Los Angeles's Neuropsychiatric Hospital in Los Angeles. She is also in private practice, specializing in group and individual treatment of childhood sexual trauma. She is a candidate member of the Institute of Contemporary Psychoanalysis and is interested in the application of modern psychoanalytic theories in cross-cultural treatment. Her publications include articles on both the treatment of adult survivors of sexual child abuse and cross-cultural issues.

Doug Arey, L.I.C.S.W., is the codirector of Lambda Resources for Women and Men, a psychotherapy practice for gays, lesbians, and bisexuals in Northampton, Massachusetts. He received his master's degree in social work at the University of Connecticut in 1984 and worked for 8 years as a clinician on the sexual abuse treatment unit in community mental health centers in western Massachusetts before beginning his private practice and cofounding Lambda Resources in 1990.

Maryellen Butke, M.S.W., is currently completing her doctoral work at Smith College School for Social Work. She is in full-time private practice at Women's Psychotherapy Associates, a group practice specializing in the treatment of women clients. She leads workshops for sexual abuse survivors as well as for therapists who were abused. She worked for 6 years at Bradley Hospital, a child and adolescent psychiatric hospital in Providence, Rhode Island, where she ran the Sexual Trauma Clinic. She is an adjunct faculty member at Boston College and Smith College School for Social Work. Her particular interests include holistic treatment that integrates mind, body, and spirit, as well as the integration of psychotherapy and spirituality.

Lillian Comas-Díaz, Ph.D., is the Executive Director of the Transcultural Mental Health Institute and maintains a private practice of clinical psychology in Washington, DC. In 1989, she was the recipient of the American Psychological Association Committee on Women in Psychology's Award for Emerging Leader for Women in Psychology. She has published extensively on cross-cultural mental health, gender and ethnic factors in psychotherapy, the treatment of torture victims, international psychology, and Latin mental health. She has edited two books, *Clinical Guidelines in Cross Cultural Mental Health* and *Women of Color: Integrating Ethnic and Gender Identities in Psychotherapy.*

Joan M. Featherman, Ed.D., is a psychologist practicing in Greenfield and Northampton, Massachusetts. In addition to her private practice of therapy and consultation on sexual abuse, sexual harassment, and related issues, she provides psychotherapy and directs the Training Psychologist Internship Program at the Outpatient Clinic of ServiceNet in Northampton, Massachusetts. She is the author of "Factors Relating to the Quality of Adult Adjustment in Female Victims of Child Sexual Abuse," an unpublished doctoral dissertation written at the University of Massachusetts at Amherst.

Eliana Gil, Ph.D., is Director of the Center for Advanced Clinical Development, a program of the Multicultural Clinical Center in Springfield, Virginia, where she provides clinical services, training, and supervision. She is founder and Senior Program Advisor of *A Step Forward,* a child abuse treatment and training program in Concord, California. She has written extensively on child abuse and related topics. Her books include *Treatment of Adult Survivors of Childhood Abuse, United We Stand: A Book for Individuals With Multiple*

Personalities, and *Outgrowing the Pain Together: A Book for Spouses and Partners of Adult Survivors*. Her most recent books include *Play in Family Therapy* and (with Toni Cavanagh Johnson) *Sexualized Children: Assessment and Treatment of Sexualized Children and Children Who Molest*. She is a well-known lecturer and a frequent guest on local and national television and radio shows. She is bilingual and bicultural, orginally from Guayaquil, Ecuador.

Patricia Heras, Ph.D., is a Filipino American clinical psychologist in private practice in San Diego with expertise in the areas of child abuse, posttraumatic stress disorder, depression, anxiety disorders, and cross-cultural assessment and treatment. She obtained her doctorate from the California School of Professional Psychology, San Diego, where she is an adjunct faculty member. She provides training and consultation for mental health providers and organizations in cross-cultural issues. She serves as a special consultant to the San Diego Juvenile Court, chairs the Cross Cultural Task Force of the San Diego Psychological Association, and serves as a board member on the California Psychological Association Foundation. She has published on cultural considerations in the treatment of sexual abuse and on the acculturation of Filipino Americans.

Theanvy Kuoch is a survivor of the Cambodian holocaust and former refugee who worked in the German Surgical Ward in Khao-I-Dang, caring for people with war injuries and leprosy. She holds a master's degree in family therapy and is the Program Director of Khmer Health Advocates, Inc., which she cofounded in 1982. As a therapist, she has treated hundreds of survivors of the Mahantdorai. As an advocate for mental health and human rights, she has spoken internationally, urging that mental health problems be addressed as a major concern in the rebuilding of Cambodia. In 1989, she helped found Cambodian Mothers for Peace as a vehicle for giving voice to the suffering and strengths of Cambodian women. She also works for the Connecticut Department of Health in the refugee and tuberculosis programs.

Richard A. Miller is a psychiatrist who has worked with Khmer Health Advocates, Inc., for more than a decade. He is part of the therapy team that offers a weekly mental health clinic for Cambodians, and he provides medical care and advocacy for KHA. He received his medical degree from Case Western Reserve Medical School in 1969, interned at Baylor Medical School in Houston, Texas, and completed his residency in psychiatry at the Institute of Living in Hartford, Connecticut. In addition to his private practice, he is also the medical director of the Child and Family Agency of Southeastern Connecticut, Inc. He has given presentations on the psychiatric problems of Cambodian refugees, and his letter on fluoxetine treatment for posttraumatic stress disorder was published in the *American Journal of Psychiatry.*

Amy Okamura, M.S.W., L.C.S.W., is a "sansei" Japanese American educator and therapist. She is a faculty member at the San Diego State University School of Social Work and also has a private practice. She is a Board Certified Diplomate in Clinical Social Work with 25 years of clinical practice with Asian Pacific and Filipino populations in San Diego. She has developed and managed comprehensive services for immigrants and refugee children and their families in child abuse and mental health, educated and encouraged many ethnic minority individuals to pursue careers in social work, and trained hundreds of professionals in providing culturally competent therapeutic services. She is a consultant to the People of Color Leadership Institute and cochair of the San Diego County Mental Health Ethnic Diversity Resource Team.

Ronnie Priest, Ph.D., has worked in the specialty area of child victimization for 10 years. He has published in nationally recognized professional journals and presented workshops, institutes, and seminars related to child sexual victimization and diversity. He is currently an Assistant Professor in the Department of Counseling, Educational Psychology and Research at the University of Memphis in Memphis, Tennessee.

Marian Schmidt, Ph.D., is a licensed psychologist working as a consultant to mental health agencies in Kennebec/Somerset counties in Maine, and holding private practice in Skowhegan, Maine. She previously authored a chapter on WASP mothers for the *Journal of Feminist Family Therapy* (1990). She originated and conducted successful art therapy programs involving parents and children in at-risk families in both New Jersey and Maine. She is a certified addictions specialist and holds clinical membership in the American Association for Marriage and Family Therapy and the American Society of Clinical Hypnosis.

Mary Scully, R.N., C.S., is a Psychiatric Nurse Specialist who has 20 years of experience in cross-cultural psychiatric nursing. She was a member of the lead medical team that opened a camp for 20,000 Cambodian refugees in 1980 and was responsible for establishing psychiatric services. In 1982, she cofounded Khmer Health Advocates, Inc., where she is currently working as Executive Director in addition to her work as therapist and advocate. She has coproduced two ATOD prevention videos for Cambodians and has been responsible for archiving thousands of original documents about the Cambodian trauma experience and Cambodian health issues.

Catherine Taylor, L.I.C.S.W., works as a family therapist at People's Bridge Action in Athol, Massachusetts, and is also in private practice. She developed and coordinates the MOSAIC Project for mothers of children who have been abused sexually. This project includes support groups, videos, an internationally distributed newsletter, consultations, and peer advocates. She teaches and consults to Seventh Day Adventists in the North Atlantic region.

Linda Wong-Kerberg is a Chinese American licensed marriage, family, and child therapist. She is currently the Executive Director of the Center of Women's Studies and Services in San Diego. She received her master's degree in counseling from San Diego State University. She has directed three multicultural child abuse treatment programs in northern and southern California, two of which served predominantly Asian and Pacific Island children and families. Her expertise is in the area of sexual abuse treatment of Asian children, and she conducts trainings in California and nationally on clinical and cultural aspects of prevention, interventions, and cultural competency in child abuse.

Printed in the United States
29056LVS00006BA/116

9 780803 954359